SIMPLY SUGAR

SS&GF

AND GLUTEN-FREE

180 Easy and Delicious Recipes You Can Make in 20 Minutes or Less

AMY GREEN

Ulysses Press

Published by Ulysses Press
P.O. Box 3440
Berkeley, CA 94703
www.ulyssespress.com

ISBN: 978-1-56975-865-6
Library of Congress Catalog Number 2010937123

Printed in Canada by Marquis Book Publishing

10 9 8 7 6 5 4

Acquisitions Editor: Keith Riegert
Managing Editor: Claire Chun
Editors: Lauren Harrison, Leslie Evans
Proofreader: Elyce Petker
Indexer: Sayre Van Young
Cover design: what!design @ whatweb.com
Cover photos: cupcake © RuthBlack/istockphoto.com; pancakes © Elena Elisseeva/shutterstock.com; pizza © Paul Matthew Photography/shutterstock.com; pasta © barbaradudzinska/shutterstock.com; fries © Robyn Mackenzie/shutterstock.com; waffle © Jiri Hera/shutterstock.com; author © Amy Twomey Photography
Production: Judith Metzener
SF&GF logo design: Rhiannon Cuang, 21RubyLane.com

Distributed by Publishers Group West

For my husband, best friend, and partner in life, Joseph Allan. You've given me the space to discover that dreams really do come true. Thank you for creating a life with me that has an ending better than any fairy tale. I love you more each passing day.

Contents

Why Eat Simply Sugar & Gluten-Free?

There are as many reasons to eat gluten-free and refined sugar–free as there are stars in the sky. Some people have celiac disease and have to cut out gluten. Others need to cut out white sugar because of health concerns like diabetes, heart disease, and obesity. Through my blog, *Simply Sugar & Gluten-Free*, I've had people share their doctor's recommendation that they greatly reduce their white sugar intake.

Still others have no official medical diagnosis but have found that they feel better without gluten or sugar. For years I thought I was the only one who had this problem. But, I've learned that I'm not as unique as I thought. I hear daily from women who struggle with their weight, intense food cravings, and finding the time to feed their family in a way that nourishes them. I'm not a doctor and have no official training in nutrition. Instead, I'm just a person who's been able to find a way of eating that makes my life work. Everything shared here is from my personal experience.

Why I Don't Eat Wheat & White Sugar

I gave up wheat and white sugar because I was just fat.

Well, maybe not *just* fat. You can add depressed, moody, irritable, and frequently in bed with a migraine. By fifth grade I was officially obese. Over the next fourteen years I got to be a world-class yo-yo dieter. I was either eating large quantities of food or trying to lose the weight I gained from binging.

Never did I let anyone see me eat a bag of chocolate chips or an entire box of animal crackers. But I did eat them. And for some reason I was always dismayed when my pants no longer fit.

At my heaviest, I was 5' 5'', over 180 pounds, and 21 years old. Most days I was unable to do what most people take for granted. Out of sheer desperation, I saw a doctor who practiced alternative medicine. After spending some time with me, he told me to quit eating sugar and wheat. His words were, "It's going to kill you." Though the change was difficult, I followed his instructions carefully. After a few weeks I started to feel better. Life felt good again.

I was young, though, and didn't understand the full implications of the changes I had made. I started eating wheat and sugar again. Soon the binging started again, and any weight that I lost was quickly regained. The next six years were a physical and emotional roller coaster.

The inevitable day came when I accepted that as long as I allowed myself to eat wheat and sugar, I would have no control of my weight. I finally understood why I had failed at every diet I ever tried.

So How Did I Do It?

It was simple—I stopped putting sugar- and gluten-laden foods in my mouth. I know, this isn't the answer anyone wants. There is no easy, magical solution. But it is simple.

Whole, nourishing foods were the perfect place for me to start. My body needed time to recalibrate. I started eating three smaller meals and one to two snacks a day, depending on how hungry I was. If I needed a sweet fix, I ate fruit. I do the same thing today as I did then. Of course, now I can throw in a gluten-free, sugar-free dessert with no problem. But it took a while to get there. Most importantly, I do it just for right now, just for the meal in front of me. I don't worry about what I'm going to eat two months from now. Yes, I take care of myself and plan ahead. But keeping the focus on right now takes away the obsession and fear that initially brought me to my knees.

I've had to learn to listen to my body and walk my own path with food. Eating this way has helped me maintain a 60-plus-pound weight loss for nearly seven years.

Rethinking Quick & Simple

As I write this, I have a pot of made-from-scratch chicken noodle soup on my stovetop for my husband who's under the weather. It took me all of 10 minutes to put it together.

I pulled some homemade chicken broth out of the freezer that I'd cooked weeks before on a lazy Sunday afternoon, and I threw it into a pot with chopped carrots and celery. Once the veggies were tender, I added noodles and shredded chicken, which was also previously cooked and frozen. (I know, you're thinking it took forever to make the chicken and broth. No, not really. Just 15 minutes or so of active kitchen time.) So when Joe needed a pot of homemade soup on a day when my to-do list had more things on it than any human could realistically get done, my stress didn't increase at all. Even better, I didn't have to feed him store-bought soup. He got the good stuff.

Let's face it, we're all busy. No one has three hours to prepare a weeknight meal. In today's world of hectic schedules and instant gratification, quick and simple has come to mean dinner from the closest fast food joint, the pizza delivery man, or a box of processed food with some browned meat. No wonder America is obese.

Eating gluten-free and refined sugar–free has caused me to rethink quick and simple. There was a day when I balked at the thought of having to plan a meal or organize a grocery list. I didn't have time, or so I thought. My hectic schedule forced me to find shortcuts in the kitchen while still preparing nutritious home-cooked meals.

I learned to organize my grocery list, keep a tidy and well-stocked pantry, and plan meals. With some practice, I started to think ahead and find creative solutions to dinner. I learned to make extra rice, quinoa, and beans and freeze them for busy nights. My slow cooker, food processor, and stand mixer have all paid for themselves a hundred times over through the precious minutes they've shaved off my kitchen time.

My goal with this book was to take the often intimidating world of gluten-free, sugar-free cooking and make it as simple as pie and, as a result, help as many people as possible live a healthier lifestyle without being chained to the kitchen.

After one of my cooking classes, a student told me a story about his grandmother, who could bake a mean loaf of bread. He'd tried over and over to replicate her recipe, and though he could get darn close, it was never quite the same. When he asked his grandmother what he was doing wrong, she lovingly replied, "The bread knows how many times you've baked it."

How true.

Give three people the exact same recipe and each will produce a different product based on their experience with the ingredients and techniques required, as well as their level of proficiency in the kitchen.

The recipes here are the result of countless hours of cooking and baking, with more failed attempts than I'd like to admit. My dad always said I was stubborn, and at least when it comes to gluten-free, sugar-free cooking and baking, I take it as a compliment. These quick, simple, and delicious recipes not only work in my kitchen, but have worked in the kitchens of my recipe testers and blog readers. I've served them to friends and family, all of whom loved every last bite.

I'm confident that these recipes will be quick and simple and turn out just as good for you as they do for me. But if not, don't throw in the towel. The bread knows how many times you've baked it.

Much love,

Amy

How to Use This Book

Quick and simple cooking requires a few things. Here are some basic guidelines for using this book and making the most out of your time in the kitchen.

1. Read the recipe all the way through before starting. When I'm doing something new in the kitchen, I read the recipe twice and make sure I understand each step along the way. It requires a little effort up front but it saves time and money, as I'm less likely to have a result worthy of only the garbage can.

2. Gather all the ingredients and equipment you need before beginning. In the culinary world, this is called *mis en place*, a French term for "everything in its place." In my kitchen, it means "set yourself up for success." My experience has taught me that it's better to be prepared than to ruin dinner. Think the recipe through from beginning to end in terms of what you'll need while you cook and what you'll need once the recipe is complete. Will you need cooling racks? What about serving dishes? Again, it takes some time, but once you practice this, it will become a habit and occur naturally.

3. After your ingredients and equipment have been gathered, it should take about 20 minutes of hands-on time to complete each recipe. I haven't accounted for baking time or unattended time on the stove. I use those periods of time to clean up the kitchen, spend time with my husband, or read my newest magazine. Likewise, I haven't included time for ingredient hunting, an impromptu trip to the grocery store, or family interruptions.

   A note about equipment: Having certain kitchen equipment, such as a stand mixer, food processor, or immersion blender, saves time. If you don't have one, you can still make nearly every recipe in this book with a little creativity. For example, a hand mixer does the same thing as a stand mixer fitted with a paddle attachment.

4. A well-stocked pantry is essential. See The Simply Sugar & Gluten-Free Kitchen Guide (page 211) for items I stock regularly. If your pantry is bare, don't worry. It took time to fully stock my pantry, but each week I added a few items until I was satisfied.

Breakfasts

Olive Oil Zucchini Muffins

Zucchini is one of my favorite veggies to add to baked goods. No one ever argues about eating an extra serving when it's tucked neatly into these muffins.

makes 12 muffins

1¾ cups Basic Flour Blend
(page 212)

¼ cup teff flour

2 teaspoons ground cinnamon

1 tablespoon gluten-free
baking powder

½ teaspoon freshly grated nutmeg

½ teaspoon ground ginger

½ teaspoon kosher salt

½ teaspoon xanthan gum

¼ teaspoon ground cloves

½ cup unsweetened applesauce

2 large eggs, lightly beaten

⅓ cup extra-virgin olive oil

½ cup agave nectar

1¾ cups coarsely grated zucchini

1 recipe Lemon Cream Cheese
(page 53), at room temperature

Preheat the oven to 350°F. Prepare a standard 12-cup muffin tin with cooking spray or line with cupcake papers.

In a large bowl, whisk together the flour blend, teff flour, cinnamon, baking powder, nutmeg, ginger, salt, xanthan gum, and cloves until uniformly combined.

In a medium bowl, whisk together the applesauce, eggs, oil, and agave until combined. Make a well in the middle of the dry ingredients. Add the wet ingredients and stir until smooth. Gently stir in the zucchini.

Use a spring-release ice cream scoop to divide the batter evenly among the prepared muffin cups. Bake for 22 to 25 minutes, until a toothpick inserted into the center of a muffin comes out clean. Let the muffins cool in the tin for 5 minutes. Remove them from the tin and carefully transfer to a wire rack lined with a paper towel to cool completely.

Serve the muffins warm, topped with room-temperature lemon cream cheese. Store in an airtight container, or wrap individually with plastic wrap and freeze.

Quick Tip: Make the lemon cream cheese the day before and take it out of the refrigerator while you assemble the muffins. By the time the muffins are ready to eat, the lemon cream cheese will be at the perfect spreading temperature.

Banana Oat Muffins

Leaving some chunks when mashing the banana adds great texture to these moist muffins.

makes 12 muffins

¾ cup low-fat milk

1 cup gluten-free rolled oats

1 large ripe banana

½ cup agave nectar

2 large eggs, lightly beaten

1 teaspoon vanilla extract

1¼ cups Basic Flour Blend (page 212)

2 teaspoons gluten-free baking powder

1 teaspoon ground cinnamon

½ teaspoon xanthan gum

¼ teaspoon kosher salt

¼ teaspoon freshly grated nutmeg

¼ cup unsalted butter, melted, or canola oil

Preheat the oven to 400°F. Prepare a standard 12-cup muffin tin with cooking spray or line with cupcake papers.

Combine the milk and oats in a medium bowl. In another bowl, mash the banana with a fork, leaving some chunks. Whisk the agave, eggs, and vanilla into the mashed banana. Stir the banana into the oats and set aside to soak.

In a large bowl, whisk together the flour blend, baking powder, cinnamon, xanthan gum, salt, and nutmeg. Whisk the butter or oil into the wet ingredients, then add the wet ingredients to the dry ingredients and stir just until blended.

Use a spring-release ice cream scoop to divide the batter evenly among the prepared muffin cups. Bake for 12 to 15 minutes, until a toothpick inserted into the center of a muffin comes out clean. Let the muffins cool for 5 minutes in the tin. Remove them from the tin and transfer to a wire rack lined with a paper towel to cool completely. Store in an airtight container, or wrap individually with plastic wrap and freeze.

Make It Dairy-Free: Use your favorite nondairy milk instead of cow's milk.

Quick Tip: If you don't have a banana on hand, try ¾ cup of another thick fruit puree, such as applesauce.

Apple Spice Muffins

The apple chunks and spices in these muffins remind me of fall, but they're delicious any time of year. **dairy-free**

makes 12 muffins

1 cup Basic Flour Blend (page 212)

1 cup quinoa flakes

½ cup plus 2 tablespoons palm sugar

2 teaspoons ground cinnamon

1½ teaspoons gluten-free baking powder

½ teaspoon baking soda

½ teaspoon freshly grated nutmeg

½ teaspoon xanthan gum

¼ teaspoon salt

⅓ cup frozen unsweetened apple juice concentrate, thawed

¼ cup canola oil

2 large eggs

1 cup finely chopped unpeeled apple

1 recipe Muffin Crumble Topping (page 12) (optional)

Preheat the oven to 400°F. Prepare a standard 12-cup muffin tin with cooking spray or line with cupcake papers.

In a medium bowl, whisk together the flour blend, quinoa flakes, palm sugar, cinnamon, baking powder, baking soda, nutmeg, xanthan gum, and salt.

In another medium bowl, whisk together the apple juice concentrate, oil, and eggs. Add the wet ingredients to the dry ingredients and mix until just barely combined. Gently stir in the apples.

Use a spring-release ice cream scoop to divide the batter evenly among the prepared muffin cups and top each one with the crumble topping, if using. Bake for 8 to 11 minutes, rotating the tin 180 degrees halfway through, until a toothpick inserted into the center of a muffin comes out clean. Allow the muffins to cool in the tin for 5 minutes. Remove them from the tin and transfer to a wire rack lined with a paper towel to cool completely. Store in an airtight container, or wrap individually with plastic wrap and freeze.

Quick Tip: To quickly core an apple, slice through the flesh just to the side of the apple core. Turn the apple 90 degrees and make your next cut. Repeat two more times until all the flesh has been cut away from the core.

Healthy Morning Muffins

I made these muffins so I'd have a healthier choice for mornings when I didn't have time to make breakfast. When I'm making them just for me, I leave out the optional add-ins and spread them with a little almond butter and any all-fruit preserve I have on hand. If you want to jazz these up, mix in your favorite dried fruit, nuts, or carob chips. Janet, one of my recipe testers, suggested adding dried cranberries and carob, which makes these muffins incredible. Note: If using add-ins, you may have batter for more than 12 muffins. **dairy-free**

makes 12 muffins

1½ cups mashed ripe banana (from about 3½ medium bananas)

⅓ cup agave nectar

¼ cup canola oil

2 large eggs

¼ cup unsweetened almond milk

1 teaspoon vanilla extract

1 cup Basic Flour Blend (page 212)

1 cup quinoa flour

2 teaspoons ground cinnamon

1½ teaspoons gluten-free baking powder

½ teaspoon baking soda

½ teaspoon xanthan gum

¼ teaspoon salt

Optional add-ins:

½ cup unsweetened carob chips; or ½ cup toasted chopped walnuts or pecans; or ½ cup dried cranberries; or combine them for a total of ½ cup

1 recipe Muffin Crumble Topping (page 12)

Preheat the oven to 350°F. Prepare a standard 12-cup muffin tin with cooking spray or line with cupcake papers.

In a medium bowl, mash the bananas roughly with a fork, measure out 1½ cups, and place the measured banana into the bowl of a stand mixer fitted with the paddle attachment. Turn the mixer on medium-low speed and add the agave and oil. Mix in the eggs one at a time. Add the almond milk and vanilla and stir on low speed until combined.

In another medium bowl, whisk together the flour blend, quinoa flour, cinnamon, baking powder, baking soda, xanthan gum, and salt until uniformly mixed. Add the dry ingredients to the wet ingredients, then stir on low speed until just combined. If using any optional add-ins, stir them in on low speed.

Use a spring-release ice cream scoop to divide the batter evenly among the prepared muffin cups. Top each muffin with the crumble topping, if using. Bake for 18 minutes, or until a toothpick inserted into the center of a muffin comes out clean.

Let the muffins cool in the tin for 5 minutes. Remove them from the tin and transfer to a wire rack lined with a paper towel to cool completely. Store in an airtight container, or wrap individually with plastic wrap and freeze.

Quick Tip: If you use frozen bananas, pop them into the microwave for 45 seconds at a time, mashing with a fork and stirring well before returning to the microwave each time. Stop when you have a nice fork-mashed puree, and don't allow the bananas to become too runny.

Chocolate Walnut Muffins

My husband makes a point of requesting a batch of these muffins when his supply in the freezer gets low. When heated up and topped with homemade vanilla ice cream, they make a fabulous dessert.

makes 16 to 18 muffins

1¼ cups Basic Flour Blend (page 212)

½ cup cocoa powder, preferably Dutch-processed

¼ cup teff flour

1½ teaspoons gluten-free baking powder

½ teaspoon baking soda

½ teaspoon decaffeinated instant coffee granules

½ teaspoon kosher salt

½ teaspoon xanthan gum

2 large eggs

1 cup buttermilk

½ cup canola oil

½ cup agave nectar

½ cup light sour cream

1 teaspoon vanilla extract

1 cup coarsely chopped toasted walnuts

Preheat the oven to 350°F. Prepare a standard 12-cup muffin tin and 6 cups of a second tin with cooking spray or line with cupcake papers.

Sift the flour blend, cocoa powder, teff flour, baking powder, baking soda, instant coffee, salt, and xanthan gum into a large bowl. Whisk until the flour is uniformly mixed.

In a medium bowl, whisk together the eggs, buttermilk, oil, agave, sour cream, and vanilla. Add the wet ingredients into the dry ingredients and mix with a spatula until just combined. Mix in the walnuts.

Use a spring-release ice cream scoop to divide the batter evenly among the prepared muffin cups. Bake for 15 to 18 minutes, until a toothpick inserted into the center of a muffin comes out clean. Let the muffins cool in the tin for 5 minutes. Remove them from the tin and transfer to a wire rack lined with a paper towel to cool completely.

Serve warm or let cool completely. Store cooled muffins in an airtight container, or wrap individually with plastic wrap and freeze.

Quick Tip: Toast the walnuts by spreading them on a baking sheet and placing them in a 350°F oven for 5 to 8 minutes, until fragrant. They'll continue to cook once removed from the oven, so it's best to take them out a minute or so before they're perfectly toasted.

Blueberry Muffins

When blueberries are at their peak, I buy them in bulk and flash freeze them by putting them in single layers on baking sheets in the freezer. Then I put them in sealable plastic bags and store them in the freezer. They keep nicely without sticking together, and I have fresh-frozen blueberries year round.

makes 12 muffins

6 tablespoons unsalted butter, at room temperature

¾ cup palm sugar

1 tablespoon grated lemon zest

1 tablespoon freshly squeezed lemon juice plus enough low-fat milk to equal ½ cup

1¾ cups Basic Flour Blend (page 212)

1 teaspoon gluten-free baking powder

1 teaspoon baking soda

½ teaspoon xanthan gum

½ teaspoon kosher salt

2 large eggs

¾ cup frozen blueberries, not thawed

1 recipe Muffin Crumble Topping (page 12) (optional)

Preheat the oven to 375°F. Prepare a standard 12-cup muffin tin with cooking spray or line with cupcake papers.

In the bowl of a stand mixer fitted with the paddle attachment, beat the butter on medium speed for about 3 minutes, until light in color and fluffy. Add half of the palm sugar, letting it mix in before adding the second half. Beat for 5 minutes longer.

While the butter and sugar are creaming together, mix the lemon zest into the lemon juice and milk. Set aside. In a medium bowl, whisk together the flour blend, baking powder, baking soda, xanthan gum, and salt. Set aside. Once the butter and sugar have creamed, add the eggs to the mixture one at a time. Let the first egg fully incorporate and scrape down the bowl before adding the second.

On low speed, beat the dry ingredients into the butter mixture in three parts, alternating with the milk mixture, starting and ending with the dry ingredients. Mix just until smooth. Fold in the blueberries.

Use a spring-release ice cream scoop to divide the batter evenly among the prepared muffin cups and top each one with the crumble topping, if using. Bake for 15 to 18 minutes, until the muffins are lightly golden brown on top and a toothpick inserted into the center of a muffin comes out clean. Let the muffins cool in the tin for 5 minutes. Remove them from the tin and transfer to a wire rack lined with a paper towel to cool completely. Store in an airtight container, or wrap individually with plastic wrap and freeze.

Quick Tip: Toss the frozen blueberries in a pinch or two of the flour mixture before adding to the muffin batter. This helps to suspend them in the muffins so that all the berries don't end up on the bottom.

Muffin Crumble Topping

Use this crumb topping as a way to jazz up Apple Spice Muffins, Blueberry Muffins, or Healthy Morning Muffins. Note that baking times will be a little longer than indicated in the recipe. Be sure to test the muffins with a toothpick to check for doneness.

makes enough for 12 muffins

½ cup Basic Flour Blend (page 212)

¼ cup palm sugar

½ teaspoon ground cinnamon

pinch of salt

3 tablespoons unsalted butter, melted

Whisk together the flour blend, palm sugar, cinnamon, and salt in a medium bowl until uniformly combined. Drizzle with the melted butter and quickly work the butter into the flour mix with your fingers until it resembles small pebbles.

Cake Donuts

Every baker should have a donut pan or two in her stock of supplies. Pulling a pan of freshly baked donuts out of the oven always sparks a sense of pride. These donuts are light but can hold up to being dunked in your morning coffee, tea, or glass of milk. Add my donut glaze for a special touch.

makes 6 donuts

1 tablespoon unsalted butter, at room temperature

1 tablespoon non-hydrogenated shortening

⅓ cup palm sugar

1 teaspoon vanilla extract

1 large egg

1¼ cups Basic Flour Blend (page 212)

½ teaspoon gluten-free baking powder

½ teaspoon baking soda

¼ teaspoon kosher salt

¼ teaspoon xanthan gum

½ cup low-fat milk

1 recipe Chocolate Glaze or Caramel Glaze (page 180) (optional)

½ cup finely chopped toasted pecans or walnuts or ½ cup toasted shredded unsweetened coconut (optional)

Preheat the oven to 350°F. Lightly mist a donut pan with cooking spray.

In the bowl of a stand mixer fitted with the paddle attachment, cream the butter, shortening, palm sugar, and vanilla on medium speed for about 2 minutes, until soft and well blended. Scrape down the bowl as needed. Add the egg and mix until combined.

In a medium bowl, whisk together the flour blend, baking powder, baking soda, salt, and xanthan gum. On low speed, beat the dry ingredients into the butter in three parts, alternating with the milk, starting and ending with the dry ingredients. Mix just until smooth.

Spoon the batter into a 1-quart sealable plastic bag or a pastry bag and squeeze it into the prepared donut pan. (If using a plastic bag, snip one corner off so you have a ½-inch opening.) Tap the pan several times on the counter to settle the batter into the pan.

Bake for 10 to 12 minutes, rotating the pan 180 degrees halfway through the baking time, until the donuts are firm to the touch and a toothpick inserted into a donut comes out clean. Let cool in the pan for 5 minutes, then transfer the donuts directly onto a wire rack lined with a paper towel and allow to cool completely.

To glaze the donuts, dip the smoother side of a donut (the side that was in contact with the donut pan) in the warm glaze of your choice, then immediately dip the glazed side of the donut into the nuts or the coconut. Set the donuts glaze-side up on waxed paper or parchment paper.

These are best the day they're made. Wrap leftover unglazed donuts individually in plastic wrap and freeze so you'll have donuts ready any time you want one.

Make It Dairy-Free: Omit the butter and use 2 tablespoons non-hydrogenated shortening and your favorite nondairy milk.

Variation—Chocolate Cake Donuts: Add 1 tablespoon sour cream with the butter, shortening, and vanilla. Reduce the Basic Flour Blend to 1 cup and add ¼ cup sifted unsweetened cocoa powder to the dry ingredients. Add an optional ¼ teaspoon instant decaf coffee granules to the flour mix to enhance the chocolate flavor. Bake and store as directed for Cake Donuts. **Make It Dairy-Free:** Omit the butter and use 2 tablespoons non-hydrogenated shortening; use unsweetened applesauce instead of sour cream; and use your favorite nondairy milk.

Variation—Apple Cider Cake Donuts: Carrie from Ginger Lemon Girl (www.GingerLemonGirl.com) tested this recipe for me. She came up with this variation, which I tried and fell in love with. Add ¼ teaspoon each of cinnamon and freshly grated nutmeg. Use ½ cup apple cider instead of milk. Top with Caramel Glaze (page 180) for the perfect fall donut. **Make It Dairy-Free:** Omit the butter and increase the shortening to 2 tablespoons.

Quick Tip: Set your pastry bag or sealable plastic bag in a cup that allows the bag to hang down over the sides. Fold the opening of the bag around the rim of the cup so it stays open. Use a rubber spatula to spoon the batter into the bag.

Rustic Cinnamon Raisin Scones

Scones are at the top of my list when it comes to baked goods—there's something about the slightly sweet, sandy texture that makes me happy. It's utter bliss in every bite. Like all scones, these are best on the day they're made. Freeze any leftovers and use them to make Hodge Podge Bread Pudding (page 191).

makes 6 scones

½ cup raisins

1 cup warm water

2 cups Basic Flour Blend (page 212)

2 teaspoons gluten-free baking powder

1 teaspoon ground cinnamon

½ teaspoon xanthan gum

¼ teaspoon kosher salt

5 tablespoons unsalted butter, chilled and diced

⅓ cup heavy cream

1 large egg, lightly beaten

1 tablespoon agave nectar

egg wash: 1 large egg, lightly beaten with 1 tablespoon water

palm sugar and cinnamon, for sprinkling

Preheat the oven to 375°F. Line a baking sheet with a silicone mat or parchment paper.

Cover the raisins with the warm water and set aside. In a food processor fitted with the steel blade, pulse the flour blend, baking powder, cinnamon, xanthan gum, and salt several times to combine well. Distribute the butter evenly around the food processor bowl, and pulse until the mixture resembles small pebbles. In a small bowl, use a fork to beat together the heavy cream, egg, and agave. Pour the wet ingredients evenly around the dough in the food processor, then pulse until nearly mixed. Add the raisins and pulse to combine.

Turn the dough out onto the prepared baking sheet and form it into a 9 x 3-inch rectangle, about 1½ inches thick. Cut it into 3 (3-inch) squares, then cut each square into 2 triangles. Space the triangles evenly on the baking sheet. Lightly brush the egg wash on top of each scone. Sprinkle the tops with palm sugar and cinnamon.

Bake for 15 to 18 minutes, until the scones are a light golden brown. Let cool on the baking sheet for 5 minutes. If not serving immediately, transfer to a wire rack lined with a paper towel to cool completely.

Make It Dairy-Free: Instead of heavy cream, use full-fat coconut milk or other nondairy heavy cream substitute; use non-hydrogenated shortening instead of butter.

Variation—Blueberry Lemon Scones: Omit the cinnamon. Decrease the heavy cream to ¼ cup and add 1 teaspoon lemon zest and 1 tablespoon lemon juice with the heavy cream. Substitute ¾ cup fresh blueberries for the raisins (there's no need to soak them). Instead of adding the blueberries to the food processor, transfer the dough to a large bowl when it's nearly formed and fold them in.

Light and Fluffy Fruit Pancakes

Who doesn't love pancakes? I've tried many different versions on my quest for the perfect pancake-house pancake, and I've found that thick batters work best. A little fresh fruit adds some nutrition and makes these extra special. Drop a few carob chips in with sliced banana for a good-enough-to-be-dessert meal.

makes 8 to 10 (4-inch) pancakes

1¼ cups Basic Flour Blend (page 212)

2 tablespoons palm sugar

1 tablespoon gluten-free baking powder

¼ teaspoon kosher salt

¼ teaspoon xanthan gum

1 cup low-fat buttermilk

2 large eggs, separated

2 tablespoons unsalted butter, melted and cooled

1 to 2 sliced bananas or 1 cup fresh berries (optional)

Maple Berry Syrup (page 19) (optional)

In a medium bowl, whisk together the flour blend, palm sugar, baking powder, salt, and xanthan gum. Make a well in the middle of the dry ingredients. Add the buttermilk, egg yolks, and melted butter. Use a fork to mix the wet ingredients together, then stir the wet ingredients into the dry ingredients with a spatula. It's OK to leave a few lumps.

In another medium bowl, beat the egg whites to soft peaks. Stir one-fourth of the egg whites directly into the batter, then fold in the rest. Preheat a nonstick skillet over medium heat and lightly mist it with cooking spray. Drop the batter onto the skillet using a spring-release ice cream scoop or a ¼-cup measuring cup. Use the back of the scoop or the bottom of the measuring cup to spread the batter out slightly.

Add the banana or berries to the pancakes by placing the fruit directly into the batter in the pan before you flip the pancakes. Flip the pancakes after about 1 minute, when the edges begin to set and the batter starts to bubble. Cook for 30 seconds longer, or until the bottom is lightly golden brown. Wipe the pan with a clean, dry paper towel between batches. To keep the pancakes warm, place them on a wire cooling rack set on a baking sheet in a 200°F oven. This keeps the pancakes from getting soggy by sitting directly on a baking sheet. Serve with syrup and fruit, if using.

Quick Tip: Using an immersion blender with a whisk attachment makes quick work of whipping the egg whites.

Easy Homemade Belgian Waffles

Waffle night is a big deal at our house. I know, it sounds silly, but having waffles for dinner is lots of fun. I'm not sure what I enjoy more—making them or eating them, especially the way the big crevices in Belgian waffles hold the syrup or fruit sauce. Top these with Poppy Seed Fruit Salad (page 81), Greek yogurt and fresh berries, or a big scoop of Vanilla Bean Ice Cream (page 197) and you have dessert.

makes 4 to 5 (6-inch) waffles

1½ cups Basic Flour Blend (page 212)

2 tablespoons palm sugar

2 teaspoons gluten-free baking powder

¼ teaspoon kosher salt

1¼ cups low-fat milk

2 large eggs, separated

3 tablespoons unsalted butter, melted and cooled

1 teaspoon vanilla extract

Maple Berry Syrup (page 19) (optional)

Preheat a waffle iron on medium-high heat.

In a large bowl, whisk together the flour blend, palm sugar, baking powder, and salt. In a medium bowl, whisk together the milk, egg yolks, melted butter, and vanilla. Add the wet ingredients to the dry ingredients and whisk until smooth.

In another medium bowl, whisk the egg whites to soft peaks. Stir one-fourth of the egg whites directly into the batter, then fold in the remaining whites.

Lightly mist the waffle iron with cooking spray. Add the appropriate amount of batter for your waffle iron and cook until golden brown and crispy. To keep the waffles warm, place them on a wire cooling rack set on a large baking sheet in a 200°F oven. This keeps the waffles from getting soggy by sitting directly on a baking sheet. Serve with syrup, if using.

Make It Dairy-Free: Use melted non-hydrogenated shortening instead of melted butter.

Quick Tip: All waffle irons cook a little differently. If your waffle iron has a variable-heat setting, increase or decrease the heat as needed to achieve a waffle with a crispy outside. I usually decrease the heat halfway through cooking because my waffle iron tends to burn the last two waffles.

Banana Walnut Belgian Waffles

Though I use bananas and walnuts here, you could just as easily use blueberries, sliced strawberries, diced pears, dried fruit, or your favorite nuts.

makes 4 to 5 (6-inch) Belgian waffles

1½ cups Basic Flour Blend (page 212)

2 tablespoons palm sugar

2 teaspoons gluten-free baking powder

1 teaspoon ground cinnamon

½ teaspoon ground ginger

¼ teaspoon kosher salt

1¼ cups low-fat milk

2 large eggs, separated

3 tablespoons unsalted butter, melted and cooled

1 teaspoon vanilla extract

5 to 6 tablespoons coarsely chopped toasted walnuts

½ large firm, ripe banana, diced

Maple Berry Syrup (page 19) (optional)

Preheat a waffle iron to medium-high heat.

In a large bowl, whisk together the flour blend, palm sugar, baking powder, cinnamon, ginger, and salt. In a medium bowl, whisk together the milk, egg yolks, melted butter, and vanilla. Add the wet ingredients to the dry ingredients and whisk until smooth.

In another medium bowl, whisk the egg whites to soft peaks. Stir one-fourth of the egg whites directly into the batter, then fold in remaining whites.

Lightly mist the waffle iron with cooking spray. Sprinkle about 1 tablespoon of chopped walnuts on the bottom of the waffle iron. Add the appropriate amount of batter for your waffle iron (you'll need a little less than usual because you're adding fruit and nuts), then top the batter with 1 generous tablespoon of diced banana. Cook until golden brown and crispy. To keep the waffles warm, place them on a wire cooling rack set on a large baking sheet in a 200°F oven. This keeps the waffles from getting soggy by sitting directly on a baking sheet. Serve with syrup, if using.

Make It Dairy-Free: Use melted non-hydrogenated shortening instead of melted butter.

Quick Tip: Premeasure the dry ingredients and place them in labeled sealable plastic bags so you'll have waffle mix ready to go anytime.

Maple Berry Syrup

With a hint of maple syrup, this pancake and waffle topping is healthy and still delicious. The sweetness of this syrup relies on the sweetness of the fruit—add more or less maple syrup to suit your taste. Pureeing the berries with their seeds in a high-powered blender rather than a mini food chopper or food processor will give the syrup an earthy taste, so I don't recommend it. **vegan**

makes about 1 cup

1 cup frozen mixed berries, thawed

1 large ripe banana

¼ cup unsweetened applesauce

1 to 2 tablespoons grade-B maple syrup

pinch of cinnamon

pinch of salt

Puree the berries in a mini food chopper or a food processor fitted with the steel blade. Push the puree through a fine-mesh strainer to remove the seeds. Return the puree to the food chopper or food processor, add the banana, and puree until smooth. Add the applesauce, 1 tablespoon maple syrup, cinnamon, and salt. Mix until smooth. Taste and add more maple syrup if desired.

Transfer the syrup to a microwave-safe bowl or serving dish and heat until warm. Serve immediately.

Variation—Pineapple Syrup Variation: Use 1 cup unsweetened canned pineapple instead of the berries. Puree the pineapple and banana together in a food processor or blender. Add 1 tablespoon maple syrup, and the cinnamon and salt, and pulse to combine. Taste and add more maple syrup as needed. Proceed as with Maple Berry Syrup.

Variation—Other Healthier Pancake and Waffle Toppings: Try your pancakes and waffles with warm applesauce with cinnamon and nutmeg; warm yogurt mixed with your favorite all-fruit preserves; or Raw Cashew Cream (page 176) pureed with a banana, ripe pear, or berries.

Quick Tip: Make this sauce several days ahead of time and store it in the refrigerator.

Buckwheat Crepes

I tried my first buckwheat crepe when my husband and I were traveling in Montreal. I was instantly hooked. We spent the rest of our time there hunting down the best crepes in the city. Crepes can be filled with almost anything, from meat and veggies to fruit and ice cream. I've included one of our favorite combinations, Summer Scrambled Egg Crepes (page 21).

makes 10 to 12 (10-inch) crepes

1½ cups low-fat milk

½ teaspoon kosher salt

2 large eggs

1 cup buckwheat flour

2 tablespoons unsalted butter, melted, plus extra for cooking

Blend the milk, salt, and eggs in a blender at medium speed for 15 to 20 seconds, until combined. Add the buckwheat flour and the measured melted butter. Mix on high for 1 minute. Refrigerate the batter for 1 hour before cooking the crepes.

Heat a 10-inch crepe pan or a 10-inch nonstick skillet over medium heat. The pan should be hot enough to make the batter lightly sizzle but not so hot that it can't spread. Often the first crepe or two is used as a way to gauge the heat. Increase or decrease the heat as needed.

Brush the pan with a thin layer of the extra melted butter. Remove the pan from the heat and hold it downward at a 45-degree angle. Pour ¼ cup of batter into the pan and quickly rotate the pan to evenly distribute the batter. Place the pan back on the heat and cook for about 1 minute, until the bottom of the crepe starts to get light golden brown in places. Flip with a wide spatula and cook for about 1 minute more, until light golden brown.

Wipe the pan with a clean paper towel before cooking the next crepe and add more butter to the pan before adding more batter. Stack the cooked crepes between sheets of waxed paper. If desired, reheat the crepes in the microwave for 10 seconds or wrap in foil and warm in the oven. To freeze the crepes, separate them with waxed paper and wrap in plastic.

Quick Tip: If you're new to making crepes, opt for a smaller pan until you're used to cooking and flipping them. If you really love making crepes, pick up special crepe tools at your local kitchen specialty store. They're inexpensive and make crepe making so much easier.

Summer Scrambled Egg Crepes

I made these one night when trying to use up leftovers. I had some basil-marinated tomatoes, and they added the perfect punch of flavor to the meal. If you don't want to make them, use freshly sliced tomatoes and add pesto or freshly chopped basil.

makes 4 crepes

4 large eggs or 2 eggs and ½ cup egg whites

1 tablespoon water

½ teaspoon kosher salt

freshly ground black pepper

1 tablespoon unsalted butter, divided

4 (10-inch) Buckwheat Crepes (page 20)

½ cup shredded mozzarella

¼ recipe Balsamic Tomatoes (page 69)

½ cup baby spinach

Heat a medium nonstick skillet over medium-low heat. Break the eggs into a medium bowl. Add the water and salt, and pepper to taste. Whisk until frothy. Melt ½ tablespoon butter in the pan. Add the eggs to the pan and cook slowly, stirring every 30 seconds or so. Remove from the heat when done and stir in the remaining ½ tablespoon butter.

Meanwhile, heat a nonstick skillet large enough to lay 1 crepe flat. Reheat each crepe quickly, then divide the scrambled eggs among the 4 crepes, covering only one-fourth of each crepe. Add 2 tablespoons cheese, 2 half slices of tomato, and one-fourth of the spinach on top of the eggs. Fold each crepe in half and then in fourths. Flip the crepes over and place them back into the pan to heat through and melt the cheese. Once heated through, serve immediately.

Quick Tip: Make a batch of crepes ahead of time and freeze them, layered with parchment paper or waxed paper. You'll have them on hand to pull out on busy nights.

Protein-Packed Breakfast Crepes

One of my blog readers shared a protein-rich breakfast pancake with me, and I started playing around with it the next day. This is my version, made with stevia and filled with a jam-sweetened ricotta. It's perfect for a healthier Sunday morning breakfast.

makes 2 (10-inch) crepes, serves 1

1 large egg

2 large egg whites

2 tablespoons water

1 tablespoon Basic Flour Blend (page 212)

15 drops of vanilla liquid stevia

pinch of salt

2 tablespoons part-skim ricotta cheese

1 tablespoon all-fruit preserves

Blend the egg, egg whites, water, flour blend, stevia, and salt in a blender on high speed for 30 seconds until the batter is thoroughly combined. It will be watery; that's how you want it. In a small bowl, mix together the ricotta and all-fruit preserves.

Heat a 10-inch nonstick pan over medium-low heat. While the pan is heating, combine the ricotta cheese and preserves in a microwave-safe bowl. Warm in the microwave for 20 seconds. Stir and set aside.

Coat the pan with cooking spray. The pan should be hot enough to make the batter lightly sizzle but not so hot that it can't spread. Remove the pan from the heat and hold it downward at a 45-degree angle. Pour ¼ cup of batter into the pan and quickly rotate the pan to evenly distribute the batter. Place the pan back on the heat and cook for about 1 minute, until the bottom of the crepe starts to get light golden brown in places. Flip with a wide spatula and cook for about 1 minute more, until light golden brown. Transfer to a plate. Wipe the pan with a clean paper towel before cooking the second crepe and coat the pan with cooking spray again if necessary. Repeat with the remaining batter.

Spread a thin layer of the ricotta mixture on each crepe. Fold the crepes in half, then in fourths to create quarter circles. Serve while still hot with a bowl of fresh fruit, if desired.

Quick Tip: Almost any flour will work with this recipe. Instead of my Basic Flour Blend, I've also used all quinoa flour or all garbanzo–fava bean flour. The flour just helps thicken the batter slightly. Keep in mind that the color of the flour will affect the color of the batter.

Apple Carrot Breakfast Cake

I found this recipe in the book that came with my high-powered blender and decided to make it sugar- and gluten-free. It's super moist and stays that way for days. Students in my cooking classes always love this cake, too. It's one of those dishes a mom can feel good about feeding her kids for breakfast. **dairy-free**

serves 6 to 9

2 cups sorghum flour

½ cup palm sugar

2 teaspoons baking soda

2 teaspoons ground cinnamon

½ teaspoon freshly grated nutmeg

½ teaspoon kosher salt

½ teaspoon xanthan gum

¾ cup egg white substitute or 3 large eggs

1 tablespoon vanilla extract

2 apples, unpeeled, cut in wedges

1 cup peeled and chopped carrots (about 3 medium carrots)

1 recipe Vanilla Whipped Cream (page 182) or 1 recipe Whipped Cream Cheese Frosting (page 172) or yogurt

Preheat the oven to 350°F. Prepare an 8 × 8-inch baking pan with cooking spray.

In a large bowl, whisk together the sorghum flour, palm sugar, baking soda, cinnamon, nutmeg, salt, and xanthan gum until evenly combined.

Combine the egg whites or eggs, vanilla, apples, and carrots in a high-powered blender or food processor. If using a high-powered blender, start on low speed and quickly increase to high until thoroughly mixed. If using a food processor, pulse many times until combined and then process until smooth. Scrape down the bowl as needed. The batter will be thick.

Add the wet ingredients to the dry ingredients and fold them in with a rubber spatula until thoroughly combined. Pour the batter into the prepared pan and bake for 25 to 30 minutes, until a toothpick inserted into the center comes out clean. Let cool completely in the pan. Top with freshly whipped cream, cream cheese frosting, or yogurt.

Quick Tip: Don't worry about how your chopped apples and carrots look—they'll get shredded in the blender. This works best in a high-powered blender because it purees the produce, but I've had many people share with me that they make this in their food processor, too.

Apple Flax Cake

My mom was vigilant about how she fed her family, as was my Grandma Ruth. I guess that's where I get it from. When our family went camping, she never took the easy route of feeding us donuts and store-bought pastries for breakfast. Instead, she'd make a breakfast cake similar to this one and serve it with scrambled eggs and fresh fruit. It's one of my favorites even today.

serves 16 to 24

¾ cup unsweetened applesauce, at room temperature

¾ cup low-fat milk

¼ cup flaxseed meal

½ cup unsalted butter, at room temperature

¾ cup palm sugar

2 cups Basic Flour Blend (page 212)

2 teaspoons gluten-free baking powder

1 teaspoon baking soda

1 teaspoon ground cinnamon

1 teaspoon xanthan gum

½ teaspoon kosher salt

½ teaspoon freshly grated nutmeg

2 large eggs

3 cups peeled diced apples (about 2½ to 3 medium apples)

1 recipe Whipped Cream Cheese Frosting (page 172)

Preheat the oven to 350°F. Prepare a 9 x 13-inch cake pan with cooking spray.

In a medium bowl, combine the applesauce, milk, and flaxseed meal. Set aside.

Place the butter in the bowl of a stand mixer fitted with the paddle attachment and beat on medium speed for about 5 minutes, until light and fluffy. Add one-third of the palm sugar at a time, letting each part mix in before adding more. Let the mixer run for about 5 minutes so the butter and sugar cream while you prepare the other ingredients.

In a medium bowl, whisk together the flour blend, baking powder, baking soda, cinnamon, xanthan gum, salt, and nutmeg. Set aside. When the butter and sugar have creamed together, add one egg at a time to the mixture. Let the egg fully incorporate and scrape down the bowl between additions. Slowly add the applesauce and flaxseed mixture on medium speed, letting it incorporate before adding more.

Stir in the dry ingredients all at once, stopping the mixer just before the flour is fully incorporated. Fold in the apples, making sure to scrape down the sides and bottom of the bowl. The batter will be thick. Turn the batter into the prepared pan, using a rubber spatula to spread it evenly. Bake for 25 to 30 minutes, until a toothpick inserted into the center comes out clean.

Let cool completely in the pan. When slicing, use a sharp serrated knife to get a clean cut.

Quick Tip: Save yourself some time and make this cake the night before. Cover and refrigerate it overnight—it's even better the second day. Make the frosting the night before and frost just before serving.

Blueberry Yogurt Crumb Cake

This dense, moist cake is great with a cup of coffee on a lazy Sunday morning. It's the kind of coffee cake that entices you to use the back of your fork to mash together every last crumb. At least that's what I do.

serves 9 to 12

Crumb topping:

½ cup Basic Flour Blend (page 212)

½ cup palm sugar

½ teaspoon ground cinnamon

pinch of salt

3 tablespoons unsalted butter, melted

Cake:

2 cups Basic Flour Blend (page 212)

2 teaspoons gluten-free baking powder

1 teaspoon xanthan gum

½ teaspoon ground cinnamon

½ teaspoon kosher salt

½ cup plain low-fat yogurt

½ cup low-fat milk

½ cup agave nectar

1 large egg, at room temperature

2 tablespoons unsalted butter, melted

1 teaspoon grated lemon zest

1 tablespoon freshly squeezed lemon juice

½ teaspoon vanilla extract

¾ cup frozen blueberries, not thawed

Preheat the oven to 350°F. Prepare an 8 x 8-inch cake pan with cooking spray.

To make the crumb topping, in a medium bowl, whisk the flour blend, palm sugar, cinnamon, and salt in a bowl until uniformly combined. Drizzle in the melted butter and quickly work the butter into the flour mix with your fingers until it resembles small pebbles. Set aside.

To make the cake, in a large bowl, whisk together the flour blend, baking powder, xanthan gum, cinnamon, and salt. Put the yogurt in a medium bowl. Whisk the milk into the yogurt a little at a time until smoothly combined. Whisk in the agave, egg, butter, lemon zest, lemon juice, and vanilla extract.

Put the frozen blueberries in a bowl, dust them with a pinch or two of the flour blend, and toss to combine. Add the wet ingredients to the dry ingredients, stirring until combined. Fold in the blueberries. Turn the batter into the prepared pan and sprinkle it with the crumb topping, pressing the crumbs into the batter. Bake for 30 to 35 minutes, until the middle of the cake springs back when lightly pressed and a toothpick inserted into the center comes out clean. Let cool in the pan.

Quick Tip: Use light sour cream if you don't have any yogurt on hand. This cake can be made one day in advance.

Seven Grain Breakfast Cereal

When one of my dogs gets an upset stomach, I soft-cook white rice for them. It gets really mushy and creamy, just like a good breakfast cereal. I came across a recipe in Not Your Mother's Slow Cooker Cookbook, *by Beth Hensperger and Julie Kaufmann that used the same idea. Here's my version, laced with yummy gluten-free grains.* **vegan, slow cooker recipe**

serves 6 to 8

½ cup short-grain brown rice

½ cup quinoa, rinsed

½ cup wild rice

½ cup millet

½ cup buckwheat groats

¼ cup stone-ground cornmeal

¼ cup teff

2 tablespoons flaxseed meal

1 teaspoon kosher salt

10 cups water

warm milk, yogurt, and toasted nuts or cinnamon and fresh berries

Stir the brown rice, quinoa, wild rice, millet, buckwheat groats, cornmeal, teff, flaxseed meal, and salt together in a large (5- to 6-quart) slow cooker. Pour the water over the grains and cook on low for 5 to 6 hours, until the water is absorbed and the grains are very tender. Serve topped with warm milk, yogurt, and toasted nuts, or sprinkled with cinnamon and fresh berries.

Quick Tip: Try other gluten-free grains in this cereal, like amaranth, montina, and other varieties of rice.

Cream of Buckwheat

You can buy cream of buckwheat at the store, but it's quite simple to make at home and much more frugal. Look for raw buckwheat groats, not kasha, which has been toasted. I like to eat this cereal sweetened with a little stevia and top it with berries and yogurt.

serves 4 to 5

½ cup raw buckwheat groats

2½ cups water

1 teaspoon salt

Whirl the buckwheat groats in a clean coffee grinder until they reach a mealy consistency. Add the ground buckwheat to a heavy-bottomed 4-quart saucepan. Whisk in the water and salt. Cover, bring to a boil over medium heat, then reduce to a simmer. Continue to cook covered for 8 to 10 minutes, until the cereal is creamy and cooked through, stirring frequently. Serve hot with toppings of your choice.

Quick Tip: Grind several batches of raw buckwheat groats at once and store in your pantry.

Griddled Cream of Buckwheat Triangles

I had some leftover cream of buckwheat and noticed that it set up in the refrigerator just like polenta. I love grilled polenta and had to find out if cream of buckwheat would be just as good. It is, complete with its delicious grainy flavor. Serve these triangles with scrambled eggs and Slow Cooker Ketchup (page 54).

makes 12 buckwheat triangles, serves 6

1 recipe Cream of Buckwheat (page 27)

buckwheat flour, for dusting

kosher salt and freshly ground black pepper

1 tablespoon unsalted butter

1 tablespoon olive oil

Transfer the cooked cream of buckwheat into an 8 x 8-inch pan. Use a rubber spatula or offset spatula to smooth the top, and give the pan a few good taps on the table to help flatten it. Cover and refrigerate overnight. The cereal will firm up just like polenta does.

The next day, run an offset spatula around the edge of the pan. Cut the buckwheat into 6 equal rectangles. Flip the pan upside down onto a cutting board and smack the bottom until the cold cereal squares fall out. Dust the squares lightly with buckwheat flour, salt, and pepper. Flip the squares and dust and season the other sides. Cut each square in half diagonally so you have 12 triangles.

Heat half of the butter and oil over medium-high heat in a large nonstick sauté pan. Cook half the buckwheat triangles for 3 minutes on each side, until crispy. Transfer to a plate and cover to keep warm. Add the remaining butter and oil to the pan and cook the remaining triangles. Serve warm.

Oat Bran Cereal with Fruit

I'm the only person who regularly eats breakfast at my house, and I need something substantial and nutritious. I make this quick cereal several mornings a week. It contains a good amount of fiber, which many people on a gluten-free diet lack. See Product Resources (page 227) for gluten-free oat bran sources.

serves 1

1/3 cup gluten-free oat bran

1/2 cup water, or more if a thinner consistency is desired

1/2 cup low-fat cottage cheese or plain low-fat yogurt

1/8 teaspoon powdered stevia, or as needed

pinch of salt

1/4 cup chopped fruit or berries

1 tablespoon chopped toasted nuts

cinnamon and/or freshly ground nutmeg

In a medium microwave-safe bowl, cover the oat bran with the water and microwave on high for 1 minute. Stir in the cottage cheese or yogurt, stevia, and salt. Microwave for 30 seconds to 1 minute longer, until heated through. Top with fresh berries and toasted nuts. Sprinkle with cinnamon and/or nutmeg to taste.

Starters & Snacks

Not Just Any Old Hummus

I've always loved hummus, but finding a recipe my husband would eat was difficult. This one he'll eat without hesitation. **vegetarian, egg-free**

makes about 2 cups

1 (15-ounce) can chickpeas (garbanzo beans), drained

¼ cup tahini

¼ cup plain low-fat yogurt

3 tablespoons freshly squeezed lemon juice

1 medium garlic clove, grated on a fine rasp grater or minced

¾ teaspoon kosher salt

½ teaspoon ground cumin

pinch of cayenne pepper

¼ cup water

veggie sticks

Oven-Baked Cumin Lime Tortilla Chips (page 35)

Place the chickpeas, tahini, yogurt, lemon juice, garlic, salt, cumin, and cayenne in the bowl of a food processor fitted with the steel blade. Pulse several times to combine. Then, with the food processor running, add the water through the feed tube and process about 45 seconds, until smooth, stopping to scrape down the bowl as needed. Taste and adjust the seasoning as needed.

This dish is best when refrigerated for several hours before serving, but you can eat it right away (I often do). Serve with veggie sticks or oven-baked tortilla chips.

Variation—Cilantro Lime Hummus: Replace the lemon juice with lime juice. Add ¼ cup cilantro leaves and ½ to 1 jalapeño, seeded and chopped (depending on the heat of the pepper).

Quick Tip: Keep a can of chickpeas in the refrigerator so you can whip up a batch of chilled hummus anytime.

Herbed White Bean Dip

Everyone enjoys the fresh flavors in this healthier, simple-to-prepare dip. **vegan**

makes about 1 cup

1 (15.5-ounce) can cannellini beans, drained, liquid reserved

1 garlic clove, grated on a fine rasp grater or minced

1 tablespoon freshly squeezed lemon juice

½ teaspoon minced fresh thyme leaves

2 fresh sage leaves, minced (about ¼ teaspoon)

¼ teaspoon ground white pepper, or as needed

kosher salt

gluten-free tortilla chips or veggie sticks

Place the beans, garlic, lemon juice, thyme, and sage into the bowl of a food processor fitted with the steel blade. Pulse several times to combine, then process until smooth. Check the consistency of the dip and, if necessary, add 1 to 2 tablespoons of the reserved bean liquid to thin it out. Season to taste with white pepper and salt. Serve with tortilla chips or veggie sticks.

Quick Tip: Dried herbs will work if you don't have fresh; use half as much as indicated in the recipe.

Seven Layer Avocado Dip

This recipe is from my mom—she's been making it since I was a little girl. I could never wait until she served it, so I would take a chip and run it around the edge of the serving dish hoping she wouldn't notice, though she always did. My mom's recipe uses taco sauce, but most taco sauces contain sugar. I use picante sauce instead—it's just as delicious. **vegetarian, egg-free**

makes 8 to 10 servings

3 ripe avocados

1½ cups light sour cream

1 (16-ounce) jar picante sauce

3 ounces Monterey Jack cheese, shredded

3 ounces sharp cheddar cheese, shredded

2 Roma tomatoes, seeded and diced

1 to 2 green onions, chopped

Peel, seed, and roughly mash the avocados. Spread on the bottom of a 7 x 11-inch glass or stoneware dish. Spread the sour cream in an even layer across the avocado. Next, spread the picante sauce across the sour cream. Refrigerate overnight. Right before serving, top with the Monterey Jack, cheddar, tomatoes, and green onions.

Quick Tip: Avocados are rarely ripe when you buy them at the grocery store. Buy firm avocados a few days before you'll use them, put them in a paper bag, and fold it closed. They'll be ripe in 3 or 4 days.

Dilled Yogurt Dip

Serve this simple, healthy dip with veggies. It's one of my childhood favorites that's gotten a makeover. If you don't have time to strain the yogurt or don't care to, use 1 cup Greek yogurt instead. It's incredibly thick, rich, and creamy, so it doesn't need to be drained. **vegetarian, egg-free**

makes about 1 cup

2 cups plain low-fat yogurt

1 teaspoon dried parsley

1 teaspoon dried dill

½ teaspoon salt

¼ teaspoon ground coriander

In a medium bowl, stir together the yogurt, parsley, dill, salt, and coriander. Line a fine-mesh strainer with a double layer of paper towels. Transfer the yogurt mixture into the lined strainer, then set the strainer in a large bowl. The strainer should not touch the bottom of the bowl. Cover and let the yogurt drain in the refrigerator for 6 hours or overnight. The yogurt will get really thick. Reserve the whey (the liquid that was drained from the yogurt). Transfer the dip to a small bowl; it will easily fall away from the paper towel. Stir. If the dip is too thick, add in spoonfuls of the whey until it reaches the desired consistency. Taste and adjust the seasoning as needed.

Quick Tip: Make this a day or two ahead of time—the flavor improves as it sits.

Oven-Baked Cumin Lime Tortilla Chips

I rarely use an entire package of tortillas before they become stale. It's against my nature to let anything go to waste, so I started making chips with the leftovers. There's nothing like hot, salty chips right out of the oven, and I especially love the lime and cumin seasoning in this recipe. **vegan**

makes 48 chips

1 tablespoon freshly squeezed lime juice

1 tablespoon neutral-flavored oil, such as canola or grapeseed

1 teaspoon ground cumin

8 (6-inch) corn tortillas

table salt or finely ground sea salt

salsa, Seven Layer Avocado Dip (page 33), Not Just Any Old Hummus (page 31), Herbed White Bean Dip (page 32)

Preheat the oven to 350°F. Line 2 baking sheets with silicone mats or parchment paper.

Whisk together the lime juice, oil, and cumin. Set aside. Cut the tortillas in half, then cut each half into thirds. Put the tortilla wedges in a medium bowl and drizzle them with the lime and oil mixture. Sprinkle with the salt and toss to coat. Working quickly so the tortillas don't get soggy, place the wedges in neat rows on the prepared baking sheets.

Bake for 20 to 25 minutes, flipping the chips after 10 to 12 minutes. The chips are done when they're no longer chewy. These are fabulous hot out of the oven with your choice of one or more dips. Store in a brown paper bag.

Quick Tip: Whenever you have corn tortillas left over from another dish, freeze them until you have enough to make a big batch of chips at once.

Blueberry Fruit Dip

When I was a kid, my friend's mom used to make a strawberry-cinnamon fruit dip—I loved it. My mom refused to make it for us because it was loaded with sugar and fat. At the time I didn't understand why, but today I do. This healthier fruit dip is one any mom would feel good about serving her kids, and it's perfect for spreading on toast, muffins, and quick breads. **vegetarian, egg-free**

makes about 1 cup

½ teaspoon unflavored gelatin

2 tablespoons water

½ cup low-fat cottage cheese

½ cup nonfat Greek yogurt

3 tablespoons blueberry all-fruit preserves, or your favorite flavor

¼ teaspoon ground cinnamon

¼ to ½ teaspoon powdered stevia

Combine the gelatin and water in a small microwave-safe bowl. Microwave for 15 to 20 seconds to dissolve. Stir and repeat if the gelatin has not dissolved. Set aside to cool.

Put the cottage cheese and yogurt in a blender or food processor. Process until completely smooth, scraping down the sides of the bowl as needed. Add the blueberry preserves, cinnamon, and ¼ teaspoon powdered stevia and process until combined. Taste and add more stevia, if desired. With the food processor or blender running, add the melted gelatin through the feed tube and blend until completely combined, scraping all of the gelatin into the mixture. Transfer to a small bowl, cover, and chill for several hours or overnight. Stir before serving.

Quick Tip: I use Greek yogurt in this recipe because it's thick. Using regular yogurt will also work; the dip will just be a little thinner.

Perfect Hard-Boiled Eggs

My Grandma Ruth makes the most amazing deviled eggs, and her secret lies in how she cooks the eggs. She'll tell you that it's about making sure the whites don't get rubbery. When working in professional kitchens, I learned to throw in an extra test egg. I save the test egg for a salad or eat it as a snack with a piece of fruit. **vegetarian, dairy-free**

makes 6 or more eggs

6 large eggs, plus 1 or 2 extra for testing

cold water to cover

Place the eggs in a saucepan large enough to accommodate them all. Cover with cold water and bring to a boil over medium-high heat. Once the water comes to a full boil, remove from the heat, cover the pot, and set a timer for 12 minutes. Prepare an ice bath for the eggs and set aside.

When the timer goes off, check an egg to see if it's cooked by cracking it open. It should be fully cooked. If it's not, leave all the eggs in the water for 1 minute longer. Place the eggs in the prepared ice bath to stop the cooking process and allow them to cool.

Quick Tip: Don't overcrowd your pan. This method is flexible, so you can use more or fewer eggs depending on your needs.

Crispy Prosciutto Deviled Eggs

This is my appetizer version of one of my husband's favorite meals—eggs and bacon.

makes 12 deviled eggs

6 Perfect Hard-Boiled Eggs (page 37), cooled and peeled

¼ cup mayonnaise

2 tablespoons plain low-fat yogurt

2 teaspoons Dijon mustard

⅛ teaspoon salt

⅛ teaspoon white pepper

3 slices prosciutto

1 tablespoon chopped fresh chives

Slice the eggs in half and place the yolks in a medium bowl. Set the whites aside. Add the mayonnaise, yogurt, mustard, salt, and white pepper. Beat with a handheld mixer or an immersion blender fitted with a whisk attachment until light and fluffy. Taste and adjust the seasoning as necessary. Spoon the filling into a pastry bag or sealable plastic bag, snip off the end, and fill the center of each egg white with the egg yolk mixture. Cover and refrigerate the filled eggs for up to 1 day.

Line a baking sheet with aluminum foil. Lay the prosciutto slices on the baking sheet and broil, turning if necessary, for 1 to 2 minutes, until crispy. Cooking time depends on how thickly your prosciutto has been cut. Let cool. Chop the prosciutto into tiny pieces. Just before serving, sprinkle the deviled eggs with prosciutto and chives.

Quick Tip: The prosciutto can be prepared and crumbed up to a day ahead of time. If you can't find prosciutto, use bacon instead.

Buckwheat Blini

Traditionally, blini (tiny savory pancakes) are topped with smoked salmon and caviar. You can also try them topped with salmon salad and fresh dill, or with white bean dip and roasted turkey. **vegetarian**

makes about 18

1 cup buckwheat flour

½ teaspoon gluten-free baking powder

½ teaspoon kosher salt

¾ cup low-fat milk

1 large egg

1 tablespoon unsalted butter, melted

Heat a large nonstick skillet over medium heat. In a medium bowl, whisk together the flour, baking powder, and salt. In another medium bowl, whisk together the milk, egg, and melted butter. Pour the wet ingredients into the dry ingredients and mix until combined.

Spray the skillet lightly with cooking spray. Drop the batter by tablespoons onto the skillet, spacing the blini about 1 inch apart in the pan so you have enough room to easily flip them. Cook the blini for 45 seconds to 1 minute, until bubbles start to form on the surface, then flip them. Cook for 30 seconds longer on the second side, or until the batter is set and the blini are golden brown on the bottom. Repeat until all the blini are cooked. Top as desired.

Make It Dairy-Free: Use your favorite nondairy milk and canola or grapeseed oil instead of butter.

Mushroom Quesadillas

I often make this appetizer into a meal because the mushrooms take on a hearty, meaty quality. If you can find canned petite diced tomatoes, their smaller size works best. ***vegetarian, egg-free***

makes 4 to 6

1 tablespoon canola oil

½ large white onion, diced

3 garlic cloves, shredded on a fine rasp grater or minced

½ jalapeño, seeded and diced

½ red bell pepper, diced

4 to 5 cups cremini mushrooms, sliced (about 16 to 20 ounces)

1 cup drained canned petite diced tomatoes

½ cup chopped cilantro leaves

1 teaspoon ground cumin

kosher salt and freshly ground black pepper

8 to 12 (6-inch) corn tortillas or 4 to 6 (8-inch) corn tortillas

4 ounces queso fresco or Monterey Jack cheese, shredded

salsa (optional)

sour cream (optional)

Heat the oil in a large nonstick sauté pan over medium heat. Add the onion and cook for about 5 minutes, until translucent. Add the garlic, jalapeño, and red bell pepper, cooking for several more minutes until slightly tender. Add the mushrooms and cook until they start to soften. Add the tomatoes, cilantro, and cumin. Cook until heated through. Taste and adjust the seasoning with salt and pepper as needed.

Heat a second large nonstick sauté pan over medium-high heat. Add as many tortillas to the pan as you can fit. If using 6-inch tortillas, spread the cooked mushroom mixture over the entire surface of half the tortillas. Sprinkle with cheese, then top each one with a second tortilla. Flip the quesadillas when the bottom tortilla is slightly browned. If using 8-inch tortillas, spread one-half of each tortilla with the mushroom mixture and top with cheese. Fold over and flip when the bottom half has browned.

Let the quesadillas stand for a few minutes before cutting. Serve with salsa and sour cream, if desired.

Quick Tip: Keep the quesadillas warm in a 200°F oven until ready to serve.

Cocoa-Roasted Nuts

Using powdered palm sugar results in a slightly sweet, crunchy, candylike coating that's utterly addictive. **vegetarian, dairy-free**

makes 1 cup

1 egg white

3 tablespoons Powdered Palm Sugar (page 185)

2 tablespoons cocoa powder, plus extra for sprinkling, preferably Dutch-processed

½ teaspoon powdered stevia

½ teaspoon kosher salt

¼ teaspoon vanilla extract

pinch of decaf instant coffee granules

1 cup raw almonds

Preheat the oven to 275°F. Line a large baking sheet with a silicone mat or parchment paper.

In a medium bowl, whisk the egg white almost to soft peaks. Sift in the powdered palm sugar, 2 tablespoons cocoa powder, and the stevia. Add the salt, vanilla, and instant coffee. Whisk until combined. Stir in the almonds and coat thoroughly. Use a fork to transfer the almonds to the prepared baking sheet, shaking off excess egg and cocoa coating. Don't let the almonds touch each other.

Bake for 20 minutes, then rotate the tray 180 degrees. Bake 20 to 25 minutes longer, until the coating is set and the almonds are toasted. Sprinkle the almonds generously with the extra cocoa powder immediately after removing from the oven, and toss to cover thoroughly. Let the almonds cool completely. Store in an airtight container.

Quick Tip: Instead of getting out your mixer, you can quickly whip one egg white to nearly soft peaks using a whisk.

Cinnamon Vanilla Granola

The crunchy, sweet-tartness of this granola is addictive. You'll love each bite and have a hard time pulling yourself away. **dairy-free, egg-free**

makes about 8½ cups

4 cups gluten-free rolled oats

1 cup sliced raw almonds

¾ cup raw pepitas

¾ cup raw sunflower seeds

½ cup flaxseed meal

1 teaspoon ground cinnamon

¾ teaspoon kosher salt

¼ cup canola oil

¼ cup plus 2 tablespoons palm sugar, divided

¼ cup unsweetened applesauce, divided

¼ cup plus 2 tablespoons honey, divided

1 tablespoon vanilla extract

¾ cup dried cranberries

¾ cup raisins

Preheat the oven to 300°F. Line a large baking sheet with parchment paper or a silicone mat.

In a large bowl, mix together the oats, almonds, pepitas, sunflower seeds, flaxseed meal, cinnamon, and salt.

In a microwave-safe bowl, combine the oil, ¼ cup palm sugar, and 2 tablespoons applesauce. Microwave for 20 to 30 seconds and stir to dissolve the palm sugar, then stir in ¼ cup honey and the vanilla. Pour the wet ingredients onto the dry ingredients and mix until the oats and nuts are coated. Make sure to scrape every last drop of the wet ingredients into the dry. Combine until evenly coated. Spread evenly onto the prepared baking sheet.

Bake for 30 minutes. While the granola is baking, mix together the remaining 2 tablespoons each of palm sugar, applesauce, and honey in a small bowl. Set aside. After 30 minutes, remove the granola from the oven and drizzle the remaining wet ingredients on top. Stir well to evenly distribute. Use a rubber spatula to press the granola down firmly into the baking pan. Bake for 30 to 35 minutes longer, until the granola is lightly golden brown. Remove from the oven and let cool completely. Break into bite-size pieces and mix in the cranberries and raisins. Store in an airtight container.

Quick Tip: Switch out the nuts, seeds, and dried fruit to suit your tastes.

Chewy Granola Bars

When I make this recipe, I double it. Then I wrap the leftovers and pop them in the freezer. That way I always have a snack that will travel and something tasty and healthy to pack in lunches. **vegetarian, dairy-free**

makes 12 (2 x 3-inch) bars

2 cups gluten-free rolled oats

2 tablespoons flaxseed meal plus enough teff flour to make ½ cup total

1 cup walnuts, chopped to desired size

½ cup dried black Mission figs, stemmed and chopped

½ cup golden raisins

½ teaspoon ground cinnamon

¼ teaspoon ground ginger

⅓ cup agave nectar

2 large eggs

1 to 2 tablespoons water

Preheat the oven to 350°F. Lightly coat a 9 × 13-inch baking pan with cooking spray.

Mix the oats, flaxseed meal and teff mixture, walnuts, figs, raisins, cinnamon, and ginger in a large bowl.

In a small bowl, whisk together the agave and eggs. Pour the wet ingredients into the dry ingredients and mix until combined. Add water 1 tablespoon at a time to help moisten the oats, until clumps form.

Put 1 cup of the mixture into a food processor fitted with the steel blade. Pulse for 3 seconds at a time until the mixture is chopped and sticks together. You don't need to make this too fine, but it needs to be a little sticky. This helps the bars stick together.

Scoop the chopped granola into the remaining granola and mix with a wooden spoon or rubber spatula until combined. Transfer to the prepared pan. Using moist fingers, press the granola into the pan until it covers the entire bottom. Check for any little gaps and push them together.

Bake for 15 to 20 minutes, until the edges are just starting to brown. Remove the granola from the oven and let cool in the pan on a wire rack for 15 to 20 minutes. Remove from the pan and transfer directly onto a rack to finish cooling completely. Once cooled, quickly flip the granola in one piece onto a cutting board. Use a very sharp knife to cut 12 (2 x 3-inch) bars. Store in an airtight container. These also freeze well.

Quick Tip: Teff is the tiniest grain in the world and contains calcium and iron. I love the flavor and the boost it gives to the nutritional profile of these granola bars.

Carob Nut Cups

My Granny Jeanne used to buy boxes of Russell Stover's chocolates, and I'd poke a hole in the bottom of each one to figure out what was inside. My favorites were the nutty coconut cups. This is my sugar-free version. **vegetarian, egg-free**

makes 10 nutty snacks

1 cup unsweetened carob chips

2 teaspoons non-hydrogenated vegetable shortening

¼ cup plus 2 tablespoons roasted salted sunflower seeds

¼ cup plus 2 tablespoons unsweetened shredded coconut, plus extra for topping

Line 10 cups in a mini-muffin pan with mini-cupcake papers.

Place the carob chips and shortening in a heatproof bowl that will fit snugly on top of a saucepan. Bring 1 inch of water to a gentle simmer in the saucepan. Place the bowl on top of the pan and turn off the heat. Let the carob and shortening sit for several minutes.

Meanwhile, place the sunflower seeds in the bowl of a mini food chopper fitted with the steel blade. Pulse until the seeds are chopped. Add the measured coconut and pulse several more times until combined.

Stir the carob and shortening until melted. Add the sunflower and coconut mixture to the carob and stir until combined. The mixture will be thick. Using two small spoons, evenly distribute the carob mixture among the cupcake papers, being careful to keep the tops of the papers clean. Tap the muffin tin several times on the countertop to level the melted carob. Sprinkle the tops with the extra coconut and press lightly into the carob. Let sit at room temperature until firm, or refrigerate to speed up the process. Store in an airtight container in the refrigerator for several weeks. Let the nut cups sit at room temperature for a few minutes before serving.

Quick Tip: Non-hydrogenated vegetable shortening works just like regular vegetable shortening, but it's healthier. Here, it helps the carob melt smoothly and maintain a nice color once it hardens.

Apricot and Carob-Stuffed Dates

I'd been thinking about making stuffed dates for weeks but kept putting it off. Then one night when my husband was out of town, I stood in our kitchen and shamelessly stuffed dates with everything in my pantry until I found the perfect combination. I love how the tartness of the apricot works with the sweetness of the creamy date. Coconut and coarsely chopped almonds give a nice crunch. This might be nature's perfect candy bar. **vegetarian, egg-free**

makes 12 to 16 dates

10 small to medium dried apricots

¼ cup sliced almonds

3 tablespoons carob chips

¼ cup finely shredded unsweetened coconut, plus extra for garnish

12 to 16 large Medjool dates

In the bowl of a food processor or mini food chopper fitted with the steel blade, chop the apricots until they're in small pieces. Add the almonds and carob chips and pulse until coarse. Put two-thirds of the mixture in a bowl and set aside. Process the remaining one-third of the mixture in the food processor until it sticks together. Transfer to the bowl with the rest of the almond mixture and combine with the measured coconut.

Use a sharp paring knife to cut a slit in the top of each date. Remove the pits. Take 1 to 1½ teaspoons of the apricot mixture at a time and form into an oblong log a little smaller than the size of the dates. When the logs are ready, put one apricot log inside each date and press the sides of the date together. Some of the apricot mixture will still be exposed. Garnish the top of each date with a sprinkle of the extra coconut. Store in an airtight container in the refrigerator and bring to room temperature before serving.

Quick Tip: Coconut should be stored in the refrigerator to prolong its shelf life. Because of its healthy, natural fats, it can go rancid at room temperature.

Raw Apple Pie Bites

This is my take on raw bars. I use dried cranberries to help balance the sweetness of the dates and raisins. Cut them into little squares for bite-size snacks, or big bars for a midday pick-me-up. Either way, they're delicious. **vegan, raw**

makes 32 (1-inch) square bites or 8 (1 x 4-inch) bars

8 ounces large pitted Medjool dates (about 18)

¼ cup almonds

¼ cup walnuts

¾ cup unsweetened dried apples

2 tablespoons dried cranberries

2 tablespoons raisins

1½ teaspoons ground cinnamon

pinch of freshly grated nutmeg

Line an 8 x 4-inch bread pan with parchment paper so that the paper hangs over the long edges of the pan.

In a large microwave-safe bowl, microwave the dates for 30 seconds. Transfer to the work bowl of a food processor fitted with the steel blade. Process until smooth. Transfer back to the first bowl. Add the almonds to the food processor and pulse until coarsely chopped, about 30 seconds. Add to the dates. Repeat with the walnuts, then with the dried apples. Add the cranberries, raisins, cinnamon, and nutmeg to the bowl with the other ingredients. Use a rubber spatula to work the ingredients together. If the mixture becomes too stiff to mix, return the bowl to the microwave for 15 to 20 seconds at a time until it softens.

Scrape the mixture into the prepared bread pan. Use a rubber spatula to press it into the bottom. Once it's mostly flat, fold the parchment paper down and press until the mixture is completely flat. Cover and let sit at room temperature until firm. Lift out of the pan and cut with a wet serrated knife into 32 (1-inch) squares or 8 (1 x 4-inch) bars. Store in the refrigerator layered with waxed paper to prevent the bars from sticking together.

Quick Tip: Look for dried cranberries sweetened with 100% fruit juice instead of corn syrup or sugar.

Spreads & Condiments

Slow Cooker Apple Butter

Apple butter brings back great childhood memories—my Grandma Ruth made the world's best. I hesitantly sent her a few jars of mine for Christmas a few years ago, a little fearful that my version might not measure up. She was thrilled with the flavor and couldn't believe I didn't use white sugar. Use apples that are naturally sweeter, like Gala, for the best result. **vegan, slow cooker recipe**

makes 5 to 6 cups

4 to 5 pounds apples, cored and sliced

½ to 1 cup unsweetened frozen apple juice concentrate, divided

½ teaspoon ground allspice

¼ teaspoon ground cloves

¼ teaspoon freshly grated nutmeg

1½ to 2 teaspoons ground cinnamon, divided

pinch of salt

Place the apples in a large (5- or 6-quart) slow cooker. Melt ½ cup apple juice concentrate in the microwave or on the stovetop and pour over the apples. Sprinkle the apples with the allspice, cloves, nutmeg, 1½ teaspoons cinnamon, and the salt. Gently stir with a large wooden spoon. Place the lid on the slow cooker and cook on low for 8 to 10 hours, or overnight.

Check the apples after 8 hours. If they need to be cooked longer, leave the slow cooker on. If the apples are soft, puree with an immersion blender while the apples are still in the slow cooker. Or you can transfer them to a food processor or blender and puree in small batches. Taste and adjust the seasoning, adding the remaining ½ cup apple juice concentrate and ½ teaspoon cinnamon for sweetness, if desired. Continue to cook on low with the lid off until the apple butter is thick.

Store in glass jars in the refrigerator for two months, or freeze. I often can my apple butter in a water bath canner, but, of course, it takes longer than 20 minutes!

Quick Tip: Don't bother peeling the apples. The skin helps create a thicker apple butter and, once the apples are pureed, you won't even know it's there.

Slow Cooker Pear Butter

The combination of orange and cardamom is one of my favorite flavor pairings. Use this spread just like you'd use apple butter. **vegan, slow cooker recipe**

makes 5 to 5½ cups

5 pounds Bartlett pears, cored and sliced

½ to ¾ cup unsweetened frozen white grape juice concentrate

3 tablespoons freshly squeezed lemon juice

1 teaspoon ground ginger

½ teaspoon ground cardamom

4 orange slices (about ½ large orange)

1 vanilla bean, split, or 1 tablespoon vanilla extract

Put the pears in a large (5- or 6-quart) slow cooker. Melt ½ cup grape juice concentrate in the microwave or on the stovetop and pour over the pears. Add the lemon juice, ginger, and cardamom. Toss with a large wooden spoon to coat the pears. Top with the orange slices and vanilla bean or extract. Cover and cook on low for 5 to 6 hours, until the pears are very tender and have cooked down.

Remove the orange slices and vanilla bean, if using. Puree with an immersion blender in the crock or transfer the pears to a conventional blender or food processor in small batches and puree. Return to the slow cooker and add the remaining ¼ cup grape juice concentrate for sweetness as needed. If the pear butter isn't thick enough, remove the lid and cook on low, stirring occasionally, until it reaches the desired consistency. It should mound up on a spoon and be spreadable.

Store in glass jars in the refrigerator for up to 2 months, or freeze. This can also be canned in a water bath canner.

Crème Fraîche

A friend shared her crème fraîche recipe with me, and I made it time and time again, but I couldn't get it to thicken. We finally figured out that it was because I was using low-fat buttermilk. If you use full-fat buttermilk, you can use a little less than 2 tablespoons. I like to spread crème fraîche on toast and muffins. Making it at home is simple and frugal—one jar from the store can easily cost $6 to $8. **vegetarian, egg-free**

makes about 1 cup

1 cup heavy cream

2 tablespoons low-fat buttermilk

Heat the heavy cream to 100°F in a heavy-bottomed saucepan. Pour into a Mason jar and stir in the buttermilk. Screw on the lid loosely and put the jar in a warm, or room-temperature, location for 12 to 24 hours, until the mixture is the thickness of sour cream. Refrigerate for up to a week.

Chocolate Almond Butter

This recipe started out as plain old almond butter. I found I didn't love the texture of homemade nut butters but just couldn't throw away the two cups of almonds I had already processed. This recipe was my solution. It's smooth, creamy, and delicious. If you want to get it as smooth as possible, use blanched almonds. You can also roast the almonds beforehand for a deeper flavor; it'll just take a little longer. **vegan**

makes about 1½ cups

2 cups raw almonds

¾ cup unsweetened almond milk

½ cup plus 2 tablespoons
Dutch-processed cocoa powder

2 to 4 tablespoons agave nectar

½ to 1 teaspoon powdered stevia

¼ teaspoon instant
decaf coffee granules

pinch of salt

Place the almonds in the bowl of a food processor fitted with the steel blade. Pulse several times, then process until the almonds start to stick together and form a mass. Scrape down the bowl as needed. Add the almond milk, cocoa powder, 2 tablespoons agave, ½ teaspoon stevia, instant coffee, and salt. Pulse a few times then process until smooth. Taste and add additional agave 1 tablespoon at a time or stevia ¼ teaspoon at a time until it's as sweet as you like. Too much stevia can bring out the bitterness in the chocolate, so add it carefully. Refrigerate in a Mason jar for up to two weeks.

Quick Tip: The coffee enhances the flavor of the chocolate. If you like mocha, increase the coffee to your taste. Or if you don't like coffee, simply leave it out.

Chocolate Hazelnut Spread

This is my healthier adaptation of store-bought chocolate hazelnut spread. I fell in love with it years ago when my friend brought me a jar from France. Today it's more of a treat than a staple in my house, but I love being able to share this on holidays or when I have company. **egg-free**

makes 1 cup

1 cup raw hazelnuts

¼ cup Dutch-processed cocoa powder

2 tablespoons agave nectar

1 tablespoon canola oil

¼ cup carob chips

½ to ¾ cup unsweetened almond milk

½ teaspoon vanilla extract

pinch of kosher salt

Preheat the oven to 350°F. Line a baking sheet with aluminum foil.

Spread the hazelnuts on the pan and toast for 5 minutes. Rotate the tray 180 degrees and toast for 3 to 4 minutes longer, until fragrant. When the nuts are toasted, wrap them in a clean dish towel and roll back and forth on the countertop to remove the skins. If a handful of skins refuse to budge, that's OK.

Place the hazelnuts in the bowl of a food processor fitted with the steel blade. Process for about 3 minutes, until the nuts start to stick together and form a dry butter. Add the cocoa powder, agave, and oil. Pulse to combine, then process to mix well.

Put the carob chips in a microwave-safe bowl and microwave for 15 seconds. Stir the chips to melt. If needed, return the chips to the microwave for 10 seconds longer and stir again. Add to the nut mixture and process. With the food processor running, add ½ cup almond milk in a steady stream. If the mixture is too thick, add the remaining almond milk 1 tablespoon at a time until the desired consistency is reached. Process for 1 minute or so longer. The spread will thicken up once it's chilled. Refrigerate in a Mason jar for up to two weeks.

Make It Dairy-Free: Use your favorite dairy-free chocolate chips instead of carob chips.

Lemon Cream Cheese

Serve this dip as a healthier spread for muffins. It's especially good on Olive Oil Zucchini Muffins (page 6). **vegetarian, egg-free**

makes about 1 cup

1 (8-ounce) package Neufchâtel cheese (light cream cheese), at room temperature

generous ½ teaspoon grated lemon zest

2 tablespoons agave nectar or honey

Combine the cream cheese, lemon zest, and agave in the bowl of a stand mixer fitted with the paddle attachment. Mix on medium-high speed until thoroughly combined and the cream cheese has lightened slightly. Serve chilled or at room temperature. Cover and refrigerate for up to two weeks.

Quick Tip: Use a fine rasp grater to make quick work of grating your lemon zest. Pick one up at your local kitchen supply store for about $20. I use mine almost daily. It's become one of my favorite tools.

Slow Cooker Ketchup

Ketchup is one of the things I've missed the most since going sugar-free, as store-bought brands typically contain some form of white sugar. This recipe has been adapted from Beth Hensperger and Julie Kaufmann's Not Your Mother's Slow Cooker Cookbook *to be sugar-free.* **vegan, slow cooker recipe**

makes about 4 cups

1 (28-ounce) can tomato puree

½ medium yellow onion, coarsely chopped

½ cup cider vinegar

¼ cup gluten-free brown rice syrup

½ teaspoon dry mustard

¼ teaspoon ground allspice

¼ teaspoon ground cinnamon

¼ teaspoon ground mace

¼ teaspoon ground ginger

¼ teaspoon ground cloves

¼ teaspoon ground red chile pepper

kosher salt and freshly ground black pepper

25 drops liquid stevia, or as needed

Combine all the ingredients except the salt and pepper in a large (4- to 6-quart) slow cooker. Stir well. Cover and cook on high for 2 to 2½ hours, stirring occasionally, until the onions are very tender. Remove the lid and puree with an immersion blender, or transfer to a regular blender or food processor and puree until smooth. Season to taste with salt and pepper. Add stevia to taste. The ketchup should be nice and thick. If necessary, return it to the slow cooker and cook on high, uncovered, stirring occasionally, for 30 minutes to 1 hour, until the ketchup has reached the consistency you want.

Transfer to Mason jars. Refrigerate for up to 2 months, or freeze.

Quick Tip: The brown rice syrup doesn't make this ketchup sweet. Instead, it balances the acid from the tomatoes.

Light Garlic Aioli

I prefer this lighter aioli to a pure olive oil aioli. It's the perfect dip for Parmesan-Crusted Sweet Potato Fries (page 113). **vegetarian**

makes 2 cups

1 egg, at room temperature

2 teaspoons Dijon mustard, at room temperature

²/₃ cup extra-virgin olive oil

1 garlic clove, grated on a fine rasp grater or minced

1 teaspoon freshly squeezed lemon juice

¼ cup low-fat cottage cheese

¼ cup nonfat or plain low-fat yogurt

kosher salt and ground white pepper

Combine the egg and mustard in the bowl of a food processor fitted with the steel blade. Process until smooth. If your food processor has a small drain hole in the plug for the feed tube, use that to slowly pour the oil into the egg mixture with the processor running. Otherwise, pour the oil through the uncovered feed tube in a thin, steady stream. It's important to incorporate the oil slowly into the egg so the mixture will emulsify. If the oil is added too quickly, the aioli will separate.

Add the garlic and lemon juice and pulse to combine. Add the cottage cheese and yogurt to the food processor and mix until absolutely smooth. Season to taste with salt and pepper.

Quick Tip: Because this aioli contains raw egg, it's best to eat it on the day it's made. Make sure to refrigerate it if you make it several hours before serving. I don't recommend serving raw egg to children, the elderly, or anyone with a compromised immune system.

Sweet and Spicy Mustard Sauce

Before I created this recipe, I tried many sauces for my Asian Lettuce Wraps (page 98), none of which quite hit the mark. I hadn't eaten Asian food in years because of the gluten and sugar involved, and I couldn't remember the exact flavor. My husband, Joe, coached me on this sauce, and we love it. **vegan (if agave nectar is used)**

makes about ½ cup

½ cup Dijon mustard

4 tablespoons honey
or agave nectar

4 teaspoons gluten-free soy sauce

4 teaspoons rice vinegar

½ teaspoon garlic powder

½ teaspoon ground white pepper

In a small bowl, stir together the mustard, honey or agave, soy sauce, vinegar, garlic powder, and pepper. Cover and refrigerate for at least 30 minutes before serving.

Quick Tip: Bragg's Liquid Aminos tastes just like soy sauce, but it's soy-free and gluten-free. It's become a pantry staple for me.

Simple Soups

Tomato Basil Soup

I grew up in Ohio, where we had cold winters and tons of snow. My mom made grilled cheese sandwiches and tomato soup to warm our bones after a long day of building snow forts and making snow angels. This soup is great on chilly days, but it's also delicious served chilled. The cinnamon just enhances the sweetness of the tomatoes—you won't be able to taste it.

makes 10 servings

2 tablespoons unsalted butter

2 tablespoons olive oil

1 large onion, diced

3 garlic cloves, grated on a fine rasp grater or minced

4 cups chicken broth

2 (28-ounce) cans peeled whole plum tomatoes, seeded and chopped

3 tablespoons chopped fresh basil, plus extra for garnish

1/8 teaspoon ground cinnamon

salt and freshly ground black pepper

Melt the butter and heat the oil in a 6-quart heavy-bottomed stockpot over medium-low heat. Add the onion and cook for about 5 minutes, until the onions are soft, stirring occasionally. Add the garlic and cook for 1 minute longer, until fragrant.

Add the broth and tomatoes. Bring to a boil, then reduce the heat to a simmer. Continue to simmer uncovered for 10 minutes, then add 3 tablespoons basil and cinnamon and simmer for 10 minutes longer, until the tomatoes and onions are very tender. Remove from the heat and cool slightly.

Puree the soup with an immersion blender or in small batches in a blender or food processor. Season to taste with salt and pepper. This soup can be served hot or chilled. Garnish with the extra basil before serving.

Make It Dairy-Free: Eliminate the butter and increase the oil to 3 tablespoons.

Make It Vegan: Eliminate the butter and increase the oil to 3 tablespoons. Replace the chicken broth with vegetable broth.

Quick Tip: Basil chiffonade makes a beautiful garnish. Chiffonade actually refers to a method of cutting herbs. It's very simple—just tightly roll several basil leaves together lengthwise and cut at an angle into thin strips. Use a very sharp chef's knife for best results.

Sweet Curried Carrot Soup

Even though carrots are on my husband's "yuck" list, he loves this soup. So does everyone I've served it to. There's something about the sweetness of the carrots and the spiciness of the curry that makes it really delicious. **egg-free**

makes 10 servings

2 tablespoons unsalted butter

1 medium onion, diced medium

2 teaspoons Curry Powder (page 60)

2 teaspoons salt

¼ teaspoon ground white pepper

2 pounds carrots, peeled and coarsely chopped into 1-inch pieces

4 cups chicken broth

2 cups water

Melt the butter in a 6-quart heavy-bottomed stockpot over medium-low heat. Add the onion, curry powder, salt, and pepper. Sauté about 5 minutes, until the onion is soft and translucent. Add the carrots, then pour in the chicken broth. Simmer for 20 minutes, or until the carrots are very tender.

Puree the soup with an immersion blender or in small batches in a blender or food processor until very smooth. Add water until the desired consistency is reached.

Make It Vegan: Use canola oil instead of butter and vegetable broth instead of chicken broth.

Quick Tip: Like many soups, this will thicken when refrigerated. Gently reheat and add water or chicken broth until you reach the desired consistency.

Curry Powder

I didn't think I liked curry powder until I tried one from Susan O'Brien's book Gluten-Free, Sugar-Free Cooking, *on which the following mix is based. Since then I've found that there are many, many ways to make a curry. While I don't know if this blend would hold up to the "authentic" curry test, it will most certainly be delicious.*

makes about ¼ cup

- 1 tablespoon ground cumin
- 2 teaspoons ancho chile powder (light or dark)
- 2 teaspoons ground cardamom
- 2 teaspoons ground cinnamon
- 2 teaspoons ground coriander
- 1 teaspoon ground cloves
- 1 teaspoon ground turmeric
- ½ teaspoon cayenne pepper (optional)

Mix the spices together in a small bowl, using cayenne as indicated or to taste. Store in an airtight container in a cool, dark place.

Quick Tip: Buy small amounts of spices from the bulk foods section of your grocery store—it's a frugal way to expand your spice collection. I store my spices in inexpensive glass spice jars, which you can find at most stores that carry kitchen supplies.

Split Pea Soup

The great thing about pureed soups is that you don't have to worry about chopping your veggies so they look nice. Just cut them up, throw them in your slow cooker, and go. **dairy-free, slow cooker recipe**

serves 8

1 cup split peas, sorted and rinsed

½ medium onion, sliced

1 cup chopped carrots

1 cup chopped celery

1 ham hock

4 cups chicken broth

1 bay leaf

1½ teaspoons chopped fresh sage

⅛ teaspoon cayenne pepper (optional)

salt and freshly ground black pepper

Place the split peas, onion, carrots, celery, ham hock, chicken broth, and bay leaf in a 4-quart slow cooker. Cover and cook on low for 6 to 8 hours. Add the chopped sage during the last 30 minutes of cooking.

Remove the crock from the slow cooker and take out the ham hock and bay leaf. Puree the soup with an immersion blender right in the crock. If you don't have an immersion blender, puree the soup in batches in a blender or food processor.

Add cayenne as indicated or to taste. Taste and adjust the seasoning with salt and pepper as needed. Reheat if necessary and serve.

Variation—Stovetop Method: Add all the ingredients except the cayenne, salt, and pepper to a large stockpot. Bring to a boil, then reduce to a simmer and cook for 30 to 45 minutes, until the split peas are very tender. Follow the directions for pureeing and seasoning.

Make It Vegetarian: Omit the ham hock and use vegetable broth instead of chicken broth.

Quick Tip: Bean soups are incredibly versatile. Instead of split peas, use 1 cup white beans that have been soaked in water overnight instead and create an entirely different soup.

Spicy 'n' Sweet Turkey Pinto Bean Chili

This chili, adapted from The Bon Appétit Cookbook: Fast Easy Fresh, *has become a day-after-Thanksgiving tradition in our family. Instead of ground turkey, I use a pound of leftover turkey from the bird I roast for the holiday.* **dairy-free**

serves 12

2 tablespoons extra-virgin olive oil

1 large onion, finely chopped

2 medium red bell peppers, seeded and diced

6 garlic cloves, grated on a fine rasp grater or minced

1 pound leftover turkey meat, shredded, or ground turkey

2 teaspoons kosher salt

3 tablespoons light ancho chile powder

2 teaspoons ground cumin

1½ teaspoons Mexican dried oregano

½ teaspoon ground cinnamon

¼ teaspoon cayenne pepper

2 (15-ounce) cans pinto beans, drained and rinsed

1 (28-ounce) can diced tomatoes

3 to 4 cups chicken broth

3 tablespoons cocoa powder

1 tablespoon agave nectar

Heat the oil in a 6- to 8-quart heavy-bottomed stockpot over medium heat until hot but not smoking. Add the onion and bell pepper and cook until soft. Add the garlic and cook until fragrant. If using ground turkey, add the turkey and cook until no longer pink, breaking apart any large pieces as it cooks. If using leftover turkey, proceed to the next step.

Stir in the salt, chile powder, cumin, oregano, and cinnamon. Add cayenne as indicated or to taste. Mix well and cook until the spices are fragrant. Add the pinto beans, tomatoes, and broth. Bring to a boil.

In a small bowl, mix the cocoa powder and agave with enough water to form a thick paste. Stir into the chili until dissolved. Reduce to a simmer, stir in the cooked turkey, if using, and cook the chili uncovered stirring occasionally for 1 hour, or until the desired consistency is reached. Serve as is or with your favorite chili toppings.

Quick Tip: Keep a digital kitchen scale handy for recipes like this so you can easily measure the quantities you need.

Shredded Chicken Tortilla Soup

Throw this soup together in less than 10 minutes, let your slow cooker do the work, and you'll have a meal that tastes like you slaved over the stovetop. **egg-free, slow cooker recipe**

serves 8

3 cups chicken broth

1 (28-ounce) can diced tomatoes

1 cup tomato salsa

3 garlic cloves, grated on a fine rasp grater or minced

½ cup chopped cilantro

1 tablespoon unsalted butter

4 carrots, peeled and sliced ¼ inch thick

2 tablespoons ground cumin

⅛ teaspoon ground cinnamon

4 bone-in, skinless chicken thighs or 2 large bone-in, skinless chicken breasts

Optional toppings:
Oven-Baked Cumin Lime Tortilla Chips (page 35) or store-bought gluten-free chips

shredded Monterey Jack cheese or queso fresco

light sour cream

sliced avocado

chopped fresh cilantro

Combine the chicken broth, tomatoes, salsa, garlic, cilantro, butter, carrots, cumin, and cinnamon in a large (4- to 6-quart) slow cooker. Mix well. Add the chicken, making sure it's completely covered. Cook on low for 4 to 6 hours.

When the chicken is easy to shred with a fork, remove it from the soup, shred, and discard the bones. Return to the slow cooker and mix well. Serve with your choice of toppings. This soup freezes well.

Quick Tip: Assemble the ingredients the night before in the crock of your slow cooker. Cover and refrigerate until you're ready to cook it the next day.

Chicken Posole Stew

Traditionally made with pork, posole is a Mexican stew that can be made many different ways. All versions have one ingredient in common: hominy, which is corn that's been soaked until the outer skin comes off. You can easily make a pork posole by using a pound of pork suitable for longer cooking times, such as pork loin or pork butt. **dairy-free, egg-free, slow cooker recipe**

serves 12

3 cups chicken broth

2 (15-ounce) cans white hominy, rinsed and drained

1 (28-ounce) can diced tomatoes

3 carrots, peeled and thinly sliced

3 scallions, both green and white parts, thinly sliced

3 garlic cloves, grated on a fine rasp grater or minced

1 tablespoon ground cumin

2 teaspoons light ancho chile powder

1½ teaspoons dried oregano

¼ teaspoon cayenne pepper

1 teaspoon salt

½ teaspoon freshly ground black pepper

4 bone-in skinless chicken thighs or 2 bone-in skinless chicken breasts

Optional toppings:
chopped fresh cilantro

shredded queso fresco or other good-quality cheese, like Monterey Jack

shredded radishes (use the large holes on a box grater)

sliced avocado

light sour cream

Oven-Baked Cumin Lime Tortilla Chips (page 35) or store-bought gluten-free chips

Combine the chicken broth, hominy, tomatoes, carrots, scallions, garlic, cumin, chile powder, and oregano in the crock of a large (4- to 6-quart) slow cooker and mix well. Add cayenne, salt, and pepper as indicated or to taste. Add the chicken, making sure that it's covered completely. Cover the slow cooker and cook on low for 5 to 6 hours, until the chicken and carrots are cooked through and tender. Remove the chicken, shred it with a fork, and discard the bones. Return the chicken to the insert and stir to combine. Serve with your choice of toppings.

Quick Tip: Dark meat stays much moister than white meat when cooked for long periods of time, and keeping the meat on the bone helps with moisture and flavor. I've included white meat as an option for those who prefer it.

French Onion Soup

This soup is so flavorful that no one will believe that it was made in a slow cooker. Adding fresh herbs in the last 20 minutes of cooking makes the flavor bright. I'm not incredibly fond of white bread, except when it comes to certain dishes. Here, I find it essential. **egg-free, slow cooker recipe**

serves 6 to 8

2 large yellow onions

2 large white onions

2 large red onions

4 garlic cloves, grated on a fine rasp grater or minced

2 tablespoons extra-virgin olive oil

4 cups chicken broth

4 cups beef broth

2 sprigs fresh flat-leaf parsley

2 sprigs fresh thyme

1 bay leaf

1 teaspoon kosher salt

½ to 1 teaspoon balsamic vinegar

6 to 8 slices gluten-free bread, preferably white

8 ounces Gruyère cheese, grated

Cut the onions in half end to end, slice off the ends, and remove the papery outer layers. Thinly slice the onions into half moons by cutting them from top to bottom. Place the onions in a large (5- to 6-quart) slow cooker. Add the garlic and toss with the oil. Cover and cook on high for 8 hours. The onions will cook down and get very sweet.

Place the chicken broth and beef broth in a microwave-safe container and microwave for about 5 minutes, until boiling. (You can also heat the broth on the stovetop.) Add the hot broth to the cooked onions in the slow cooker. Do not pour the broth into the slow cooker until it has stopped boiling. Use kitchen twine to tie the parsley and thyme together and add the bundle to the soup along with the bay leaf. Cover and cook on high for 20 minutes longer. Remove the herbs and bay leaf. Add salt and balsamic vinegar as indicated or to taste. If you want more broth, simply add more broth or thin out the soup with a little hot water.

Preheat the broiler. Just before serving the soup, toast the bread and slice off the crust. Place individual broiler-safe bowls onto a baking sheet. Ladle the soup into the bowls and top with the toasted bread and cheese. Put under the broiler for 30 seconds to 1 minute, until the cheese melts. Serve immediately.

Quick Tip: Line your baking sheet with aluminum foil to make cleanup quick and simple.

Black Bean Soup

There's nothing simpler than a pureed bean soup. Just toss the ingredients into the pot, let them cook, then puree. It's frugal, too, especially when cooking the beans from scratch. **dairy-free, egg-free**

serves 10 to 12

1 pound dried black beans

3 cups chicken broth

3 cups water

1 large onion, diced

½ cup chopped cilantro

3 garlic cloves, grated on a fine rasp grater or minced

1 jalapeño, seeded and chopped

1 teaspoon cumin

2 teaspoons kosher salt

½ teaspoon freshly ground black pepper

For serving:
Oven-Baked Cumin Lime Tortilla Chips (page 35) or store-bought salsa

light sour cream

Sort and rinse the black beans. Place in a large bowl and cover with water. Let sit for 6 hours or overnight. Drain the beans, rinse well, and place in a large Dutch oven or stockpot. Add the chicken broth and water. Cover, bring to a boil, then reduce the heat to a simmer. Skim any foam that rises to the top. Once there is no more foam, add the onion, cilantro, garlic, jalapeño, and cumin. Cover and simmer for 1½ hours or until the beans are very tender.

Remove from the heat and puree with an immersion blender until very smooth. Season with salt and pepper as indicated or to taste.

Serve with tortilla chips, salsa, and light sour cream.

Variation—Rustic Black Bean Soup: If desired, remove half of the beans before pureeing. Puree the remaining beans in the pot then return the whole beans to the soup and stir to combine.

Make It Vegan: Use vegetable broth instead of chicken broth.

Quick Tip: Using an immersion blender will make quick work of pureeing this soup. They're relatively inexpensive, about $30 to $40. If you don't have one, this soup can be pureed in batches in your food processor or blender.

Cauliflower Soup

If you call my mom during the winter months and ask what she's doing, chances are that she's either getting ready to make soup, making soup, or just finished cooking a big pot. She shared this recipe when my husband and I started dating because she knew he liked cauliflower. It was the first thing I made for him that he asked me to make again—and then later asked me to make for his family.

serves 10 to 12

4 cups chicken broth

2 tablespoons olive oil

1 medium onion, diced

1 large head cauliflower or
1½ small heads (about 2 to 2½ pounds total)

2 teaspoons dried parsley

½ teaspoon dried thyme

3 cups low-fat or whole milk

1 teaspoon kosher salt

¼ teaspoon ground white pepper

4 ounces Gruyère cheese, grated

4 ounces Swiss cheese, grated

Put the chicken broth in a saucepan and bring to a boil, then reduce to a simmer.

While the chicken broth is warming up, heat the oil in a large stockpot over medium-low heat. Add the onion and cook 3 to 5 minutes, until translucent. While the onion is cooking, chop the cauliflower into bite-size pieces. Add the cauliflower to the onion and then very carefully pour in the hot chicken broth. Add the parsley and thyme and cook until the cauliflower is tender.

Right before serving, add the milk and heat through. Season with salt and white pepper as indicated or to taste. Once the soup is hot, stir in the cheese and serve immediately. Do not boil the soup once the milk and cheese have been added.

Quick Tip: This soup can be prepared up to one day ahead of time. Cook up to the point when the cauliflower is tender. Refrigerate overnight. When you're ready to serve, heat the soup, add the milk, and proceed as directed.

Salads

Balsamic Tomatoes

Sometimes simple is best. ***vegan***

serves 2 to 4

2 medium vine-ripened tomatoes

1½ teaspoons good-quality balsamic vinegar

1 garlic clove, grated on a fine rasp grater or minced

1 tablespoon fresh basil chiffonade

kosher salt and freshly ground black pepper

Core the tomatoes, cut them in half, and slice ¼ inch thick. Toss with the vinegar, garlic, and basil. Season to taste with salt and pepper.

Quick Tip: The quality of the balsamic vinegar affects the flavor of this dish. Ask your specialty grocer about their selection and choose a few to take home. Decide which one you like best and stick with it. Keep in mind that more expensive brands don't necessarily taste better.

Fruited Curry Chicken Salad

This chicken salad tastes labor intensive, but it's quick and simple. Make it the night before and let the flavors fully develop. I love to eat this salad on fresh spinach, and my husband puts it on a sandwich with Swiss cheese.

serves 2

1 cup shredded cooked chicken

¼ cup mayonnaise

¼ cup plain low-fat yogurt

½ medium pear or apple, diced

⅓ cup raisins, regular or golden

⅓ cup seedless red grapes, cut in half

1 stalk celery with leaves, thinly sliced

1 green onion, thinly sliced

¾ teaspoon Curry Powder (page 60)

¼ cup toasted pecans, coarsely chopped, or sunflower seeds

1 (9-ounce) bag baby spinach (or your favorite lettuce)

kosher salt and freshly ground black pepper

Place the chicken in a medium bowl. Add the mayonnaise, yogurt, pear or apple, raisins, grapes, celery, green onion, and curry powder and stir until combined. Season to taste with salt and pepper. Refrigerate for 2 hours, if desired, to let flavors develop, then add pecans or sunflower seeds just before serving. Serve over a bed of baby spinach or your choice of lettuce, or make into sandwiches.

Quick Tip: If you can find quality canned chicken, keep some in your refrigerator for nights when you need a quick meal. Otherwise, use Make Ahead Chicken (page 97).

Salmon Salad

I was in a pinch for dinner one night and decided to use canned salmon to make a salad. It was a hit. I love the milder flavor from the salmon and how well it goes with fresh dill and capers.

serves 2 to 4

¼ cup mayonnaise

¼ cup plain low-fat yogurt

1½ tablespoons capers, drained and coarsely chopped

1 tablespoon chopped fresh dill or ¾ teaspoon dried dill

2 (6-ounce) cans salmon (preferably wild-caught)

1 Perfect Hard-Boiled Egg (page 37), chopped

1 stalk celery with leaves, thinly sliced

kosher salt and freshly ground black pepper

Mix together the mayonnaise, yogurt, capers, and dill in a medium bowl. Drain the salmon, add it to the bowl, and break into pieces. Add the egg and celery. Stir to combine. Season to taste with salt and pepper. This keeps for a day or two in the refrigerator.

Quick Tip: Keep canned salmon in the refrigerator so it's chilled and ready for a meal.

Chicken and Cannellini Bean Salad with Spinach

I learned to love tarragon from watching Barefoot Contessa. It wasn't an herb I was familiar with until I made Ina Garten's chicken salad. Though this salad is nothing like hers, every time I eat this I'm grateful for all I've learned watching her show. **egg-free**

serves 4

1 (14.5-ounce) can cannellini beans, drained and rinsed

1 (12-ounce) can chicken packed in water or 2 cups shredded cooked chicken

4 Roma tomatoes, seeded and diced

1 garlic clove, grated on a fine rasp grater or minced

1 tablespoon capers, coarsely chopped

juice from ½ lemon, or as needed

1 tablespoon chopped fresh flat-leaf parsley

2 teaspoons chopped fresh tarragon

¼ cup plain low-fat yogurt

2 tablespoons extra-virgin olive oil

salt and freshly ground black pepper

1 (9-ounce) bag baby spinach

Gently combine the beans, chicken, tomatoes, garlic, capers, lemon juice, parsley, and tarragon in a medium bowl. In a small bowl, whisk together the yogurt and oil. Pour the dressing over the chicken and bean salad and fold it in. Season to taste with salt and pepper. Divide the spinach among 4 plates and top with chicken and bean salad.

Quick Tip: If you don't have fresh parsley or tarragon on hand, start with ¾ teaspoon dried parsley and ½ teaspoon dried tarragon. Let the salad sit for several hours and taste. Add more herbs if desired.

Chickpea and Summer Veggie Salad

Chickpeas, also called garbanzo beans, are one of my favorites because of their dense, firm texture and flavor. You can serve this as is or pile it on top of a bed of leafy greens, which is what I do. Of course, I'll put a pile of raw spinach under just about anything. **vegan**

serves 2 as a main course, 4 as a side

1 (14.5-ounce) can chickpeas, drained, not rinsed

1 medium zucchini

1 medium tomato

2 tablespoons chopped fresh flat-leaf parsley

1 tablespoon capers, chopped

¼ cup extra-virgin olive oil

2 tablespoons freshly squeezed lemon juice

10 drops of liquid stevia

kosher salt and freshly ground black pepper

Put the chickpeas in a medium bowl. Slice the zucchini in half, then cut each half lengthwise into four strips. Slice thinly and add to the beans. Cut the tomato in half and then in quarters. Remove the seeds and cut the flesh into strips, then into small pieces. Add to the bowl along with the parsley and capers. Mix well.

In a small bowl, whisk together the oil, lemon juice, and stevia. Taste and add more stevia if needed. The dressing shouldn't be too sweet—just sweet enough to balance the acid of the lemon juice. Drizzle over the chickpea salad and toss. Season to taste with salt and pepper. For the best flavor, cover and chill for 2 hours or more. Serve alone or on a bed of lettuce.

Quick Tip: For a little variety, swap out the zucchini for broccoli and use cherry tomatoes cut in half.

Broccoli and Raisin Salad

I loved broccoli salad as a kid, especially the way the florets soaked up the sweet-tart dressing. This is my spin on that classic, using stevia instead of sugar. If you want a sweeter dressing, add more stevia in ¹/₈-teaspoon increments until it's perfectly sweet for you.

serves 4 to 6

4 cups broccoli florets, cut into bite-size pieces

¼ cup raisins

¼ cup mayonnaise

¼ cup plain low-fat yogurt

1 tablespoon freshly squeezed lemon juice

½ teaspoon powdered stevia

salt and freshly ground black pepper

¼ cup roasted sunflower seeds

Combine the broccoli florets and raisins in a medium bowl. In a small bowl, whisk together the mayonnaise, yogurt, lemon juice, stevia, and a pinch of salt. Pour the dressing over the broccoli and raisins and toss well. Cover and refrigerate overnight. Just before serving, toss in the sunflower seeds. Taste and adjust the seasoning with salt and pepper as needed.

Quick Tip: Combining low-fat yogurt and mayonnaise makes a healthier dressing that still has great body and flavor to it.

Pear and Spinach Salad with Lemon Truffle Vinaigrette

Joe, my husband, and I had the most amazing salad with pears and truffle oil while at dinner with some friends. Here's my version. It's simple enough to make every night and elegant enough to serve to guests.

serves 4

1 ripe Bartlett pear

2 tablespoons freshly squeezed lemon juice

2 tablespoons truffle oil

1/8 to 1/4 teaspoon powdered stevia

pinch of kosher salt

6 cups baby spinach

2 tablespoons coarsely chopped toasted walnuts

Put 4 salad plates in the refrigerator to chill. Cut the pear in half and remove the core with a melon baller. Slice the halves lengthwise into 1/4-inch strips. Whisk together the lemon juice, truffle oil, 1/8 teaspoon stevia, and salt. Add more stevia if needed. Divide the spinach among the prepared salad plates. Top each bed of spinach with one-fourth of the pear. Drizzle lightly with 1 tablespoon of the dressing. Sprinkle each salad with 1 1/2 teaspoons chopped walnuts.

Quick Tip: If you're in a hurry to ripen up your pears, place them in a paper bag and roll it shut. The fruit gives off a natural gas as it ripens, and keeping it closed in the bag speeds the process. If you're really pressed for time, add an overripe banana to the bag.

Carrot and Jicama Slaw

After having a similar slaw at a Mexican restaurant, I decided to create my own version. Serve this with black beans, as a topping for burritos, or my personal favorite—on Sweet Potato and Black Bean Tacos (page 89). **egg-free**

makes about 4 cups

2 cups shredded carrot
(about 3 medium carrots)

2 cups shredded jicama
(about ½ medium bulb)

¼ cup light sour cream

¼ cup plain low-fat yogurt

juice of ½ lime

1 tablespoon chopped fresh cilantro

1 teaspoon kosher salt

½ teaspoon ground cumin

½ teaspoon ground coriander

¼ teaspoon ground red
chile pepper

freshly ground black pepper

Place the carrot and jicama in a medium bowl and toss to combine. In another medium bowl, mix together the sour cream, yogurt, lime juice, cilantro, salt, cumin, coriander, and red chile pepper. Pour the dressing over the carrots and jicama and mix until combined. Season to taste with black pepper. Cover and chill for 2 hours before serving.

Quick Tip: Use the feed tube on your food processor to make fast work of grating the carrot and jicama. Instead of inserting the vegetables vertically, cut them so they lie in the feed tube horizontally. This will create long strands of carrots and jicama and makes a much more interesting presentation.

Buttermilk Dill Ranch Dressing

I started making homemade salad dressing a long time ago because most store-bought dressings contain white sugar. To re-create dressings, I often read labels so I know what ingredients are used and then work from there. Though I use mostly dried herbs, the fresh dill brightens the entire dressing. **egg-free**

makes about 1 cup

½ cup plain low-fat yogurt

½ cup low-fat buttermilk

2 tablespoons mayonnaise

¼ teaspoon onion powder

¼ teaspoon ground black pepper

¼ teaspoon dried marjoram

¼ teaspoon celery salt

¼ teaspoon dried savory

¼ teaspoon dried parsley

⅛ teaspoon garlic powder

1½ teaspoons chopped fresh dill (fronds from 1 stem of dill)

Whirl all the ingredients in a blender until thoroughly combined. Let rest, covered, in the refrigerator for at least 1 hour before serving.

Quick Tip: Make this a dip by replacing half of the buttermilk with mayonnaise or yogurt.

Pesto Salad Dressing

I came up with this recipe one night when I was out of oil and couldn't make my usual salad dressing. Now I use it for my grilled chicken salads or drizzled on tomatoes, and sometimes I even omit the water and use it as a dip for raw veggies. **egg-free**

makes about 1½ cups

½ cup pesto

½ cup plain low-fat yogurt

¼ to ½ cup water

freshly ground sea salt and black pepper

Place all the ingredients in a 1-pint Mason jar and shake to combine well, or whisk them together in a small bowl. Start with ¼ cup water and add up to ¼ cup more, or until desired consistency is reached. Season to taste with salt and pepper. This will keep in the refrigerator for a week or so.

Quick Tip: Be creative when topping salads. Instead of croutons, use your favorite roasted, salted seeds and nuts. Try toasted pepitas (hulled pumpkin seeds), sunflower seeds, or sliced almonds.

Balsamic Dijon Vinaigrette

This is my favorite dressing—I make an individual serving nearly every night for my own salad. When my mom was visiting, she tried it and immediately insisted I make a big batch for both of us to share. I'm sure you'll like it as much as we do. **vegan**

makes about ½ cup

¼ cup balsamic vinegar

¼ cup extra-virgin olive oil

1 generous tablespoon Dijon mustard

¼ teaspoon liquid stevia

kosher salt and freshly ground black pepper

Whisk together the balsamic vinegar, oil, mustard, and stevia. Taste and adjust the seasoning with salt, pepper, or more stevia. Store in the refrigerator for up to 1 week

Quick Tip: Stevia is a simple, no-calorie way to balance the acids in your salad dressings. Always start with a little and add in small increments, tasting as you go along. A little stevia goes a long way.

Cottage Cheese and Fruit Salad

I eat this almost every day for breakfast or lunch. It's simple to make, filling, and versatile. I've packed this salad for lunch and taken it on road trips because it travels so well. My freezer always has a few cold ice packs ready to go so I can easily pack a cooler and have a sugar-free, gluten-free meal wherever I go. **egg-free**

makes 1 serving

1 cup chopped baby spinach

1 to 1½ cups chopped fresh fruit

½ cup low-fat cottage cheese

¼ teaspoon powdered stevia

1 teaspoon ground cinnamon

1 tablespoon chopped nuts

Place the spinach in a single-serving salad bowl. Place the fruit on top of the spinach, followed by the cottage cheese. Sweeten by sprinkling the stevia on top of the cottage cheese. Sprinkle the cinnamon on top, followed by the nuts. Add more cinnamon, if you like.

Quick Tip: Keep a variety of fresh and frozen fruits on hand for snacks and meals. One day I was totally out of fresh fruit and tried this with frozen berries. It was surprisingly delicious and is now a favorite of mine on hot summer days.

Poppy Seed Fruit Salad

When I was little, my Grandma Ruth used to make Waldorf salad. It was one of my favorites. She made her salad dressing with Miracle Whip, a little vinegar, and sugar. This is my version sans white sugar. I love how the poppy seeds complement the fruit. **egg-free**

serves 4 to 6

2 cups plain low-fat yogurt

1 tablespoon honey or agave nectar

1 tablespoon freshly squeezed orange juice

1 teaspoon poppy seeds

2 bananas, cut in half lengthwise and sliced

2 apples, cored and chopped

1½ cups red grapes, cut in half

½ cup raisins

¼ cup toasted walnuts (optional)

Set a mesh strainer in a bowl large enough to surround it. Line the strainer with a double thickness of paper towels. Place the yogurt into the strainer and cover it with plastic. Let the yogurt drain in the refrigerator overnight. To drain the yogurt quicker, place plastic wrap directly on the yogurt and put a small plate on top of the plastic. Set a 15-ounce can of beans (or whatever you have on hand) on top of the plate. This will press down on the yogurt and drain it in several hours.

Transfer the strained yogurt (it should have reduced by half and will be thick) to a medium bowl and mix in the honey or agave, orange juice, and poppy seeds. Combine the bananas, apples, grapes, and raisins in another bowl. Use a rubber spatula to scrape all of the yogurt dressing over the fruit and gently fold it in. Let the fruit salad sit for several hours before serving. Top with walnuts, if using.

Quick Tip: If you don't have time to strain the yogurt or don't care to, use 1 cup Greek yogurt instead. It's incredibly thick, rich, and creamy.

Berry Quinoa Salad

Quinoa, a protein-packed seed (often referred to as a grain), is delicious in both sweet and savory applications. Add the berries to the salad just before serving to keep the berry juice from dying the quinoa pink. **egg-free**

serves 4 to 6

½ cup plain low-fat yogurt

juice of 1 small lime, divided

2 teaspoons chopped fresh mint

2 cups cooked quinoa

kosher salt and freshly ground black pepper

1½ cups fresh berries and grapes

stevia, as needed

2 tablespoons sliced toasted almonds

In a small bowl, stir together the yogurt, half the lime juice, and the mint. Stir the dressing into the cooked quinoa. Season to taste with salt and pepper. Set aside. Place the berries and grapes in a bowl, add the remaining lime juice, and sweeten to taste with stevia. Cover each bowl and refrigerate for 2 hours or longer to let the flavors develop. Add the fruit to the quinoa and top the salad with the toasted almonds just before serving.

Quick Tip: When making quinoa or rice for a meal, cook extra. Freeze it in 2-cup portions and reheat as needed in the microwave, adding a little water if necessary. It makes for a quick and nutritious side dish on busy evenings.

Main Dishes

Socca Pizza

I've been making socca, a type of chickpea flatbread, to go with my ratatouille for years, but I never thought to use it as a pizza crust until I had it for dinner while traveling in New York. I came home and started playing with my socca recipe until I had the perfect crust. My husband is the pizza fan in our house, and he says this is one of the best crusts he's ever had.

To make socca pizzas, you'll need a hot oven and a cast iron skillet. My skillet is 12 inches, but you can most certainly make the socca in a smaller pan. (My friend and recipe tester Cara, from Cara's Cravings—CarasCravings.blogspot.com—gave me a heads-up about pan size: A 9-inch pan has about half the surface area of a 12-inch pan, so if you use a smaller skillet, cut the batter recipe in half and adjust the cooking time accordingly.) I also use a pizza stone to finish the crust on—this makes it much crispier. If you have one, great. If not, this will still be a delicious dish.

Socca can be topped with almost anything. I've included three of my favorite socca pizza recipes. Try those and then have fun inventing your own. To make a socca pizza, first make your batter, then your socca pizza of choice. Serve with a big green salad. **egg-free**

makes 1 (12-inch) pizza

Socca pizza batter:

1 cup garbanzo bean flour

1½ cups cold water

1 tablespoon extra-virgin olive oil

½ teaspoon kosher salt

Socca pizzas:

Pepperoni and Cheese Socca Pizza
(page 85)

Tomato, Pesto, and Fresh Mozzarella
Socca Pizza (page 88)

Veggie, Onion, and Prosciutto
Socca Pizza (page 86)

To make the batter, combine the garbanzo bean flour, water, olive oil, and salt in a blender and blend on medium speed for 20 to 30 seconds until thoroughly combined and smooth. Put the batter into the refrigerator until ready to use.

Pepperoni and Cheese
Socca Pizza

Add any of your favorite traditional pizza toppings to this. I like mushrooms, sliced tomatoes, and olives. **egg-free**

makes 1 (12-inch) pizza

1 tablespoon extra-virgin olive oil

1 tablespoon chopped onion

1 garlic clove, grated on a
fine rasp grater or minced

1 (8-ounce) can tomato sauce

¼ teaspoon ground black pepper,
or as needed

¼ teaspoon dried basil or
3 fresh basil leaves

¼ teaspoon dried oregano

¼ teaspoon dried parsley

¼ teaspoon kosher salt,
or as needed

5 drops of liquid stevia

1 tablespoon unsalted butter

1 recipe cold Socca Pizza Batter
(page 84)

1 cup shredded mozzarella cheese
(about 4 ounces)

1½ ounces sliced pepperoni

To make the sauce, heat the oil in a small saucepan over medium heat. Add the onion and cook until translucent, then add the garlic and cook about 30 seconds to 1 minute, just until fragrant. Stir in the tomato sauce, pepper, basil, oregano, parsley, salt, and stevia. Bring the sauce to a boil, reduce to a simmer, and let cook for 10 minutes.

Rub a 12-inch cast iron skillet with a thin layer of oil. Place the pan in the oven and preheat the oven to 475°F. If you're using a pizza stone, place it on the rack below the skillet.

When the oven is preheated, carefully add the butter to the cast iron pan while it's still in the oven. Once the butter has melted, carefully remove the cast iron skillet from the oven. Pour the batter into the pan. It should sizzle.

Bake for 15 to 20 minutes, until the top of the socca has started to lightly brown in places.

Spread the desired amount of sauce on the baked pizza crust. Top with the cheese and pepperoni and any other toppings you'd like. Return the pizza to the 475°F oven for 10 to 15 minutes, until the cheese has melted and the toppings are cooked through. If you're using a pizza stone, carefully remove the cast iron pan from the oven, transfer the socca to the stone, add your pizza toppings, and place the pizza back in the oven for 10 to 15 minutes, until the cheese is melted and the toppings are cooked through. Let the pizza rest for 5 minutes before slicing and serving.

Veggie, Onion, and Prosciutto Pizza

Throw your favorite green veggies into this recipe. I've used broccoli, asparagus, okra, spinach, green beans, and shaved Brussels sprouts. They're all delicious in their own way. Oaxaca is a mozzarella-like cheese from Mexico. It melts nicely without being greasy. I prefer prosciutto on this but if you can't find any, bacon is great, too. **egg-free**

makes 1 (12-inch) pizza

1 tablespoon extra-virgin olive oil

½ medium onion, thinly sliced in half moons from top to bottom

1 garlic clove, grated on a fine rasp grater or minced

1 cup diced canned tomatoes, with juice

1 cup chopped fresh green veggies

½ teaspoon kosher salt

¼ teaspoon ground cumin

$1/8$ teaspoon cayenne pepper, or as needed

1 tablespoon unsalted butter

1 recipe cold Socca Pizza Batter (page 84)

1 cup grated mozzarella or Oaxaca cheese

4 slices prosciutto or 4 slices bacon, cooked and sliced into pieces

To make the sauce, heat the oil in a medium nonstick sauté pan over medium-low heat. Add the onion and cook for 3 to 5 minutes, until the onion starts to soften. Stir in the garlic and cook for about 1 minute, until fragrant. Add the tomatoes, veggies, salt, cumin, and cayenne. Increase the heat to medium and cook uncovered for about 3 minutes, until the tomatoes start to release their juices. Cover and cook for another 5 minutes, until the veggies are soft. Remove the lid and cook, stirring occasionally, for about 5 minutes, until the juices have evaporated and the tomatoes start to stick to the bottom of the pan. Taste and adjust the seasoning as needed.

Rub a 12-inch cast iron skillet with a thin layer of oil. Place the pan in the oven and preheat the oven to 475°F. If you're using a pizza stone, place it on the rack below the skillet.

When the oven is preheated, carefully add the butter to the cast iron pan while it's still in the oven. Once the butter has melted, carefully remove the cast iron skillet from the oven. Pour the batter into the pan. It should sizzle.

Bake for 15 to 20 minutes, until the top of the socca has started to lightly brown in places. Spread the cheese on the baked pizza crust. Add the veggie and tomato sauce, then top with the prosciutto or bacon. Return the pizza to the 475°F oven for 10 to 15 minutes, until the cheese is melted and the crust is slightly brown around the edges. If you're using a pizza stone, carefully remove the cast iron pan from the oven, transfer the socca to the stone, add your pizza toppings, and place the pizza back in the oven for 10 to 15 minutes, until the cheese is melted and the toppings are cooked through. Let the pizza rest for 5 minutes before slicing and serving.

Quick Tip: Start preparing this topping when you put your socca pizza crust in the oven. It will be ready well before the crust is cooked.

Tomato, Pesto, and Fresh Mozzarella Socca Pizza

Using pesto as the sauce is not only delicious but it makes this dish so quick and simple. I like to cut this pizza into small wedges and serve it as an appetizer at parties. **egg-free**

makes 1 (12-inch) pizza

1 tablespoon unsalted butter

1 recipe cold Socca Pizza Batter (page 84)

2 to 3 tablespoons pesto, or as needed

2 ounces fresh mozzarella, sliced

1 medium tomato, sliced

4 slices prosciutto, very thinly sliced

Rub a 12-inch cast iron skillet with a thin layer of oil. Place the pan in the oven and preheat the oven to 475°F. If you're using a pizza stone, place it on the rack below the skillet.

When the oven is preheated, carefully add the butter to the cast iron pan while it's still in the oven. Once the butter has melted, carefully remove the cast iron skillet from the oven. Pour the batter into the pan. It should sizzle.

Bake for 15 to 20 minutes, until the top of the socca has started to lightly brown in places.

Spread a thin layer of pesto on the baked pizza crust. Top with the mozzarella, sliced tomatoes, and prosciutto. Return the pizza to the 475°F oven for 10 to 15 minutes, until the cheese is melted and the crust is slightly brown around the edges. If you're using a pizza stone, carefully remove the cast iron pan from the oven, transfer the socca to the stone, add your pizza toppings, and place the pizza back in the oven for 10 to 15 minutes, until the cheese is melted and the toppings are cooked through. Let the pizza rest for 5 minutes before slicing and serving.

Sweet Potato and Black Bean Tacos

My husband and I both love this meal, but we prefer it with different toppings. I like mine topped with Carrot and Jicama Slaw. Joe likes his with salsa and sour cream. We do agree on the queso fresco, though. Try the tacos both ways and decide what version you like best. **vegan**

makes 8 to 10 tacos

1 large sweet potato, peeled and diced ¼ inch

1 tablespoon canola oil

½ large onion, diced

1 (14.5-ounce) can black beans, drained, liquid reserved

½ teaspoon ground cumin

¼ teaspoon light ancho chile powder

10 corn tortillas

kosher salt and freshly ground black pepper

Optional toppings:

Carrot and Jicama Slaw (page 76)

queso fresco

light sour cream

salsa

Preheat the oven to 200°F.

Place the sweet potato in a steamer and cook for 10 minutes, or until cooked through but still a bit al dente. Meanwhile, heat the oil in a large nonstick sauté pan over medium-low heat. Add the onion and cook for 5 to 8 minutes, until soft. Add the beans, cumin, chile powder, and about ¼ cup of the reserved bean liquid. Mash some of the beans in the pan and add more liquid as necessary.

Meanwhile, heat a medium nonstick sauté pan over medium-high heat and toast the tortillas until they're warm and a little brown on each side. Wrap the tortillas in aluminum foil and keep warm in the oven.

When the sweet potatoes are cooked but still firm, add them to the beans and stir. Add more liquid if necessary. The taco filling shouldn't be dry, but it shouldn't be runny either. Taste and adjust the seasoning as needed. Spoon the filling into the center of each tortilla. Serve with your choice of toppings. Serve hot.

Quick Tip: Keep an extra bowl out on your countertop when you're cleaning veggies and fruits. Throw any scraps in to make clean up quicker and simpler.

Black Bean Tostadas

I like to use black beans for this dish because of the color contrast, but pinto beans would be just as delicious. **vegetarian, egg-free**

makes 6 tostadas

1 large onion, thinly sliced in half moons from top to bottom

2 red bell peppers, seeded and thinly sliced

2 to 4 tablespoons canola oil

salt and freshly ground black pepper

2 cups Refried Beans (page 119) or 1 (15-ounce) can refried black beans

1 teaspoon ground cumin

6 (6-inch) corn tortillas

½ cup crumbled queso fresco

¼ cup chopped fresh cilantro

Optional toppings:
salsa

light sour cream

guacamole

Preheat the broiler. Line 2 baking sheets with aluminum foil. Set one pan aside and spread the onion and bell peppers on the second pan. Drizzle with 2 tablespoons canola oil, season with salt and pepper, and toss to coat. If necessary, add a little more oil. Roast for 10 to 12 minutes, until the vegetables are soft.

Meanwhile, heat the refried beans in a medium saucepan over medium-low heat, stirring frequently. Taste the beans and season as indicated or to taste with the cumin. This adds a little punch of flavor.

While the veggies are roasting and the beans are heating, heat a large sauté pan over medium-high heat. Toast each tortilla for a minute or so on each side until brown and crisp, then arrange the tortillas in rows on the second baking sheet. Spread the beans on the tortillas, then top with the roasted veggies and queso fresco. Place the pan under the broiler just until the cheese is melted. Cut each tortilla into 4 or 6 wedges. Serve with your choice of toppings.

Variation—Chicken and Black Bean Tostadas: After you spread the beans on the tortillas, divide 1 cup of Make Ahead Chicken (page 97) among the tortillas, then top with the veggies and the queso fresco. Proceed as directed.

Quick Tip: Quickly seed and slice a bell pepper by cutting off the top and bottom. Then set the pepper on one end and use your knife to slice down one side. Lay the pepper on its side, open it up, and use your knife to cut the seed pods away by slicing through the ribs.

Black Bean Veggie Burgers

This is a slight variation on my sister Marcia's favorite bean burger. She and I share a love of healthier food, and these burgers fit the bill. She loves heat, while I'm more conservative with it. Use the jalapeño or leave it out to suit your taste. Serve these burgers topped with sliced fresh tomatoes or salsa, queso fresco, avocado slices, and a little sour cream. **dairy-free**

makes 6 burgers

1 (14.5-ounce) can black beans, drained and rinsed or 2 cups home-cooked beans

½ medium onion, diced

½ cup frozen corn kernels, thawed

2 garlic cloves, grated on a fine rasp grater or minced

½ to 1 jalapeño, seeded and diced (optional)

1 large carrot, peeled

½ red bell pepper

4 cremini mushrooms

1 teaspoon ground cumin

1 teaspoon salt

¼ to ½ teaspoon freshly ground black pepper

1 large egg, lightly beaten

½ cup brown rice bread crumbs or other gluten-free bread crumbs, or more

In a large bowl, mash the beans with the back of a wooden spoon or a potato masher. Add the onion, corn, garlic, and jalapeño, if using. Fit a food processor with the shredder attachment and shred the carrot, bell pepper, and mushrooms. Add the shredded veggies to the beans along with the cumin, salt, and pepper. Stir to combine. Stir in the egg and the bread crumbs. If the mixture seems a little runny, add more bread crumbs 1 tablespoon at time until the mixture is firm enough to hold a burger patty shape.

Heat a large nonstick sauté pan over medium-high heat. Put a long piece of waxed paper on your countertop. Scoop the burger mixture in ⅓-cup portions onto the waxed paper and shape them into burger patties. Cook the burgers for 3 minutes on each side, or until they're nicely browned. Be patient when cooking these burgers and don't try to flip them too early—they need time to set up and cook or they will fall apart when turned.

Quick Tip: Using a food processor saves time when shredding vegetables. If you don't have one, use a box grater to shred the carrot and finely chop the bell pepper and mushrooms.

Grilled Balsamic Dijon Chicken

Grilled chicken with a quick, simple marinade for summer nights. **dairy-free, egg-free**

serves 4 to 6

⅓ cup extra-virgin olive oil

3 tablespoons good-quality balsamic vinegar

1½ tablespoons Dijon mustard

1½ teaspoons fresh thyme leaves

1 teaspoon kosher salt

½ teaspoon freshly ground black pepper

4 boneless, skinless chicken breasts

In a small bowl, whisk together the oil, balsamic vinegar, mustard, thyme leaves, salt, and pepper until combined. Place one chicken breast between 2 pieces of plastic wrap and use a mallet or the bottom of a heavy sauté pan to pound the breast to a uniform thickness. Repeat with the remaining chicken breasts. Place the chicken in a 1-gallon sealable plastic bag, pour in the balsamic-Dijon marinade, and marinate in the refrigerator for several hours or overnight, turning once.

Preheat a grill over medium-high heat. Drain the chicken breasts and discard the marinade. Grill for about 6 minutes per side, until cooked through. If you're using an instant-read thermometer, the chicken should reach 165°F. Let the chicken rest for 5 minutes before serving.

Quick Tip: When marinating chicken in a plastic bag, always place it on a baking sheet or in a baking dish, just in case it leaks.

Slow Cooker Chicken and Wild Rice

Chicken broth adds a lot of flavor to this dish. If you don't have any on hand, use vegetable broth or water. Brown rice can be used in place of wild rice. **dairy-free, egg-free, slow cooker recipe**

serves 4 to 6

1 cup sliced carrots, about ¼ inch thick

1 cup wild rice

1 cup sliced cremini mushrooms, about ¼ inch thick

½ cup frozen peas

½ small onion, diced

1 teaspoon dried tarragon

2 cups chicken broth

1 teaspoon kosher salt

6 boneless, skinless chicken thighs

½ teaspoon freshly ground black pepper

1½ tablespoons white wine vinegar (optional)

Bring a small pan of water to a boil over high heat. Add the carrots and blanch for 3 minutes. Drain the carrots and add them to a large (4- to 6-quart) slow cooker. Add the wild rice, mushrooms, peas, onion, tarragon, chicken broth, and ½ teaspoon salt.

Trim any large pieces of extra fat from the chicken thighs. Rub the thighs with the remaining ½ teaspoon salt and the pepper. Nestle the chicken into the rice and vegetables. Cover and cook on low for 4 to 6 hours. The chicken will fall apart. For a little punch of acidity to bring depth to the dish, stir in the vinegar 30 minutes before serving, if desired. Taste and adjust the seasoning as needed.

Quick Tip: Frozen vegetables can be used in this recipe to shave off preparation time.

Spicy Stuffed Southwest Chicken

In Texas, there's a yearly celebration of Hatch chiles when the crop comes in from Mexico. My favorite grocery store roasts huge quantities of the chiles outside the store. I wasn't born in Texas, so it took a few years for me to embrace the occasion and roast the chiles myself. This dish highlights one of the many ways I now love to use Hatch chiles. Canned green chiles work as well as fresh.

serves 4

4 ounces light cream cheese, at room temperature

1 cup canned drained petite diced tomatoes

½ cup frozen sweet corn kernels

2 tablespoons chopped roasted Hatch green chiles

kosher salt and freshly ground black pepper

4 boneless, skinless chicken breasts

olive oil

Preheat the oven to 350°F.

In a medium bowl, stir together the cream cheese, tomatoes, corn, and chiles. Add salt and pepper to taste. Set aside.

Trim any big pieces of fat from the chicken. With a sharp knife held horizontally to the work surface, slice open the thick part of each chicken breast so it opens up like a book. Place a double layer of plastic wrap over the chicken and pound it with a meat mallet or heavy skillet until it's about ¼ inch thick. If any of the breasts are really large after they're pounded out, cut them in half.

Season one side of each chicken breast with salt and pepper. Spread the cream cheese filling evenly on the seasoned sides of the chicken breasts. Roll up each breast and place it seam side down into a stoneware or glass baking dish. Season the tops of the chicken with salt and pepper. Drizzle with the oil, rubbing it over the chicken to coat. Bake, covered, for 35 minutes. Remove the cover, baste the chicken with the juices in the pan, and bake for 10 to 15 minutes longer, until cooked through. The chicken should reach 165°F on an instant-read thermometer. Let rest for 5 minutes before serving.

Quick Tip: Prepare this dish up to one day ahead. After you roll up the chicken, cover and refrigerate it until you're ready to bake.

Roasted Chicken

There are so many different ways to roast a chicken. I've fussed over them, turned them on their sides, baked them at low temperatures for long periods of time. You can season a chicken a thousand different ways, too. This is my current favorite, especially because I can get it in the oven in less than 10 minutes and don't have to worry about having any fresh herbs on hand. Herbes de Provence is usually a mix of dried fennel, savory, basil, and thyme, and sometimes lavender. **egg-free**

serves 4 to 6

1 roasting chicken (about 3 pounds)

1 tablespoon herbes de Provence, divided

1½ teaspoons kosher salt, divided

1 teaspoon freshly ground black pepper, divided

1 small lemon, cut in half

5 garlic cloves, cut in half

2 tablespoons unsalted butter, melted

Preheat the oven to 425°F. Line a roasting pan with heavy-duty aluminum foil for easy clean up.

Season the inside of the chicken with a little herbes de Provence, salt, and pepper. Place the lemon and the garlic in the center of the chicken. Tuck the wing tips behind the chicken so they stay in place. Use kitchen twine to tie the legs together, crossing them at the ends.

Put the chicken in the prepared roasting pan. Rub the melted butter on the outside of the chicken, then season it with the remaining herbes de Provence, salt, and pepper. Roast for 50 minutes to 1 hour, until the thickest part of the thigh reaches 180°F and the juices run clear. Let the chicken rest for 10 minutes before carving.

Quick Tip: To get a really moist chicken, rub the cavity and the outside of the chicken with 1 teaspoon salt at least 1 hour before roasting, or preferably the night before. This helps the meat hold more juice.

Easy Chicken Cacciatore

I like to use dark chicken meat when I'm cooking in the slow cooker because it stays moister than white meat. If you don't like dark meat, choose bone-in chicken breasts, as the bone helps keep the meat from drying out. Serve with gluten-free pasta, Simple Oven-Baked Brown Rice (page 120), or Oven-Baked Polenta (page 121), and roasted vegetables (page 109). **dairy-free, egg-free, slow cooker recipe**

serves 4

4 large or 6 small bone-in or boneless, skinless chicken thighs or 2 to 3 large bone-in chicken breasts, skins removed

1 teaspoon kosher salt

½ teaspoon freshly ground black pepper

½ large onion, sliced in half moons from top to bottom

¾ cup sliced carrots, ¼ inch thick

4 ounces mushrooms, quartered

1 red bell pepper, seeded and sliced ¼ inch thick

1 (14 ½-ounce) can diced tomatoes, drained

3 tablespoons tomato paste

2 garlic cloves, grated on a fine rasp grater or minced

2 teaspoons dried parsley

Rub the chicken with salt and pepper. Set aside.

Place the onion, carrots, mushrooms, and bell pepper in the bottom of a large (4- to 6-quart) slow cooker. Arrange the seasoned chicken on top. In a medium bowl, combine the tomatoes, tomato paste, garlic, and dried parsley and put on top of the chicken. Cover and cook on low for 4 to 6 hours, until the chicken reaches an internal temperature of 165°F and the carrots are tender.

Remove the chicken from the slow cooker and pour the vegetables into a large saucepan. Spoon some of the cooking liquid over the chicken and cover to keep warm. Bring the sauce to a boil, then reduce it to a simmer. Let the sauce reduce for 10 minutes uncovered, or until it's thickened. Serve the chicken topped with the sauce.

Quick Tip: Next time you open a can of tomato paste, wrap the leftovers in 1 tablespoon portions and keep them in the freezer. You'll have tomato paste on hand whenever you need it.

Make Ahead Chicken

This is a trick I have up my sleeve at all times. My friend Helen calls this a stewed chicken, and I call it my Make Ahead Chicken, but really, it doesn't matter what you call it. It's just smart. Make this on a Sunday afternoon when you're relaxing at home—it requires almost no supervision. I use classic seasonings so that the meat and broth will work well with any other recipe. If you have a specific purpose in mind, there's no reason why you can't add your favorite herbs. **dairy-free, egg-free**

makes 4 to 5 cups shredded chicken meat and 3 quarts chicken broth

1 whole chicken, about 3 pounds

3 carrots, cut into 1-inch pieces

2 celery stalks, cut into 1-inch pieces

6 garlic cloves, cut in half

½ large onion, cut into quarters

3 sprigs flat-leaf parsley

10 black peppercorns

1 teaspoon kosher salt

Rinse the chicken, making sure to remove any giblets that might be in the cavity. Cut off any large pieces of fat around the cavity opening. Put the chicken in a large stockpot and add the carrots, celery, garlic, onion, parsley, peppercorns, and salt. Cover the chicken with water and bring it to a boil, uncovered. Reduce the heat to a bare simmer, so that the bubbles just barely break the surface of the water. Let simmer for 3 hours.

Move the chicken to a large bowl to cool. It will be very tender and fall apart. When the chicken is cool enough to handle, separate the meat from the bones. Divide it into 1- or 2-cup portions depending on your intended use, transfer the portions to freezer-safe bags, label them, and freeze for future use.

Once the broth cools slightly, carefully strain it into a large container. Cover it well and place it in the refrigerator overnight. The next day, the fat will be solidified at the top, and it's easy to just skim it off. Transfer the broth to freezer-safe containers, label them, and freeze for future use.

Quick Tip: Use Make Ahead Chicken in chicken salads, add it to Mac and Cheese (page 124) with some frozen peas to make a casserole, use it in Black Bean Tostadas (page 90), top a quick green salad with it, or add it to any dish where you need already-cooked chicken.

Asian Lettuce Wraps

One of the cuisines I miss the most is Asian. Most of the sauces contain sugar, and the soy sauce contains gluten. Bragg's Liquid Aminos has always worked as a soy sauce substitute, but I'm sure there are others on the market that will work just as well. My husband, Joe, and I have played around with this recipe a lot, and we like this version the best. **dairy-free, egg-free**

serves 4

1 tablespoon sesame oil

½ large onion, diced

2 garlic cloves, grated on a fine rasp grater or minced

1 cup sliced cremini mushrooms

1 to 1½ pounds ground turkey

1 cup chicken broth, divided

3 tablespoons gluten-free soy sauce

1 tablespoon cornstarch

½ cup chopped bamboo shoots

½ cup chopped water chestnuts

kosher salt and freshly ground black pepper

12 to 16 iceberg lettuce leaves

1 recipe Sweet and Spicy Mustard Sauce (page 56) (optional)

Heat the sesame oil in a large nonstick skillet over medium heat. Add the onion and sauté for 5 minutes, or until soft. Add the garlic and cook for about 1 minute, until fragrant. Add the mushrooms and cook for several minutes, until they begin to soften. Increase the heat to medium-high, add the turkey, and cook until no longer pink.

While the turkey is cooking, combine ¾ cup chicken broth and the soy sauce in a medium bowl. Combine the remaining ¼ cup chicken broth and the cornstarch in a small bowl.

When the turkey is cooked, add the bamboo shoots and water chestnuts. Pour the chicken broth and soy sauce mixture into the pan. Bring it to a simmer, then stir in the cornstarch mixture and simmer until the sauce thickens. Taste and adjust the seasoning as needed.

Serve the filling in the lettuce leaves. Accompany with Sweet and Spicy Mustard Sauce, if using.

Quick Tip: To easily remove the leaves from a head of lettuce, remove the core by slamming it onto the counter. You'll be able to pull the core right out. Then cut the head of lettuce in half lengthwise from the core to the top. Peel the leaves off one by one.

Turkey Meat Loaf

When you're craving comfort food, make this meat loaf. It's moist and has a lightness to it. The secret is using a fork to gently work the ingredients together so that the meat isn't compacted. Leftovers make delicious sandwiches for lunch the next day. If you can't find sugar-free ketchup in the store, use the recipe on page 54. **dairy-free**

serves 4

¼ cup quinoa, rinsed

½ cup chicken broth

1½ pounds ground turkey

½ medium onion, diced small

¼ cup finely chopped
flat-leaf parsley

2 large eggs, lightly beaten

1 tablespoon tomato paste

2 garlic cloves, grated on a
fine rasp grater or minced

1 teaspoon kosher salt

1 teaspoon light
ancho chile powder

½ teaspoon freshly ground
black pepper

½ teaspoon dried oregano

¼ teaspoon ground cumin

½ cup Slow Cooker Ketchup (page
54), divided

Preheat the oven to 350°F.

Place the quinoa and chicken broth in a small saucepan over medium-high heat. Cover, bring to a boil, then reduce the heat to a simmer and let cook for 15 minutes, or until all the liquid is absorbed.

Meanwhile, place the ground turkey in a large bowl. Add the onion, parsley, eggs, tomato paste, garlic, salt, chile powder, pepper, oregano, and cumin. Add the cooked quinoa and use a fork to gently mix the ingredients. Do not compact the meat. Transfer the mixture into an 8 x 4-inch loaf pan and gently shape it with a rubber spatula. Spread ¼ cup ketchup over the top. Bake for 45 to 55 minutes, until the internal temperature reaches 165°F.

As the meat loaf bakes, the liquid from the turkey will surround it and keep it moist. When the meat loaf has finished cooking, carefully spoon off the excess liquid. Then top the meat loaf with the remaining ¼ cup ketchup and broil for 1 to 2 minutes, until the ketchup is hot and has set up on top. Let the meat loaf rest for 5 minutes before serving.

Quick Tip: Take a few extra minutes to make a big batch of quinoa and freeze the leftovers for another meal. Or be a little frugal and freeze your leftovers from other meals, even if it's just ¼ cup, and use them in recipes like this one.

Herb-Crusted Pork Loin

Roasted pork loin is an easy way to feed a crowd. It pairs well with a fresh green salad, Parmesan Mashed Cauliflower (page 116), and roasted vegetables (page 109). **dairy-free, egg-free**

serves 6 to 8

1 (2 to 3-pound) pork loin

¼ cup fresh thyme leaves

¼ cup fresh flat-leaf parsley leaves

4 garlic cloves, peeled

2 teaspoons kosher salt

1 teaspoon freshly ground black pepper

2 to 4 tablespoons extra-virgin olive oil

Preheat the oven to 350°F. Rinse the pork, pat it dry, and place it in a foil-lined roasting pan.

Pile the thyme, parsley, garlic, salt, and pepper on a cutting board. Drizzle with 2 tablespoons oil and chop until fine to make a paste. Add more oil if necessary. Rub the herb paste over the entire surface of the pork. Roast for 45 to 50 minutes, until the internal temperature reaches 155°F. Let rest for 10 minutes before slicing.

Quick Tip: Season the pork ahead of time, cover it, and pop it back in the refrigerator. Pull it out 20 minutes before roasting to let it come to room temperature.

Stuffed Bell Peppers

My Grandma Ruth made the best stuffed bell peppers with ground beef and rice. To make this quick and simple, I use canned white beans, but you can substitute whatever you have on hand. **egg-free**

serves 4 to 6

1 tablespoon extra-virgin olive oil

1 medium onion, diced

¾ pound ground turkey

2 cups canned or home-cooked cannellini beans

1 (14.5-ounce) can diced tomatoes

¼ cup chicken broth

1½ teaspoons dried basil

1 teaspoon dried parsley

½ teaspoon kosher salt, or more

¼ teaspoon freshly ground black pepper, or more

4 large or 6 small red bell peppers

¼ to ½ cup grated Parmesan cheese

Preheat the oven to 350°F.

Heat the oil in a large nonstick pan over medium heat. Add the onion and cook for 3 to 5 minutes, until translucent. Add the turkey and cook until browned. Add the beans, tomatoes, chicken broth, basil, parsley, salt, and pepper. Heat through. Taste and adjust the seasoning as needed.

While the meat is browning, cut the tops off the bell peppers. Use a paring knife to cut the ribs so that you can easily pull out the seeds. Gently tap the bell peppers to remove any stray seeds. Once the meat and bean mixture is heated through, stuff each bell pepper as full as you can get it. Nestle the peppers into a baking dish.

Bake for 35 to 45 minutes, until the peppers are soft. Top with the cheese and place the pan under the broiler just until the cheese melts and browns slightly. Serve hot.

Variation—Slow Cooker Method: Nestle the stuffed peppers in a large (4- to 6-quart) slow cooker. Cook on low for 4 to 6 hours, until the peppers are soft. Remove the crock from the slow cooker and top each pepper with cheese. Cover until the cheese melts, or place the crock under the broiler just until the cheese melts and browns slightly. Serve hot.

Quick Tip: To make this a freezer meal, blanch the peppers in boiling water for 3 minutes. Let them drain and cool before stuffing with the cooked meat mixture. Arrange in a freezer-safe dish, wrap, label, and freeze. To cook, remove the peppers from the freezer 1 to 2 days before needed and let thaw in the refrigerator. Cook in the oven or slow cooker as directed above.

Antipasto Platter

This is one trick every cook should have in her back pocket, gluten-free or not. It's really just a variety of tasty deli meats, cheeses, olives, and other pickled items. You can use as little or as much as you want. Presentation counts with this dish, so use a variety of colors and textures, taking care to arrange the items with finesse. Here's a list of my favorites. Of course, read package labels and check about gluten-free status at the deli counter.

Meats	Fruits and Veggies
• proscuitto di Parma, salami, such as Genoa	• seedless red grape clusters
• sliced pepperoni	• fresh figs, stemmed and cut in half
• serrano ham	• fresh berries
• capocollo	• sliced carrots, radishes, or mushrooms
• smoked salmon	• pickled or lightly steamed asparagus
	• hearts of palm
	• Greek olives
	• artichoke hearts
	• roasted red peppers
	• slow-roasted tomatoes
	• pepperoncini
Cheeses	**Other Favorites**
• shaved Parmesan	• Marcona or plain roasted almonds
• Gruyère	• chickpeas in a light vinaigrette
• Brie	• marinated fava beans
• Gouda	• crackers or bread sticks
• Havarti	
• fresh mozzarella	
• bocconcini	

Quick Tip: Keep a supply of your favorite canned or jarred items on hand so when you need to put together an impromptu meal, you'll just have to stop by the deli and get a few items.

Parchment Paper–Baked Fish

I learned how to make this dish when I was working at a little upscale diner. For some reason, I had trouble folding the parchment paper so that it would hold steam and bake the fish. Luckily, the chef was a great teacher, too. He insisted I cut and fold the parchment paper until I'd perfected the seal. Don't worry if it takes more than one try. **dairy-free, egg-free**

serves 2

2 (6-ounce) fish fillets, such as salmon or halibut

1 tablespoon unsalted butter, melted

kosher salt and freshly ground black pepper

1 tablespoon chopped fresh flat-leaf parsley

1 tablespoon finely chopped shallots

4 thin lemon slices

Preheat the oven to 450°F. Cut 2 pieces of parchment paper about 6 inches longer than the fish fillets. Fold each piece of parchment in half and cut it into a heart shape. Open up the hearts. Place each fillet on one side of a heart and brush it with the melted butter. Season lightly with salt and pepper, then sprinkle with the parsley and shallots. Top each fillet with 2 lemon slices.

To seal the parchment paper by crimping the edges, fold the paper over so it covers the fish. Start at the top of the heart and carefully fold the edges closed, overlapping as you go so that the steam can't get out when the fish cooks. When you reach the bottom of the heart, fold the point under so that it stays in place. Bake for 5 to 8 minutes, until the paper is puffed and brown. If your fillets are very thin, bake them for a shorter time. If you have very thick pieces of fish, you'll need to bake them longer.

If for some reason your paper doesn't brown and you want a dramatic presentation, pop the parchment-wrapped fillets under the broiler for a few seconds. Don't walk away from the oven, though, or the fish will overcook and you'll ruin your dinner. Serve immediately, with the fish in the paper. Cut the paper open with kitchen shears at the table for a dramatic presentation.

Quick Tip: The general rule of thumb for baking fish is 10 minutes for every inch of thickness.

Swiss Chard and Mushrooms with Linguini

In order to cook a pasta dish with 20 minutes active time or less, you have to get the pasta water boiling first. Salting the water will not only help it boil quicker but will also season the pasta.

serves 4

salt

3 slices bacon, cut into ¼-inch strips

½ medium onion, sliced into half moons from top to bottom

3 garlic cloves, grated on a fine rasp grater or minced

12 medium to large cremini mushrooms, sliced thinly

1 bunch Swiss chard, thick ribs removed and coarsely chopped

2 cups chicken or vegetable broth

12 ounces brown rice linguini

freshly ground black pepper

½ cup freshly grated Parmesan cheese

Fill a large stockpot with water and season with 1 tablespoon salt. Cover, bring to a boil, and reduce to a simmer. Leave the pot simmering until you're ready to cook the pasta.

Heat a large sauté pan over medium heat and cook the bacon until crispy. Remove from the pan and drain on paper towels.

Wipe out some of the bacon fat with a paper towel, if desired. Add the onions and sauté for about 5 minutes, until soft. Add the garlic and cook for about 1 minute, until fragrant. Add the mushrooms and cook until soft. Add half of the chard and when wilted, add the second half.

Once all the chard is wilted, add the broth and bacon. Simmer uncovered until the chard is tender.

Cook the pasta until al dente, checking 3 minutes earlier than indicated on the package. Once the pasta is cooked, transfer it directly into the pan of chard. Toss to combine. Add a little of the pasta cooking water as needed. Taste and adjust the seasoning as needed. Serve with the cheese.

Make It Dairy-Free: Omit the Parmesan cheese. Instead, stir 1 teaspoon nutritional yeast into the sauce while the chard is simmering.

Quick Tip: Bacon is easiest to slice when it's frozen. Make sure to use a sharp knife.

Shrimp in Spicy Tomato Sauce with Linguini

Quick yet elegant, this dish is company-worthy. The stevia balances out the acid in the tomatoes and keeps the sauce sugar-free. **dairy-free, egg-free**

serves 4

kosher salt

2 tablespoons extra-virgin olive oil

½ medium yellow onion, diced

2 garlic cloves, grated on a fine rasp grater or minced

1 (28-ounce) can diced tomatoes

1¼ teaspoons red pepper flakes

½ teaspoon dried basil

½ to ¾ cup fish or vegetable broth

10 drops of liquid stevia

3 tablespoons chopped fresh flat-leaf parsley

freshly ground black pepper

1 pound shrimp, peeled and deveined

¾ pound gluten-free linguini

Fill a large stockpot with water, add 1 tablespoon kosher salt, cover, and bring to a boil. Reduce to a simmer. Leave the pot simmering until you're ready to cook the pasta.

Heat the oil in a large sauté pan over medium-low heat. Add the onion and cook for about 5 to 8 minutes, until soft. Add the garlic and cook for about 1 minute, until it begins to brown. Add the tomatoes, red pepper flakes, basil, ½ cup broth, and stevia. Bring to a simmer and allow to reduce by about 25 percent, or until the desired consistency is reached, stirring frequently and mashing the tomatoes with the back of your spoon. Add the remaining broth if the sauce gets too thick. Stir in the parsley. Taste and adjust the seasoning with salt and pepper as needed. Keep the sauce warm.

Cook the pasta according to the package directions, but check for doneness 3 minutes before the time indicated. Continue to check the pasta every minute until al dente. Bring the sauce to a simmer and add the shrimp to the sauce several minutes before the pasta is ready to serve. Cook for 1 to 3 minutes depending on the size of your shrimp, just until the shrimp turn pink. Transfer the pasta to a serving bowl and top with the sauce.

Variation—Chicken in Spicy Tomato Sauce with Linguini: Use chicken broth instead of vegetable or fish broth and use 1 cup Make Ahead Chicken (page 97) instead of shrimp.

Quick Tip: If you can find peeled and deveined shrimp, that's the quickest way to prepare this recipe. If the shrimp haven't yet been peeled, ask the fishmonger to peel and devein them while you finish the rest of your grocery shopping.

Deep Dish Lasagne

I'd been trying to figure out how to throw together a quick lasagne without quick-cooking noodles when I saw a veggie lasagne post from Stephanie O'Dea at A Year of Slow Cooking (CrockPot365.blogspot. com). This slow-cooker lasagne is beautiful—it slices well, stays stacked up high, and is not greasy at all. Don't worry about having to break the pasta to make it fit. Just fill in the gaps and it somehow magically fuses itself back together. I recommend using Tinkyada Organic Brown Rice Lasagne noodles with this recipe. **egg-free, slow cooker recipe**

serves 6 to 8

1 tablespoon extra-virgin olive oil

½ large onion, diced

3 garlic cloves, grated on a fine rasp grater or minced

1 pound ground turkey

8 ounces tomato sauce, divided

1 (28-ounce) can diced tomatoes with juice

1¼ teaspoons salt, divided

1 teaspoon dried basil

1 teaspoon dried oregano

1 teaspoon dried parsley

¾ teaspoon freshly ground black pepper, divided

2 cups part-skim ricotta cheese

1 (10-ounce) package frozen spinach, thawed and drained

8 to 10 gluten-free brown rice lasagne noodles

2 cups shredded part-skim mozzarella cheese

¼ cup water

Prepare the insert of a large (5- to 6-quart) oval-shaped slow cooker with cooking spray.

Heat the oil in a large nonstick sauté pan over medium heat. Add the onion and cook for 3 to 5 minutes, until translucent. Add the garlic and cook about 1 minute, until fragrant. Increase the heat to medium-high. Add the turkey and cook until it's no longer pink, breaking it up with a wooden spoon.

While the turkey is cooking, spread 2 tablespoons tomato sauce in the bottom of the crock. Once the turkey is cooked, add the remaining tomato sauce, tomatoes with juice, 1 teaspoon salt, the basil, oregano, parsley, and ½ teaspoon pepper to the sauté pan. Stir to combine and cook until heated through.

Place the ricotta cheese in a medium bowl. Squeeze the spinach dry and stir it into the ricotta. Season the ricotta mixture with the remaining ¼ teaspoon salt and ¼ teaspoon pepper.

Arrange one layer of noodles in the bottom of the insert, breaking the noodles as needed. Spread one-third of the cooked meat mixture on top of the noodles. Top with one-third of the ricotta mixture. Add two more layers of noodles, meat, and ricotta, ending with the ricotta mixture on top. Sprinkle the mozzarella over the ricotta. Pour the water all the way around the edge of the slow cooker. Cover and cook on low for 3 to 5 hours, until cooked through and the noodles are tender. Once cooked, the lasagne will keep nicely on the warm setting for 1 hour until served.

Side Dishes

Slow Cooker Winter Squash

It doesn't get any easier than this when it comes to preparing a winter squash. I like the convenience of throwing it in the slow cooker and cutting through the skin effortlessly once it's cooked. Make sure the squash fits into your slow cooker without touching the sides of the crock so it doesn't scorch. Butternut, acorn, and spaghetti are some of my favorite varieties of winter squash to cook in my slow cooker. **vegan, slow cooker recipe**

serves 4 to 6, depending on size of squash

1 winter squash (about 2 pounds)

½ cup water

salt and freshly ground black pepper

Put the squash and water in a large slow cooker big enough to accommodate it, making sure the squash doesn't touch the sides of the crock. Cover and cook on low for 4 to 5 hours. The squash is cooked when you can easily pierce the skin with a fork.

After the squash cools enough to handle comfortably, cut it in half. Use a large metal spoon to remove the seeds. Scrape the squash from the shell into a serving dish. Season to taste with salt and pepper and serve.

Quick Tip: Cook a spaghetti squash this way and use it like pasta—the flesh pulls apart in noodlelike strands.

Oven-Roasted Cauliflower

This is my surefire way of getting people to eat vegetables. When roasted in the oven, vegetables caramelize; they get slightly sweet and very soft. You can roast almost any vegetable using this method. You'll just need to watch the oven so you'll know when they're done. **vegan**

serves 4

1 head cauliflower

2 to 3 tablespoons extra-virgin olive oil

2 garlic cloves, grated on a fine rasp grater or minced

1 teaspoon Curry Powder (page 60)

kosher salt and freshly ground black pepper

Preheat the oven to 425°F. Line a large baking sheet with aluminum foil.

Cut the cauliflower into even-size florets. Drizzle with the oil, sprinkle the garlic and curry powder over, and season with salt and pepper. Toss with a rubber spatula to evenly coat the florets. Roast for 20 to 25 minutes, stirring halfway through. The cauliflower is done when it's soft and caramelized in places.

Variation—Other Roasted Veggie Combos: To roast other vegetables, use the method above. Try any of these:

turnips, fresh thyme sprigs, and garlic

broccoli and garlic tossed in a squeeze of fresh lemon juice before serving

carrots and cumin tossed in a squeeze of fresh orange juice before serving

zucchini, garlic, and thyme sprigs

okra sliced into ½-inch pieces, and salt and pepper

sweet potatoes, onions, and fresh rosemary sprigs

fingerling potatoes, thyme or rosemary, and garlic, topped with freshly grated Parmesan cheese

Brussels sprouts, garlic, and fresh thyme sprigs tossed in a squeeze of lemon juice before serving

Slow-Roasted Tomatoes

When you have out-of-season tomatoes that aren't bursting with flavor or a few tomatoes that are about to expire, this is the recipe to reach for. Slow roasting creates lots of flavor and brings out the tomatoes' natural sweetness. This recipe calls for Roma tomatoes, but you can use any variety you'd like. **vegan**

serves 2 to 4

4 Roma tomatoes

2 garlic cloves

2 tablespoons extra-virgin olive oil, or more

kosher salt and freshly ground black pepper

Preheat the oven to 300°F.

Stem the tomatoes and cut them in half lengthwise. Put the halves in an 8 x 8-inch glass or stoneware baking dish seed-side up. Grate the garlic on a fine rasp grater directly over the tomatoes, or mince the garlic and sprinkle it over. Drizzle with the oil and toss to coat the tomatoes. If necessary, add a little more oil. Season to taste with salt and pepper. Bake for 2 hours, or until the tomatoes are tender, rotating the pan 180 degrees after 1 hour. Slip the skins off the tomato halves before serving.

Quick Tip: Make a big batch of roasted tomatoes and keep them refrigerated in an airtight container for up to 1 week. They're fabulous in pasta, hummus, salsa, sauces, and dips.

Green Beans with Red Peppers

I wish I could take credit for this recipe because it's so simple and full of flavor, but it's my mom's. She and I could eat the entire pound of beans by ourselves. **vegan**

serves 4

2 cups chicken broth, divided

½ large onion, diced

½ red bell pepper, cut into thin strips

1 pound green beans, cleaned

kosher salt and freshly ground black pepper

Heat ½ cup chicken broth in a large saucepan over medium heat. Add the onion and cook for about 5 minutes, until slightly tender. Add the bell pepper and cook for about 1 minute. Add the green beans, cover, and cook for about 10 minutes, until crisp-tender, stirring occasionally and adding more stock as needed. Season to taste with salt and pepper.

Quick Tip: Occasionally I'll find cleaned, ready-to-cook green beans at the market. I love the convenience they offer. Look for them in the produce section of your grocery store.

Pan-Grilled Zucchini

My husband loves when I pan-grill zucchini because of the taste. I love it because it's simple and easy. Make sure to cut the zucchini at least ¼ inch thick so they retain their shape when you cook them. **vegan**

serves 3 to 4

4 to 6 zucchini or yellow summer squash

2 to 3 tablespoons extra-virgin olive oil

1 tablespoon fresh thyme leaves, chopped

1 garlic clove, grated on a fine rasp grater or minced

kosher salt and freshly ground black pepper

Holding the knife at a 45-degree angle, slice the zucchini ¼ inch thick. Place the slices in a large bowl, drizzle with oil, then season to taste with the thyme, garlic, salt, and pepper. Toss well to coat and set aside to marinate while the pan is heating.

Heat a nonstick grill pan over medium-high heat. Place the zucchini slices in rows across the grill pan and let them cook for several minutes on each side. Turn only once so that they have nice grill marks on each side. Serve immediately.

Quick Tip: The zucchini can be sliced hours ahead of time and left at room temperature until you're ready to season it.

Parmesan-Crusted Sweet Potato Fries

My husband didn't think he liked sweet potatoes until I made these fries. The sweetness of the potato plays perfectly with the saltiness of the Parmesan cheese. Make Light Garlic Aioli (page 55) to use as a dipping sauce.

serves 4

2 large egg whites

½ teaspoon freshly ground sea salt

2 large sweet potatoes

1 cup freshly grated
Parmesan cheese

freshly ground or coarse salt and
freshly ground black pepper

Preheat the oven to 425°F. Line a baking sheet with parchment paper or aluminum foil. If using foil, lightly mist it with cooking spray.

Beat the egg whites with the sea salt until foamy. Set aside. Chop the sweet potatoes into steak fry wedges. Dip the wedges into the egg whites, gently shaking to remove any excess egg. Lightly dip one side of each wedge into the Parmesan cheese. Set the fries on the prepared baking sheet with the cheese facing up. Season to taste with salt and pepper. Bake for 25 to 30 minutes, until crispy on the outside but tender when pierced with a fork.

Quick Tip: Set up a mini assembly line to quickly assemble these fries. From left to right, line up your raw fries, beaten egg whites, grated cheese, and the prepared baking sheet.

Sprouted Lentils

These lentils take a few days to sprout, but they're virtually hands-off. Make sure to cook these thoroughly before serving, as uncooked sprouted beans can make you ill. **vegan**

makes 1 ½ cups

1 cup green lentils

water as needed

kosher salt and pepper (optional)

Equipment:

1-quart glass Mason jar with a lid

cheesecloth, rinsed and squeezed dry

shallow bowl or pie plate

Place the lentils in the Mason jar and cover with filtered water. Put the lid on the jar and soak overnight. Drain and rinse the lentils, rinse the jar, and place the lentils back into the jar. Remove the insert from the Mason jar lid and set it aside. Cover the top of the jar with the cheesecloth then screw the outer rim of the lid onto the jar, securing the cheesecloth in place.

Run water through the cheesecloth directly into the jar, covering the lentils with water. Drain the jar by turning it upside down and letting the water run out through the cheesecloth. Invert the jar in a shallow bowl or pie plate so that excess water can run out into the bowl. If necessary, shake the lentils around so that they're in an even layer in the jar. Rinse and drain the lentils 3 times a day for about 2 days, until they have sprouts about ¼ to ½ inch long.

Place the sprouted lentils in a steamer and cook for about 20 minutes, until tender. Season to taste with salt and pepper if desired and serve warm.

Quick Tip: Cooked and cooled sprouted lentils make a tasty addition to green salads.

Simple Sautéed Swiss Chard

When chard is in season, I can't resist bringing it home from the market. My favorite variety is red chard, not only for its flavor when sautéed but for the beautiful red veins and stems. ***vegan***

serves 2 to 4

1 bunch red Swiss chard

1 tablespoon extra-virgin olive oil

½ medium onion, diced

¼ to ½ cup chicken broth,
or more

freshly ground sea salt and freshly
ground black pepper

1 tablespoon butter,
for the chard stems

Rinse the chard thoroughly and leave the water on the leaves. Remove the tough stems by folding the leaves in half and carefully cutting along the edge of the stems. Set the stems aside. Once all the stems are removed, cut the leaves into ½-inch strips.

Heat the oil in a medium nonstick saucepan over medium-low heat. Add the onion to the pan and cook for about 3 minutes, until translucent. Add the chard leaves and about ¼ cup broth. Cover and cook for 3 to 5 minutes, until the leaves are wilted. Season to taste with salt and pepper. If you prefer your chard to be more tender, add more broth and continue cooking until the desired consistency is reached.

The chard stems can be cooked much like asparagus. Holding your knife at a 45 degree angle to the stems, cut them into ½-inch pieces. Heat a small nonstick sauté pan over medium-high heat. Cover the bottom of the pan with broth. Once the broth simmers, add the sliced chard stems and cook until tender. Season to taste with salt, pepper, and butter.

Quick Tip: Stack 4 to 5 chard leaves so the stems line up, carefully fold them over, and slice along the stem to quickly prepare the leaves.

Parmesan Mashed Cauliflower

Try this recipe instead of mashed potatoes the next time you serve roasted chicken or pork. When cooked and mashed, cauliflower is silky smooth. **egg-free**

serves 4

½ large head cauliflower

3 to 4 cups chicken broth, divided

¼ cup low-fat milk

¼ cup low-fat sour cream

¼ cup freshly grated Parmesan cheese

kosher salt and freshly ground black pepper

Cut the cauliflower into florets and place them in a large saucepan or small stockpot. Add enough broth to cover the cauliflower, then cover the pot and bring it to a boil. Reduce the heat to a simmer and cook for 15 to 20 minutes, until the cauliflower is fork tender. Drain and reserve the broth. Return the cooked cauliflower to the pot and add ¼ cup chicken broth and the milk, and puree with an immersion blender. Once the cauliflower starts to get smooth, add the sour cream and continue to puree. Add additional hot broth to achieve the desired consistency. Stir in the cheese and season to taste with salt and pepper.

Quick Tip: If I know I'm going to use an immersion blender, I use stainless steel pots. It's easy to damage the Teflon coating on nonstick pans with the metal immersion blender.

Restaurant-Style Black Beans

We didn't eat a lot of beans growing up, so cooking them at home was a little foreign to me. I learned how to add lots of flavor to beans from cooking Martha Rose Shulman's Tasty Pot of Beans in The Best Vegetarian Recipes, *from which this recipe has been adapted.* **vegan**

*makes about 6 cups,
6 to 8 servings*

1 pound dried black beans

1 medium onion, diced small

3 garlic cloves, grated on a fine rasp grater or minced

2 teaspoons ground cumin

¼ cup chopped cilantro

2 to 3 teaspoons kosher salt

Rinse and sort the beans. Cover the beans with water and soak overnight.

Drain the beans, discard the soaking water, and place the beans in a large stockpot or Dutch oven. Add enough fresh water to cover the beans by 1 inch. Bring to a boil, then reduce to a simmer. Skim off the foam as it rises. Once there is no more foam, add the onion, garlic, and cumin. Let the beans simmer for 45 minutes, or until they start to soften. Add the cilantro.

Continue cooking for 30 to 45 minutes longer, until the beans are very soft but still intact and the broth has thickened. Taste, add salt, and adjust the seasoning as needed. Serve warm. Refrigerate or freeze any leftovers. When reheating, add water as needed to get the right consistency.

Quick Tip: Freeze the beans in 2-cup portions with their cooking liquid. Put them in 1-quart sealable plastic bags, stack them on a baking sheet, and put the entire tray in the freezer. Once frozen, they'll stack neatly on your freezer shelves.

Leek and White Bean Gratin

This dish takes ordinary white beans and elevates them to a company-worthy dish. The beans get almost creamy after they're baked with chicken broth and fresh herbs. Serve these flavorful beans instead of potatoes with your favorite roasted meat dish. **egg-free**

serves 6 to 8

2 leeks, white and light green parts only

3 tablespoons extra-virgin olive oil, divided

2 (15.5-ounce) cans cannellini beans, rinsed and drained

2 cups chicken broth

2 teaspoons chopped fresh sage

kosher salt and freshly ground black pepper

½ cup gluten-free bread crumbs

½ cup freshly grated Parmesan cheese

2 tablespoons chopped fresh flat-leaf parsley

Preheat the oven to 350°F.

Cut the leeks in half lengthwise and slice thinly. Clean the slices thoroughly by placing in a large bowl and covering with water. Swirl the leeks in the water and let sit. Any dirt will fall to the bottom of the bowl. Lift the leeks out of the water without disturbing the dirt at the bottom of bowl. Repeat if necessary.

Heat 1 tablespoon oil in a wide, deep sauté pan over medium heat. Add the leeks and cook for 8 to 10 minutes, until soft. Add the beans, broth, and sage. Mash one-third to one-half of the beans with the back of a wooden spoon. Cover and let the beans cook until the broth thickens slightly. Season to taste with salt and pepper.

While the beans are cooking, combine the bread crumbs, cheese, and parsley in a medium bowl. Drizzle with the remaining 2 tablespoons oil and mix until moist. Transfer the beans to a 1½-quart stoneware or glass baking dish. Top with the bread crumb mixture. Bake for 30 minutes, or until the bread crumbs are golden brown and the bean liquid is bubbling in a few places around the edges. Let rest for 5 minutes before serving.

Quick Tip: The beans and leek mixture can be prepared one day ahead. Top them with the bread crumb mixture right before baking.

Refried Beans

You can most certainly purchase refried beans to save time, but after you make these you'll never use the prepared ones again. These beans have more flavor, and you'll know exactly what's in them. My personal favorites for this recipe are black beans, but you can use whatever suits your fancy. I use bean liquid and broth because broth adds tons of flavor, but water will work too. **vegan**

serves 4 to 6

1 tablespoon canola oil

½ large onion, diced

2 garlic cloves, grated on a fine rasp grater or minced

1 (14½-ounce) can beans, drained and liquid reserved or 2 cups home-cooked beans with cooking liquid

1 to 2 cups chicken broth, vegetable broth, or water

2 to 3 tablespoons chopped cilantro

1 teaspoon ground cumin

kosher salt and freshly ground black pepper

Heat the oil over medium heat in a large nonstick pan. Sauté the onion for about 5 minutes, until tender. Add the garlic and cook for 1 minute, until fragrant. Add the beans to the pan and add a little bean liquid. Mash the beans with the back of a spoon. Continue adding bean liquid and broth or water and mashing until the desired consistency is reached. Stir in the cilantro and cumin and season to taste with salt and pepper.

Quick Tip: These beans can be made ahead of time, reheated, and thinned to a desired consistency with broth or water.

Simple Oven-Baked Brown Rice

This recipe is adapted from The New Best Recipe *by Cook's Illustrated. The proportion of liquid to rice is perfect. I use broth instead of water to give the rice more flavor, but be as creative as you want in choosing your liquid—try coconut milk, vegetable juice, or even your favorite nondairy milk.* **egg-free**

serves 4 to 6

2⅓ cups chicken, beef, or vegetable broth

1 tablespoon unsalted butter

1½ cups long-grain brown rice

1 teaspoon kosher salt, or as needed

freshly ground black pepper

Preheat the oven to 375°F.

Put the chicken broth and butter in a microwave-safe container and bring to a boil in the microwave.

Meanwhile, combine the rice and salt in a 1½-quart baking dish, preferably with a glass lid. When the broth is hot, carefully pour it over the rice. Cover the rice with a double layer of aluminum foil, taking care to get the tightest seal possible, then place the lid, if you have one, on top of the foil.

Place the baking dish on a baking sheet and bake for 55 minutes, or until the rice is tender and the liquid has been absorbed. Remove the foil from the baking dish and fluff the rice with a fork. Let stand for 5 minutes. Season to taste with additional salt and freshly ground black pepper.

Quick Tip: Make a batch of this rice on a day when your oven is free. Divide it into 2-cup portions and freeze in sealable plastic bags. You'll have nutritious brown rice at the ready on busy nights.

Oven-Baked Polenta

There's a standard ratio for polenta: 1 part cornmeal to 4 parts liquid. I've found, though, that the amount of water needed varies from brand to brand. Through some experimentation, I've found that using a little less water is a good place to start. If necessary, I add more water once my polenta is out of the oven. **egg-free**

serves 4 to 6

¾ cup stone-ground cornmeal

1 teaspoon kosher salt

¼ teaspoon freshly ground black pepper

2½ cups water, or more

¼ cup low-fat milk

1 tablespoon unsalted butter

Preheat the oven to 425°F.

Combine the cornmeal, salt, and pepper in a 2- to 3-quart casserole dish. Whisk in the water. Cover the dish with its lid or aluminum foil. Bake for 20 minutes, then remove the dish from the oven and carefully whisk the polenta. Return it to the oven and bake for 15 minutes longer. Remove the polenta from the oven and stir in the milk and butter. Add additional hot water as needed to reach the desired consistency.

Variations: Stir in freshly grated Parmesan cheese, oil-packed sun-dried tomatoes, drained, or fresh herbs.

Quick Tip: Put polenta leftover from dinner in a baking dish and spread it out ½ to ¾ inch thick. Let it sit overnight in the refrigerator. Grill it the next morning for breakfast, like I do in Griddled Cream of Buckwheat Triangles (page 28).

Zucchini and Brown Rice Gratin

This dish might take a little longer than 20 minutes, but it's worth every second. It's one of my favorite ways to use leftover brown rice. Whenever I make Simple Oven-Baked Brown Rice (page 120), I freeze the leftovers for dishes like this. **egg-free**

serves 4 to 6

1 tablespoon extra-virgin olive oil

½ medium onion, diced

1 cup sliced cremini mushrooms

2 medium zucchini, cut in half lengthwise and sliced ¼ inch thick

2 cups cooked long-grain brown rice

1 tablespoon freshly sliced basil

1 tablespoon unsalted butter

1 tablespoon tapioca flour

½ cup heavy cream

1 cup chicken broth

½ cup freshly grated Parmesan cheese, divided

kosher salt and freshly ground black pepper

Preheat the oven to 350°F.

Heat the oil in a large nonstick skillet or a deep sauté pan over medium heat. Add the onion and sauté for about 3 to 5 minutes, until it begins to soften. Add the mushrooms and sauté for about 5 minutes longer, until cooked through. Transfer the mixture into a 1½- to 2-quart gratin dish or other stoneware or glass dish. In the same sauté pan, cook the zucchini for about 5 minutes, until it's just beginning to soften. Add the zucchini, brown rice, and basil to the baking dish and stir to combine.

In the same sauté pan, melt the butter over medium heat and add the tapioca flour. It should sizzle when it hits the butter. Cook the flour and butter together until it's fragrant but not brown. Whisk in the cream and broth. Bring the sauce to a gentle simmer and cook until it thickens and will coat the back of a spoon. Stir in ¼ cup cheese. Season to taste with salt and pepper.

Pour the cream sauce over the rice and vegetables. Top the gratin with the remaining ¼ cup cheese. Bake for 30 to 45 minutes, until the gratin is slightly browned on top and bubbly. If desired, place the dish under the broiler for 15 to 30 seconds to add color to the top of the gratin.

Quick Tip: This recipe can be prepared several hours ahead of time. Reserve the final ¼ cup Parmesan cheese and sprinkle it on top of the gratin right before baking.

Potato Latkes

I'd never had latkes before making these, but my husband kept talking about them. My sister-in-law is an incredible cook and often makes holiday meals for thirty to forty people. She shared her secret for simple and oh-so-perfect potato latkes—Ore-Ida Hash Browns. Though I don't often eat fried foods, these latkes are better than any hash browns I've ever had. Traditionally, they're served with sour cream or applesauce, but I like them with my Slow Cooker Ketchup (page 54). **dairy-free**

makes 10 latkes

canola oil for frying

2 cups frozen hash brown potatoes, thawed

1 tablespoon finely chopped onion

2 large eggs

2 tablespoons buckwheat flour

¼ teaspoon gluten-free baking powder

pinch of salt

Optional toppings:
sour cream

warm applesauce

Slow Cooker Ketchup (page 54)

Heat ⅛ inch of oil in a deep skillet or large Dutch oven over medium-high heat. While the pan is heating, toss together the potatoes and onion in a medium bowl. Make a well in the center of the potatoes, add the eggs, and beat them with a fork. Add the buckwheat flour, baking powder, and salt and mix with the eggs until combined. Stir the potatoes into the egg mixture until coated.

Drop spoonfuls of the potato mixture into the oil and flatten with a spoon. Cook for 2 minutes on each side, or until golden brown. Drain on a plate lined with paper towels. Serve immediately with your choice of toppings. Or keep warm in a 200°F oven.

Quick Tip: Make sure the oil is hot before adding the latkes. Look for little bubbles forming around the edges. If the oil isn't hot enough, the potatoes will soak up oil instead of cooking in it and you'll have greasy latkes.

Mac and Cheese

This recipe is an adaptation of Ina Garten's mac and cheese from Barefoot Contessa Family Style, which taught me the delicious pairing of sharp white cheddar, Gruyère, and nutmeg. I've made many variations of her recipe, but this version is the one my husband declared his favorite. He had no idea I'd lightened it up with cottage cheese. I have to agree—it's creamy and full of flavor. **egg-free**

serves 6

1 tablespoon plus 1½ teaspoons kosher salt

1 tablespoon extra-virgin olive oil

8 ounces gluten-free penne pasta

3 tablespoons unsalted butter, divided

¼ cup Basic Flour Blend (page 212)

2 cups low-fat milk

1 cup shredded Gruyère cheese

1 cup shredded sharp white cheddar cheese

1 cup low-fat cottage cheese

¼ teaspoon freshly ground black pepper

¼ teaspoon freshly grated nutmeg

½ cup gluten-free bread crumbs

2 to 3 Roma tomatoes, sliced

Preheat the oven to 350°F. Coat a 1½-quart baking dish with cooking spray.

Fill a large stockpot three-quarters full of water. Add 1 tablespoon kosher salt, cover, and bring to a boil. Once the water is boiling, add the oil and pasta to the water and stir. Cook until al dente, checking the pasta several minutes before the suggested time on the package. Drain the pasta.

Meanwhile, melt 2 tablespoons butter in a heavy-bottomed saucepan over medium heat. Add the flour blend and cook for 3 to 5 minutes, until the flour stops foaming, whisking constantly. Slowly whisk in the milk, pouring in a steady stream. If the flour starts to seize up, continue adding milk and keep whisking until smooth. Continue whisking until the sauce has thickened and will coat the back of a spoon.

Remove the milk mixture from the heat. Stir in the cheeses, the remaining 1½ teaspoons salt, and the pepper and nutmeg. Continue stirring until the cheese has melted. Add the cooked pasta and stir to combine. Transfer the pasta and cheese to the prepared baking dish.

Melt the remaining 1 tablespoon butter in the microwave and toss it with the bread crumbs. Sprinkle the bread crumbs across the top of the pasta and cheese, then lay the sliced tomatoes on top. Place the dish on a baking sheet and bake for 30 to 35 minutes, until the bread crumbs are a beautiful golden brown and the cheese is bubbly around the edges. Let rest for 5 minutes before serving.

Quick Tip: This dish can be prepared ahead of time and refrigerated. Add the bread crumbs and tomatoes right before baking.

Light and Moist Cornbread

Cornbread is one of the simplest ways to add gluten-free bread to a meal. I love it with soups, chili, and herbed pork loin.

makes 8 generous wedges

1 cup Basic Flour Blend (page 212)

2 tablespoons palm sugar

2½ teaspoons gluten-free baking powder

¾ teaspoon xanthan gum

½ teaspoon kosher salt

2 tablespoons non-hydrogenated shortening

¾ cup cornmeal

1 cup low-fat buttermilk

2 large eggs

2 tablespoons unsalted butter, melted, plus 1 tablespoon for the pan

Preheat the oven to 400°F. Place a 9- to 10-inch stoneware or glass baking dish in the oven.

In a large bowl, whisk together the flour blend, palm sugar, baking powder, xanthan gum, and salt. Use your fingers to cut the shortening into the flour mixture until its consistency resembles peas. Whisk in the cornmeal. Set aside.

Whisk the buttermilk, eggs, and melted butter together in a medium bowl. Place the 1 tablespoon butter in the hot baking dish to melt while you finish mixing the ingredients.

Add the wet ingredients to the dry and mix until just combined. Carefully remove the baking dish from the oven and swirl the butter to coat the bottom and sides. Pour the cornbread batter into the hot dish and bake for 15 to 20 minutes, until the top is golden brown and a toothpick inserted into the center comes out clean.

Let cool slightly before slicing. Serve warm with room-temperature butter. Wrap and freeze leftovers.

Quick Tip: Freeze leftover cornbread and make cornbread croutons for salads and soups. Simply cut the bread into the desired shape, let it dry on a pan for a day or so, then drizzle it lightly with olive oil and season with salt and pepper. Toast in a 350°F oven until crispy. These are more delicate than store-bought croutons, but they're delicious.

Cookies & Bars

Carob Chip Cookies

Carob is my alternative to chocolate. I've shared these cookies with friends on countless occasions, and two things are always the same: No one ever mentions that they don't taste the chocolate, and the plate is always empty in no time. I prefer to use parchment paper when baking these cookies because the carob bakes well on it, but silicone baking mats will work, too.

makes 2 dozen cookies

½ cup unsalted butter, at room temperature

1 cup palm sugar

1 large egg

1½ teaspoons vanilla extract

1¾ cups Basic Flour Blend (page 212)

1 teaspoon gluten-free baking powder

½ teaspoon xanthan gum

¼ teaspoon kosher salt

1 cup unsweetened carob chips

½ cup coarsely chopped toasted walnuts (optional)

Preheat the oven to 350°F. Line 2 baking sheets with silicone baking mats or parchment paper.

In the bowl of a stand mixer fitted with the paddle attachment, beat the butter on medium speed for about 5 minutes, until light and fluffy. Add the palm sugar one-half at a time, letting it fully incorporate before adding more. Continue beating until light and fluffy. (The palm sugar won't fully dissolve at this point the way white sugar would.) Add the egg and vanilla and mix until incorporated.

While the butter and sugar are creaming, whisk the flour blend, baking powder, xanthan gum, and kosher salt together in a medium bowl until uniform. Add the dry ingredients to the butter mixture in one addition and mix until just incorporated. Add the carob chips and walnuts, if using, in one addition and mix just enough to evenly distribute them through the dough.

Use a spring-release cookie scoop or 2 soup spoons to drop heaping tablespoons of dough onto the prepared baking sheets about 2 inches apart. Bake 1 sheet at a time for 8 to 12 minutes, rotating the sheet 180 degrees halfway through, until the edges and tops are lightly golden brown.

Let the cookies cool on the baking sheet for 5 minutes or until set. Transfer to a wire rack lined with a paper towel to cool completely. Store in an airtight container or wrap and freeze.

Variation—Make Ahead: Use waxed paper to form the dough into a long cylinder 2½ inches in diameter. Wrap and freeze. When you want to bake the cookies, remove the dough from the freezer and let it sit at room temperature for a few minutes to soften. Slice the cookies ¼ to ½ inch thick and bake as directed above. The cookies may bake 2 or 3 minutes faster this way.

Quinoa Chip Cookies

This is my play on classic chocolate chip oatmeal cookies. Quinoa flakes are made from quinoa, a nutritious protein-packed seed.

makes 20 cookies

½ cup unsalted butter,
at room temperature

¾ cup palm sugar

1 large egg

1½ teaspoons vanilla extract

2 tablespoons water

1 cup Basic Flour Blend (page 212)

1 teaspoon baking soda

½ teaspoon xanthan gum

¼ teaspoon kosher salt

1 cup quinoa flakes

1 cup unsweetened carob chips

Preheat the oven to 325°F. Line 2 baking sheets with silicone baking mats or parchment paper.

In the bowl of a stand mixer fitted with the paddle attachment, cream the butter medium speed for about 5 minutes, until light and fluffy. Add the palm sugar one-half at a time, letting it incorporate before adding more. Continue beating until light and fluffy. (The palm sugar won't fully dissolve at this point the way white sugar would.) Add the egg and vanilla and mix until fully incorporated, then add the water.

While the butter and sugar are creaming, whisk the flour blend, baking soda, xanthan gum, and kosher salt together in a medium bowl until uniform. Add the dry ingredients to the butter mixture in one addition and mix until just incorporated. Add the quinoa flakes and mix on the lowest speed until incorporated. Mix in the carob chips.

Use a spring-release cookie scoop or 2 soup spoons to drop heaping tablespoons of dough onto the prepared baking sheets about 2 inches apart. Bake 1 sheet at a time for about 12 minutes, rotating the sheet 180 degrees halfway through, until the edges and tops are lightly golden brown.

Let the cookies cool on the baking sheet for 5 minutes or until set. Transfer to a wire rack lined with a paper towel to cool completely. Store in an airtight container, layered with waxed paper, or wrap and freeze.

Quick Tip: If you forget to take your butter out of the refrigerator ahead of time to soften it, there's a simple solution. Cut the butter into chunks and throw it into the bowl of a stand mixer fitted with the paddle attachment. Mix on medium speed, scraping down the bowl a few times, until the butter is light and fluffy.

Double Chocolate Cherry Cookies

These cookies use the luscious flavor pairing of chocolate and cherry. Look for dried cherries that are either unsweetened or sweetened with fruit juice.

makes about 2 dozen cookies

½ cup dried cherries

½ cup unsalted butter, at room temperature

½ cup palm sugar

¼ cup agave nectar

1 large egg

1½ teaspoons vanilla extract

1 cup sorghum flour

½ cup garbanzo bean flour

¼ cup Dutch-processed cocoa powder

1 teaspoon baking soda

½ teaspoon instant espresso powder

½ teaspoon xanthan gum

¼ teaspoon kosher salt

¾ cup carob chips

Preheat the oven to 350°F. Line 2 baking sheets with silicone baking mats or parchment paper.

In a microwave safe bowl, cover the dried cherries with water and microwave for 45 seconds. Set aside.

In the bowl of a stand mixer fitted with the paddle attachment, beat the butter on medium speed for about 3 minutes, until light and fluffy. Add the palm sugar one-half at a time, letting the first part incorporate before adding more. Continue beating until light and fluffy. Add the agave, and once it's mixed in, add the egg and vanilla. Beat until fully incorporated. Scrape the bowl down if needed.

Meanwhile, sift together the sorghum flour, garbanzo bean flour, cocoa powder, baking soda, espresso powder, xanthan gum, and kosher salt in a medium bowl. Whisk until uniformly combined. Add the dry ingredients to the wet ingredients in one addition. Mix on the lowest speed until the dough comes together. Drain the soaked cherries and chop them into small pieces. Add the carob chips and dried cherries to the dough and mix on the lowest speed until barely combined.

Use a spring-release cookie scoop or 2 soup spoons to drop round balls of dough onto the prepared baking sheet about 2 inches apart. Bake 1 sheet at a time for 12 to 14 minutes, rotating the baking sheet 180 degrees after 6 minutes, until the cookies are set on the edges. Let cool on the baking sheet until firm, then transfer to a wire rack lined with a paper towel to cool completely. Store in an airtight container.

Quick Tip: Make sure to chop the dried cherries into small pieces. Large cherry pieces will expand in the oven and blow out the side of the cookies.

Almond Butter and Jelly Cookies

I thought I could eat just a bite of a cookie when testing this recipe, but one bite turned into three cookies and I still wanted more. They're moist, chewy, and perfectly sweet. Like a PB&J but even better. These take a little longer than 20 minutes to make because of the assembly, but I had to include them because they're so good.

makes 2 dozen cookies

¼ cup unsalted butter,
at room temperature

½ cup agave nectar

¾ cup creamy almond butter

½ cup unsweetened applesauce

2 cups Basic Flour Blend
(page 212)

½ teaspoon xanthan gum

½ teaspoon baking soda

½ teaspoon cream of tartar

⅛ teaspoon salt

about ¼ cup sugarless all-fruit
preserves

In the bowl of a stand mixer fitted with the paddle attachment, cream the butter on medium speed for about 3 minutes, until light. Slowly pour in the agave with the mixer running. In a microwave-safe bowl, microwave the almond butter for 20 to 30 seconds, until soft but not hot. Add the almond butter to the butter mixture in several additions, mixing on medium speed, allowing it to fully incorporate before adding more. Add the applesauce in several large spoonfuls, allowing each addition to fully mix in before adding more.

In a medium bowl, whisk together the flour blend, xanthan gum, baking soda, cream of tartar, and salt. Add the dry ingredients to the wet ingredients in two additions, mixing on the lowest speed until combined. Cover the dough and refrigerate for 30 minutes.

Preheat the oven to 350°F. Line 2 baking sheets with silicone baking mats or parchment paper. Use a spring-release cookie scoop or 2 soup spoons to scoop the dough. Roll each scoop into a ball and place the balls on the prepared baking sheet about 1 inch apart. Using your thumb, press down into the center of each cookie, then fill each indentation with ½ teaspoon preserves.

Bake 1 sheet at a time for 12 to 18 minutes, until lightly golden brown, rotating the baking sheet 180 degrees halfway through. Let cool on the baking sheet for 10 minutes, then transfer to a wire rack lined with a paper towel to cool completely. Store in an airtight container at room temperature.

Make It Dairy-Free: Omit the butter and use vegan butter instead. It doesn't whip up as nicely, but just beat it as best you can, then pour in the agave slowly, scraping down as needed until the two are well combined.

Almond Anise Biscotti

Biscotti are simple and elegant cookies. Maybe their appearance makes people think they're difficult to bake, but they're not. This classic flavor combination is my favorite. It's perfect with a late afternoon cup of coffee or with ice cream. Biscotti have a 2-week shelf life, so they're a simple way to add class to a dinner party while keeping your sanity.

makes about 2 dozen cookies

2 tablespoons unsalted butter, melted

1/3 cup agave nectar

2 1/3 cups Basic Flour Blend (page 212)

1 teaspoon gluten-free baking powder

1 teaspoon anise seed

1/2 teaspoon xanthan gum

pinch of kosher salt

2 large eggs

1/2 teaspoon vanilla extract

1/2 cup almonds, coarsely chopped

Preheat the oven to 325°F. Line a baking sheet with a silicone baking mat or parchment paper.

In the bowl of a stand mixer fitted with the paddle attachment, mix the butter and agave on medium speed for 2 minutes, or until combined and uniform in color. Add the eggs to the butter mixture one at a time, mixing well between each addition and scraping down the bowl as needed. Add the vanilla and mix.

Whisk the flour blend, baking powder, anise seed, xanthan gum, and kosher salt in a medium bowl until uniform. Add the dry ingredients to the butter mixture in one addition and mix on the lowest speed until almost combined. Add the almonds and mix on the lowest speed just until they're evenly distributed through the dough.

Use wet hands to form the dough into 2 logs, each about 9 x 3 inches. Transfer the logs to the prepared baking sheet. Bake for 20 to 25 minutes, until the logs are set and lightly golden brown. Remove from the oven and let cool for 15 to 20 minutes. Turn the oven down to 300°F.

Cut the logs into 1/2-inch slices with a sharp serrated knife at a 45-degree angle. Lay the slices flat on the baking sheet and return them to the oven for 12 to 15 minutes, until lightly browned. Flip the cookies and bake for another 12 to 15 minutes. When they're done, the biscotti should be firm all over and yield very slightly to gentle pressure in the center. Let cool on a wire rack. Store at room temperature in an airtight container for up to 2 weeks.

Quick Tip: Make sure to use an extremely sharp serrated knife when slicing biscotti, and allow the knife to do the work. If you press down into the baked biscotti log with your knife, it will crumble.

Chocolate Hazelnut Biscotti

I love chocolate and hazelnuts, which is why I put them together in these biscotti. If you don't have hazelnuts on hand, use almonds or walnuts.

makes about 2 dozen cookies

2 tablespoons unsalted butter, melted

⅓ cup agave nectar

2 large eggs

½ teaspoon vanilla extract

½ teaspoon instant espresso powder

2 cups Basic Flour Blend (page 212)

⅓ cup Dutch-processed cocoa powder

1 teaspoon gluten-free baking powder

½ teaspoon xanthan gum

pinch of kosher salt

½ cup hazelnuts, coarsely chopped

2 tablespoons palm sugar

Preheat the oven to 350°F. Line a baking sheet with a silicone baking mat or parchment paper.

In the bowl of a stand mixer fitted with the paddle attachment, mix the butter and agave on medium speed for 2 minutes, or until combined and uniform in color. Add the eggs one at a time, mixing well between each addition and scraping down the bowl as needed. Add the vanilla and espresso powder and mix.

Sift the flour blend, cocoa powder, baking powder, xanthan gum, and kosher salt into a medium bowl and whisk until uniform. Add the dry ingredients in one addition to the butter mixture and mix on the lowest speed until almost combined. Add the hazelnuts and mix on the lowest speed just until they're evenly distributed through the dough.

Use wet hands to form the dough into 2 logs, each about 9 x 3 inches. Sprinkle each log with 1 tablespoon palm sugar, lightly pressing it into the dough. Transfer the logs to the prepared baking sheet. Bake for 25 to 30 minutes, until the logs are set and firm to the touch. Remove from the oven and let cool for 15 to 20 minutes. Turn the oven down to 300°F.

Cut the logs into ½-inch slices with a sharp serrated knife at a 45-degree angle. Lay the slices flat on the baking sheet and return them to the oven for 12 to 15 minutes, until lightly golden brown. Flip the cookies and bake for another 12 to 15 minutes. When done, they should be firm all over and yield very slightly to gentle pressure in the center. Let cool on a wire rack. Store at room temperature in an airtight container for up to 2 weeks.

Quick Tip: Wet your hands before handling the dough to keep it from sticking to your fingers.

Lemon Cornmeal Biscotti

Helen has been my mentor and friend for years. She and I share many interests, baking included, and she was generous enough to share her favorite biscotti recipe with me. Of course, I made it gluten- and sugar-free. I love how the bright lemon and cornmeal complement each other. This is the perfect biscotti for an afternoon cup of tea. **dairy-free**

makes about 30 cookies

3 eggs

¾ cup palm sugar

1 tablespoon grated lemon zest

2 cups Basic Flour Blend (page 212)

¾ cup stone-ground cornmeal

1½ teaspoons gluten-free baking powder

¾ teaspoon xanthan gum

½ teaspoon salt

¾ cup almonds, chopped

Preheat the oven to 325°F. Line a baking sheet with a silicone baking mat or parchment paper.

In a stand mixer fitted with the paddle attachment, beat the eggs on medium speed until combined. Add the palm sugar one-third at a time, letting it incorporate between additions. Let the mixer run until the palm sugar has mostly dissolved, about 2 minutes. Add the lemon zest and mix to combine.

In a medium bowl, whisk together the flour blend, cornmeal, baking powder, xanthan gum, and salt. Add the dry ingredients to the egg mixture in one addition and mix on the lowest speed, scraping down the bowl as needed. When the dough starts to come together, add the almonds all at once and mix on the lowest speed just until they're evenly distributed through the dough.

Use wet hands to form the dough into 2 logs, each about 12 x 3 inches. Transfer the logs to the prepared baking sheet. Bake for 25 to 30 minutes, until the logs are set and lightly golden brown. Remove from the oven and let cool for 15 to 20 minutes. Turn the oven down to 300°F.

Cut the logs into ½-inch slices with a sharp serrated knife at a 45-degree angle. Lay the slices flat on the baking sheet and return them to the oven for 12 to 15 minutes, until lightly golden brown. Flip the cookies and bake for another 12 to 15 minutes. When they're done, the biscotti should be firm all over and yield very slightly to gentle pressure in the center. Let cool on a wire rack. Store at room temperature in an airtight container for up to 2 weeks.

Quick Tip: Slicing biscotti into cookies of equal width helps them to bake evenly.

Fudge Brownies

These brownies are cakey, with a fudgey, melt-in-your-mouth bite, and are a little healthier than most. Instead of tons of butter and chocolate, I've used applesauce and cocoa powder. The best part is that the texture and taste feels like full-fat.

makes 16 (2 x 2-inch) brownies

¼ cup unsalted butter

1 ounce unsweetened baking chocolate

½ cup unsweetened applesauce

¾ cup palm sugar

1 teaspoon vanilla extract

1 large egg

2 large egg whites

¼ teaspoon kosher salt

½ cup Basic Flour Blend (page 212)

½ cup cocoa powder (not Dutch-processed)

Preheat the oven to 350°F. Lightly mist an 8 x 8-inch baking dish with cooking spray.

In a microwave-safe bowl, microwave the butter and chocolate for 1 minute, stir, then microwave for another 30 seconds if necessary. Stir to melt completely. Set aside.

In a large bowl, beat the applesauce, palm sugar, vanilla, egg, egg whites, and salt with an electric mixer on medium speed until combined. Stir in the melted chocolate and butter.

In a medium bowl, sift the flour blend and cocoa powder. Whisk until evenly combined. Fold the dry ingredients into the wet. Turn the brownie batter into the prepared pan. Bake for 18 to 20 minutes, until a toothpick inserted into the center comes out clean and the brownies pull away slightly from the edge of the pan. Cool on a wire rack. Cover and store at room temperature. These also freeze well.

Quick Tip: When separating egg yolks and egg whites, crack the egg on the counter, not on the edge of the bowl that you're mixing in. This will avoid getting small pieces of shell in your bowl. Gently pull the two shells apart and transfer the yolk back and forth between the two halves of the shell, letting the white fall below into a bowl.

Chewy Chocolate Date Brownies

These wholesome date-filled bars are reminiscent of brownies but have a delightful chewy texture. They're a little sticky and tons of fun to eat. Let these brownies sit for an hour or two before you serve them—they're best that way. Layer them between sheets of waxed paper, wrap them up, and pop them in the freezer. They freeze just solid enough so you can still bite into them and are a perfect way to soothe your afternoon sweet tooth. **vegan**

makes 16 (2 x 2-inch) brownies

1 cup pitted Medjool dates

¾ cup hot water

2 teaspoons vanilla extract

2 teaspoons instant decaf coffee granules

½ cup Dutch-processed cocoa powder

½ cup Basic Flour Blend (page 212)

¼ cup palm sugar

½ teaspoon gluten-free baking powder

¼ teaspoon kosher salt

¼ teaspoon xanthan gum

Preheat the oven to 350°F. Lightly mist an 8 x 8-inch baking dish with cooking spray.

Combine the dates, hot water, vanilla, and coffee granules in a heatproof bowl. Let sit while preparing the remaining ingredients.

Sift the cocoa powder into a medium bowl to remove any lumps. Add the flour blend, palm sugar, baking powder, salt, and xanthan gum. Whisk to combine.

Place the dates and soaking liquid into the bowl of a food processor fitted with the steel blade. Pulse several times to combine, then process until smooth, scraping down the bowl as needed. Add the dry ingredients to the date paste and process until smooth. The batter will be thick.

Turn the batter into the prepared pan, scraping as much batter as possible from the bowl. Smooth the top with a spatula and bake for 15 to 20 minutes, until the brownies are set. A toothpick inserted into the center won't come out completely clean for these brownies. Let cool on a wire rack. Cover and store at room temperature.

Quick Tip: Coffee enhances the flavor of chocolate. You won't be able to taste it in the final product, but if you're not fond of coffee, feel free to leave it out. The brownies will still taste fabulous.

Chocolate Walnut
Black Bean Brownies

This version of black bean brownies gets rave reviews in all my cooking classes and is more figure-friendly than most. The moist, fudgelike texture will fool everyone. No one will know they're made with black beans, nor will they suspect that these are healthier than traditional brownies. The walnuts are optional, but I find they add a tasty textural contrast.

makes 24 (2 x 3-inch) brownies

¼ cup unsalted butter

1 teaspoon instant decaf coffee granules

¼ teaspoon kosher salt

2 cups canned black beans, drained and rinsed very well

1 very ripe banana

1 tablespoon vanilla extract

4 large eggs, divided

¾ cup Dutch-processed cocoa powder

¼ cup agave nectar

¼ cup plain low-fat yogurt

½ teaspoon liquid stevia

1 cup chopped toasted walnuts, divided (optional)

Preheat the oven to 325°F. Spray a 9 x 13-inch baking pan with cooking spray, then line with parchment paper and spray the paper.

In a small microwave-safe bowl, microwave the butter for 60 to 90 seconds. Stir to melt completely. Stir in the coffee granules and salt. Mix well. Set aside.

In the bowl of a food processor fitted with the steel blade, add the beans, banana, vanilla, and 1 egg. Process for about 2 to 3 minutes, until completely smooth, scraping down the bowl as needed. Add the cocoa powder and melted butter mixture. Pulse a few times to combine, then process again until smooth.

In a large bowl, beat the remaining 3 eggs with an electric mixer on medium speed for about 1 to 2 minutes, until light and fluffy. Add the agave, yogurt, and stevia and mix for another 1 to 2 minutes, until light. Add the bean mixture and mix on medium speed until thoroughly incorporated. Gently stir in ½ cup walnuts if using. Pour the batter into the prepared pan and smooth it out. Top with the remaining ½ cup walnuts if using, pressing them lightly into the batter. Bake for 25 to 35 minutes, until a toothpick inserted into the center comes out clean. Let the brownies cool. Cover and store in the refrigerator.

Quick Tip: Part of the sweetness in these brownies comes from the banana. Make sure to use a very, very ripe banana. I keep a stash of overripe bananas in my freezer, which works great for this recipe because the sweetness of bananas continues to increase once they're frozen.

Fig and Date Bars

My recipe testers unanimously said these taste like fig newtons. They're great cookie bars for kids and grown-ups alike. The crust on these cookies melts in your mouth. **egg-free**

makes 16 (2 x 2-inch) bars

½ cup pitted Medjool dates

½ cup dried black Mission figs, stemmed and cut in half

½ cup walnuts

1 cup sorghum flour

½ teaspoon ground cinnamon

¼ teaspoon baking soda

¼ teaspoon xanthan gum

pinch of kosher salt

¼ cup cold butter, diced

2 tablespoons honey or agave nectar

1 teaspoon freshly grated orange zest

1 tablespoon freshly squeezed orange juice

Preheat the oven to 375°F. Lightly mist an 8 x 8-inch baking pan with cooking spray.

In a medium heatproof bowl, cover the dates and figs with hot water. Set aside. Or, cover the dates and dried figs with water and microwave for 1 minute.

In a food processor fitted with the steel blade, chop the walnuts until they are in small pieces but not mealy. Add the sorghum flour, cinnamon, baking soda, xanthan gum, and kosher salt. Process for 30 seconds, or until the mixture is combined and the walnuts are a little finer. Sprinkle the butter evenly across the walnut mixture and drizzle in the honey or agave. Pulse until a dough forms. Turn the dough out into a large bowl.

Using a slotted spoon, transfer the dates and figs to the food processor, reserving the soaking liquid; there's no need to wash the processor bowl. Add ¼ cup of the soaking liquid, the orange zest, and orange juice. Let process for several minutes, until smooth.

While the food processor is running, use wet hands to firmly press two-thirds of the dough into the bottom of the prepared pan. Once the date and fig mixture is smooth, spread it evenly across the dough. Break the remaining dough into marble-size pieces, sprinkle them across the fig and date paste, and lightly press in.

Bake for 15 to 18 minutes, rotating the pan 180 degrees halfway through, until the top becomes lightly golden brown. Let cool completely on a wire rack. Cover and store in the refrigerator. These also freeze well.

Quick Tip: Always zest your citrus fruit before juicing.

Banana Oat Bars

This is a little fancier than your standard oat bar. It's chewy, moist, and earthy. If you don't have maple syrup on hand, try another liquid sweetener such as agave nectar or honey. **vegan**

makes 16 (2 x 2-inch) bars

½ cup pitted Medjool dates

2 cups gluten-free rolled oats, divided (not quick-cooking)

½ cup walnuts

¼ teaspoon baking soda

1/8 teaspoon kosher salt

1/3 cup unsweetened applesauce

2 tablespoons grade-B maple syrup

1 teaspoon ground cinnamon, divided

1 large ripe banana, sliced

½ teaspoon grated lemon zest

1 teaspoon freshly squeezed lemon juice

½ teaspoon freshly ground nutmeg

Preheat the oven to 375°F. Lightly mist an 8 x 8-inch baking pan with cooking spray.

In a medium heatproof bowl, cover the dates with hot water. Set aside. Or, cover the dates with water and microwave for 45 seconds.

In the bowl of a food processor fitted with the steel blade, process 1½ cups oats for several minutes until you have a coarse oat flour. Add the remaining ½ cup oats, the walnuts, baking soda, and salt. Pulse 10 to 12 times, for 1 second each, until the walnuts and oats are chopped but not fine. Add the applesauce, maple syrup, and ½ teaspoon cinnamon. Process until a dough forms. Transfer to a large bowl and set aside.

Use a slotted spoon to transfer the dates to the food processor, reserving the soaking liquid; there's no need to wash the processor bowl. Add 1 tablespoon of the soaking liquid, the banana, lemon zest, lemon juice, remaining ½ teaspoon cinnamon, and the nutmeg. Pulse several times to combine, then process until smooth. The paste should be thick but still liquid. Add a little more soaking liquid as needed.

While the food processor is running, use wet hands to press two-thirds of the dough firmly into the bottom of the prepared pan. Once the banana paste is smooth, spread it evenly across the dough. Break the remaining dough into marble-size pieces, sprinkle them across the banana paste, and lightly press in.

Bake for 16 to 18 minutes, until the oat topping is golden brown. Let cool on a wire rack. Cover and store in the refrigerator. These also freeze well.

Blueberry Quinoa Crumble Bars

I made these for a gluten-free ladies' brunch and everyone loved them. They're light enough for even the most conscientious eater to enjoy without feeling guilty.

makes 16 (2 x 2-inch) bars

1½ cups quinoa flakes

1 cup Basic Flour Blend (page 212)

¼ cup palm sugar

½ teaspoon xanthan gum

¼ teaspoon kosher salt

¼ teaspoon baking soda

½ teaspoon ground cinnamon

⅛ teaspoon freshly grated nutmeg

⅓ cup canola oil

¼ cup water

1 teaspoon grated lemon zest, divided

¼ cup sliced almonds

½ cup fresh blueberries

¾ cup all-fruit blueberry preserves

Preheat the oven to 350°F. Lightly mist an 8 x 8-inch baking pan with cooking spray.

In a large bowl, whisk together the quinoa flakes, flour blend, palm sugar, xanthan gum, kosher salt, baking soda, cinnamon, and nutmeg. Set aside.

In a medium bowl, whisk together the canola oil, water, and ½ teaspoon lemon zest. Make a well in the dry ingredients and add the wet ingredients. Stir until combined. Fold in the almonds and blueberries.

Press three-quarters of the dough into the bottom of the pan. Mix the blueberry preserves with the remaining ½ teaspoon lemon zest. Spread evenly on top of the dough. Break the remaining dough into marble-size pieces, sprinkle them across the preserves, and lightly press in.

Bake for 35 to 40 minutes, rotating 180 degrees halfway through, until the edges are bubbling and the top is a light golden brown. Allow the bars to cool completely in the baking pan on a wire rack. Run a sharp paring knife or offset spatula around the edges of the pan to loosen the cookie before cutting into bars. Cover and store at room temperature.

Quick Tip: When measuring xanthan gum, it's always important to level it off with a straight edge. It's a powerful little ingredient, so you want to make sure to measure correctly.

Raw Date Truffles

Simple to make, these truffles are a perfect addition to a box of Christmas cookies. They're also healthy enough to be a midday snack. I roll half of my truffles in coconut and half in cocoa powder, but if you prefer, you can make them all one type. You'll just need more of whatever you're rolling them in. **vegan**

makes about 2 dozen truffles

1 cup raw almonds

1 cup Medjool dates, pitted and coarsely chopped

1 cup golden raisins

½ cup dried black Mission figs, stemmed and coarsely chopped

¼ cup unsweetened finely shredded coconut

¼ cup cocoa powder
(not Dutch-processed)

In the bowl of a food processor fitted with the steel blade, process the almonds for 2 to 3 minutes until finely chopped but not mealy. Add the dates, raisins, and figs. Process again for 3 to 5 minutes, until the mixture sticks together and forms a coarse dough.

Remove the steel blade from the food processor, then scoop the dough into truffles right out of the food processor bowl using a spring-release cookie scoop for large truffles or the large end of a melon baller for smaller truffles. Roll each scoop of dough between your hands to form balls and set the truffles on a plate or tray.

After all the truffles are rolled, spread the coconut on one plate and the cocoa powder on another. Roll half of the truffles in the coconut to coat. Roll the remaining truffles in the cocoa powder to coat. When rolling in cocoa powder, it's OK to have a really good layer on the outside, because the moistness of the truffle soaks it up a bit.

Store in an airtight container in the refrigerator.

Quick Tip: If your coconut isn't finely shredded, quickly blend it in a clean coffee grinder or spice grinder. It will coat the truffles best this way.

Cobblers, Crisps, & Pies

Strawberry Rhubarb Cobbler

My earliest memories of rhubarb center on my Grandma Ruth cutting it from a friend's garden and making pies. Whenever someone else had extra they couldn't use, my grandma always found a way to create a delicious dish, letting nothing go to waste. I don't have any neighbors who grow rhubarb, but Grandma's frugal nature has become part of my everyday life.

serves 4 to 6

2 cups frozen rhubarb, thawed

3 cups sliced fresh strawberries

1 tablespoon tapioca starch

1 teaspoon freshly squeezed lemon juice

½ cup plus 1 tablespoon palm sugar, divided

¾ cup Basic Flour Blend (page 212)

½ teaspoon gluten-free baking powder

¼ teaspoon xanthan gum

⅛ teaspoon salt

¼ cup unsalted butter, at room temperature

1 egg

1 teaspoon vanilla extract

¼ cup plus 2 tablespoons low-fat buttermilk

Preheat the oven to 375°F.

Combine the rhubarb and its juice and the strawberries in an 8 x 8-inch baking dish. Add the tapioca starch, lemon juice, and ¼ cup palm sugar. Mix well and set aside.

In a medium bowl, whisk together the flour blend, baking powder, xanthan gum, and salt. In the bowl of a stand mixer fitted with the paddle attachment, beat the butter on medium speed until smooth. Add 2 tablespoons palm sugar, allow it to incorporate, then add another 2 tablespoons and mix until incorporated. Add the egg and vanilla and mix until thoroughly combined. On low speed, beat in the dry ingredients in three parts, alternating with the buttermilk, starting and ending with the dry ingredients. Mix until smooth.

Spread the batter evenly over the fruit mixture. Sprinkle the remaining 1 tablespoon palm sugar over the batter. Bake for 35 to 40 minutes, until the top is golden brown and the fruit is bubbly.

Quick Tip: Use a tomato corer (also known as a tomato huller) to quickly remove only the stem from your ripe berries. Don't spend more than $2 to $3 on this tool. The cheap ones work just as well as the more costly versions.

Pear and Blackberry Crisp

When learning to cook healthier, I devoured the work of Martha Rose Shulman, one of my personal food heroes and someone I consider to be among the greatest health-conscious chefs and authors. This crisp recipe, as well as my Raspberry Peach Crisp (page 144) and Plum Quinoa Crumble (page 145), were inspired by Chef Shulman's crisp recipes in her Light Basics Cookbook. *I've created gluten-free, refined sugar–free versions with my favorite fruit combinations.* **egg-free**

serves 4 to 6

2½ pounds firm but ripe pears

1 cup blackberries

¼ cup plus 2 tablespoons palm sugar, divided

1 tablespoon tapioca starch

1 tablespoon freshly squeezed lemon juice

1 teaspoon ground cinnamon

½ teaspoon ground ginger

¾ cup quinoa flakes

½ cup Basic Flour Blend (page 212)

¼ cup chopped pecans

½ teaspoon grated lemon zest

¼ teaspoon kosher salt

⅛ teaspoon xanthan gum

6 tablespoons cold unsalted butter, diced

Preheat the oven to 375°F.

Peel the pears, cut in half, and remove the seeds with a melon baller. Cut the halves lengthwise into 6 to 8 slices. Spread in an 8 × 8-inch baking dish. Add the blackberries. Sprinkle in 2 tablespoons palm sugar and the tapioca starch, lemon juice, cinnamon, and ginger. Toss to coat.

In a medium bowl, whisk together the remaining ¼ cup palm sugar, the quinoa flakes, flour blend, pecans, lemon zest, salt, and xanthan gum. Cut in the butter using your fingers, or put the mixture into the bowl of a stand mixer fitted with the paddle attachment and mix on the lowest speed until the butter is cut in and the mixture is the consistency of coarse, mealy pebbles.

Spread the topping evenly across the fruit. Place the dish on a baking sheet and bake for 35 to 45 minutes, until the top is lightly golden brown and the fruit is bubbly. Let cool slightly before serving.

Quick Tip: Placing your cobblers, crisps, and pies on a baking sheet and then sliding them into the oven increases ease of handling when removing them from the oven and also protects your oven floor just in case the dessert happens to bubble over the edges of the baking dish.

Raspberry Peach Crisp

This crisp is my spin on peach Melba, a dish originally created in the late 1800s by Escoffier, who is known as the father of twentieth-century cooking.

serves 4 to 6

1½ pounds peaches, pitted and sliced

1½ cups fresh raspberries

¼ cup plus 2 tablespoons palm sugar, divided

1 tablespoon freshly squeezed lemon juice

½ teaspoon vanilla extract

¼ teaspoon ground cinnamon

¾ cup gluten-free oats (not quick-cooking)

¾ cup Basic Flour Blend (page 213)

¼ cup sliced almonds

1 teaspoon grated lemon zest

¼ teaspoon ground cinnamon

¼ teaspoon kosher salt

⅛ teaspoon xanthan gum

6 tablespoons cold unsalted butter, diced

2 to 3 cups Vanilla Bean Ice Cream (page 197), for serving

Preheat the oven to 375°F. Butter a 1½-quart baking dish.

Place the peaches and raspberries in a medium bowl. Sprinkle with 2 tablespoons palm sugar and the lemon juice, vanilla, and cinnamon. Gently toss to coat the fruit. Set aside.

In a large bowl, whisk together the remaining ¼ cup palm sugar, oats, flour blend, almonds, lemon zest, cinnamon, salt, and xanthan gum. Add the butter to the dry ingredients and toss to coat the cubes. Use your fingers to rub the butter into the flour until the mixture resembles coarse, mealy pebbles.

Transfer the fruit mixture into the buttered baking dish. Top with the flour and butter mixture. Place the baking dish on a baking sheet and bake for 35 to 45 minutes, until it's light golden brown on top and bubbly on the edges. If the topping browns too quickly, cover it with a piece of aluminum foil. Let stand for 5 minutes before serving. Serve each portion warm with ½ cup Vanilla Bean Ice Cream.

Quick Tip: For a stunning presentation, divide this among 4 to 6 individual baking ramekins. Place ramekins on a large baking sheet and bake them for 20 to 30 minutes, depending on the size of your ramekins.

Plum Quinoa Crumble

I've made this dish with both unpeeled and peeled plums, and I enjoy the texture without the skins so much more. When the plums are ripe, the skin easily pulls away and makes the job of peeling them simple.

serves 4 to 6

2 pounds ripe but firm plums

½ cup large pitted Medjool dates (about 8)

¼ cup water or 1 tablespoon freshly squeezed orange juice plus 3 tablespoons water

1 tablespoon tapioca starch

¾ teaspoon ground cinnamon, divided

¾ cup Basic Flour Blend (page 212)

¾ cup quinoa flakes

½ cup palm sugar

1 teaspoon grated orange zest

¼ teaspoon xanthan gum

⅛ teaspoon kosher salt

6 tablespoons cold unsalted butter, diced

Vanilla Bean Ice Cream (page 197), Vanilla Whipped Cream (page 182), or Raw Cashew Cream (page 176), for serving

Preheat the oven to 350°F.

Quarter, pit, and peel the plums. Cut each quarter section in half lengthwise. If the plums are very large, cut each quarter into thirds. Cut the dates into 4 pieces lengthwise. Toss the plums and dates together in a 1½-quart baking dish. Mix the water, or water and orange juice, with the tapioca starch. Pour over the plums and dates. Sprinkle with ½ teaspoon cinnamon. Set aside.

In a medium bowl, whisk together the flour blend, quinoa flakes, palm sugar, orange zest, xanthan gum, salt, and the remaining ¼ teaspoon cinnamon. Add the butter to the dry ingredients and toss to coat the cubes. Use your fingers to cut the butter into the flour until the mixture resembles coarse, mealy pebbles.

Spread the crumble mixture evenly over the fruit. Place the baking dish on a baking sheet and bake for 30 to 35 minutes, until the juices bubble around the edge and the top is a light golden brown. Serve warm with ice cream, whipped cream, or cashew cream.

Quick Tip: Medjool dates can be expensive when purchased in small quantities. I buy them in a 2-pound container at my local wholesale club. They stay fresh for several months in the refrigerator.

Ruthie's Apple Crisp

This dish is near and dear to my heart—it was a childhood favorite made by my Grandma Ruth. She used to look at me with a sly grin on her face and say, "Amy, I did something to make you mad . . . I made an apple crisp." It's now a favorite of my husband, who says this is the best fruit dessert I make. The crisp part of this dessert is darker in color because of the palm sugar.

serves 4 to 6

5 medium baking apples, such as Granny Smith or Gala (about 2½ pounds)

¼ cup raisins or currants (optional)

¼ cup water

1 teaspoon ground cinnamon

⅛ teaspoon kosher salt

⅓ cup plus 1 tablespoon cold unsalted butter, diced, plus extra for the pan

¾ cup Basic Flour Blend (page 212)

¾ cup palm sugar

¼ teaspoon xanthan gum

Vanilla Bean Ice Cream (page 197) or Vanilla Whipped Cream (page 182)

Preheat the oven to 350°F. Prepare a 1½-quart baking dish by rubbing the bottom and sides with butter.

Peel and core the apples. Cut them into even slices, a little less than ¼ inch thick. Combine the apple slices and raisins or currants, if using, in the prepared baking dish and pour the water into the bottom. Sprinkle the fruit with the cinnamon and salt. Dot the fruit with 1 tablespoon butter. Set aside.

In a medium bowl, whisk together the flour blend, palm sugar, and xanthan gum. Toss the remaining ⅓ cup butter in the flour blend to coat. Use your fingers to cut the butter into the flour until the butter is the consistency of coarse, mealy pebbles. Spread the crisp topping over the apples. Place on a baking sheet, loosely cover the dish with foil, and bake for 25 minutes. Uncover and bake another 15 to 25 minutes, until the topping has browned, the apples are soft, and the juices are bubbling around the edge. Let cool for 5 minutes before serving warm with ice cream and/or whipped cream.

Variation—Make Ahead: Toss the sliced apples in 1 tablespoon lemon juice in the baking dish. Top with the cinnamon and salt and cover. Do not add the water until right before baking. Prepare the topping, place it in a bowl, cover, and refrigerate. Add the water to the apples right before baking, top them with the crisp mixture, and bake.

Quick Tip: Fill a bowl large enough to accommodate all the apples and enough water to cover. Add 1 tablespoon freshly squeezed lemon juice. Place the sliced apples in the bowl to keep them from turning brown until you're ready to top them with the crisp mixture.

Currant and Sunflower Seed Stuffed Apples

I remember my Granny Jeanne baking apples when I was little. She had a small ceramic apple dish that would perfectly bake one apple at a time. I was amazed at the way the apple's taste and texture transformed, which is what inspired this dish. The currants plump and the sunflower seeds become nutty and soft after hours of slow cooking. This is a comforting, nut-free dessert, but feel free to use almonds, walnuts, or pecans instead. **slow cooker recipe**

serves 4

4 baking apples, preferably a sweet variety like Gala or Golden Delicious

1 tablespoon freshly squeezed lemon juice

⅓ cup currants

⅓ cup roasted salted sunflower seeds

1 tablespoon palm sugar, plus extra for sprinkling

1 teaspoon ground cinnamon, divided

¼ teaspoon freshly grated nutmeg

2 teaspoons unsalted butter

½ cup water

Spray a large (5- to 6-quart) slow cooker that will comfortably hold all the apples with cooking spray.

Core the apples with an apple corer without cutting through the bottom. With a small spoon, scrape out any remaining seeds, then rub lemon juice in the cavity to prevent browning. Peel the top third of the apple with a vegetable peeler, and coat the exposed flesh with lemon juice.

In a medium bowl, toss together the currants, sunflower seeds, 1 tablespoon palm sugar, ½ teaspoon cinnamon, and the nutmeg. Stuff the currant and sunflower seed mixture into the cavities of the apples. Don't be afraid to pack it in. Set the apples into the slow cooker and top with the remaining filling so there is a little dome on top of each apple. Quarter the butter and place 1 piece on top of each apple. Sprinkle with the remaining ½ teaspoon cinnamon and a little palm sugar.

Add the water to the bottom of the slow cooker. Cover and cook on low for 4 to 6 hours, until the apples are fork tender.

Make It Dairy-Free: Omit the butter and use vegan butter instead.

Cinnamon Vanilla Poached Pears

There's nothing simpler or more elegant than poached pears. The agave nectar helps keep the fruit firm while it's gently poaching. For flavor variations, try palm sugar, honey, or grade-B maple syrup instead.

serves 4

4 ripe but firm pears

¼ cup agave nectar

2 to 3 cups water

1 teaspoon vanilla extract

1 cinnamon stick

1 recipe Whipped Ricotta Cream (page 178)

cinnamon, for sprinkling

Peel the pears, leaving the stems intact. Cut the pears in half and remove the cores with a melon baller. Arrange the halves in a single layer in the bottom of a large stockpot. In a medium bowl, combine the agave and 2 cups water. Add to the pears, and add more water to cover the fruit as needed. Add the vanilla and cinnamon stick.

Cover the stockpot and bring the pears to a very gentle simmer over medium heat. Cook for 10 to 15 minutes, until the pears are fork tender. Let cool for several minutes before serving. Serve the pears with ricotta cream sprinkled with cinnamon.

Quick Tip: If you have 10 extra minutes, you can make a luscious syrup for your poached pears with almost no effort. Remove the cooked pears from the poaching liquid and cover them to keep warm. Reduce the poaching liquid by one-half to three-quarters by letting it gently simmer, uncovered. Remove the cinnamon stick and strain the sauce before serving. Spoon over the pears.

Pecan Pie Crust

Being a vintage-cookbook junkie, I've learned that there's not much that's new in the world of cooking. Nut crusts have been around for ages. My mother-in-law, whom I adore, has generously handed down many of her old cookbooks, including The Community Cook Book *(1947) and* The Good Housekeeping Illustrated Cookbook *(1980). Both include nut crust recipes. I love the way this type of crust adds lots of flavor and a rustic feel to pies. Press the dough into the bottoms of ramekins for individual desserts.* **egg-free**

makes 1 (8- or 9-inch) pie crust

2 cups pecans

3 large pitted Medjool dates

2 tablespoons unsalted butter, melted

pinch of salt

Preheat the oven to 350°F. Spray an 8- or 9-inch tart pan or pie pan with cooking spray.

In the bowl of a food processor, pulse the pecans and dates until finely chopped. Add the melted butter and process until a dough forms. Press the dough into the prepared pan. Bake for 10 to 15 minutes, until light golden brown. The crust will puff slightly. Let the crust cool completely before filling.

Variation—Walnut Pie Crust: Follow the directions for the pecan pie crust, but replace the pecans with 2 cups walnuts.

Quick Tip: This can be made a day ahead of time, cooled, wrapped, and refrigerated overnight.

Flaky Pie Crust

This crust is fragile and requires tender loving care and a little patience. It's worth the effort, though. The combination of butter and shortening creates a buttery, flaky crust. Make sure that the shortening, butter, and egg are cold for best results.

makes 1 (9-inch) pie crust

1 cup Basic Flour Blend (page 212)

2 tablespoons sweet rice flour, plus more for dusting

2 tablespoons potato starch

pinch of salt

3 tablespoons cold non-hydrogenated shortening, diced

3 tablespoons cold unsalted butter, diced

1 cold large egg

1 teaspoon cider vinegar

In a medium bowl, whisk together the flour blend, 2 tablespoons sweet rice flour, potato starch, and salt until uniform. Add the shortening and butter, toss the cubes in the flour to coat, then quickly work them into the flour with your fingertips until the mixture resembles coarse peas.

In a small bowl, beat the egg and vinegar together. Mixing with a fork, add enough of the egg mixture to the flour and butter mixture to form a shaggy dough. You may not use all the egg mixture.

Cover your work surface with a large silicone pastry mat, which works well, or you can also use parchment paper. Dust with sweet rice flour. Turn the dough onto the work surface, gather the pieces together, and form a ball. Press the dough into a flat circle, fold it in half, and rotate it 45 degrees counterclockwise. Repeat 3 to 4 more times, adding flour as needed to keep the dough from sticking. You'll know you can stop kneading when the dough doesn't crack in half when your fold it over. Wrap in waxed paper and refrigerate for 20 minutes.

When the dough is cold, preheat the oven to 375°F. Lightly dust both sides of the dough with a little sweet rice flour. Between 2 pieces of parchment paper, roll out the dough to a 10- to 12-inch circle about $1/8$ inch thick. Transfer the crust to an 8- or 9-inch pie pan by peeling the top piece of parchment paper off the dough, turning the pie pan upside down on the dough, and quickly flipping the dough and pie pan over. Gently peel back the parchment paper.

Press the dough into the edges of the pan. Dip your fingertips as needed into a bowl of ice water, using moist fingertips to repair any cracks by pressing the dough back together. Use a knife or pastry wheel to cut off any excess. Use your fingertips to smooth the edge.

If your pie recipe calls for blind baking the crust, prick the bottom and sides of the crust with a fork. Use coffee filters to line the crust and fill it completely with dried beans to prevent the crust from shrinking. Bake for 10 to 15 minutes, until the crust is set. Remove the beans with a large spoon, then return the crust to the oven and bake until the bottom is lightly golden brown and cooked through.

Quick Tip: If the dough becomes too stiff in the refrigerator, allow it to stand at room temperature for 10 to 15 minutes before you try to roll it out.

Chocolate Cream Pie

Chocolate and walnut is a classic flavor pairing, so I didn't think twice about pouring this filling into a luscious nut crust.

makes 1 (8- or 9-inch) pie, serves 8 to 12

¾ cup low-fat milk

1 packet (about 2¼ teaspoons) unflavored gelatin

¼ cup agave nectar

¼ cup Dutch-processed cocoa powder

1 teaspoon vanilla extract

½ teaspoon instant decaf coffee granules

1 cup heavy whipping cream

1 handful carob chips, grated or finely chopped

1 (8- or 9-inch) Walnut Pie Crust (page 149), baked and cooled

Pour the milk into a medium saucepan and sprinkle it with the gelatin. Let sit for a few minutes to soften the gelatin, then heat the mixture over medium-low heat and stir in the agave. Whisk in the cocoa powder, vanilla, and coffee granules. Let the mixture heat until it nearly boils, then remove from the heat and strain through a fine-mesh strainer into a heatproof bowl. Cover and refrigerate for 20 minutes, or until cooled and slightly thickened. It should be the consistency of runny pudding. Don't chill it too long or it will be too thick to incorporate whipped cream. (Note: If by chance your chocolate mixture gets too thick, use an immersion blender or a regular blender to smooth it out.)

While the chocolate mixture is chilling, whip the heavy cream using a stand mixer or handheld mixer on medium-high speed until stiff peaks form. Cover and refrigerate until the chocolate mixture has cooled and thickened.

Stir one-fourth of the whipped cream right into the chocolate. Fold the remaining cream into the chocolate in 2 or 3 additions, adding more when the previous addition has started to incorporate. Once you add the last of the cream, sprinkle the carob chips over the mousse and fold them in. Resist the temptation to stir. Just keep folding until the mousse is homogeneous. Turn into the cooled pie crust, cover, and chill for several hours or overnight.

Quick Tip: Heavy cream has reached the stiff-peaks stage when you lift your beater or whisk out of the cream and it forms a peak that doesn't fall over. If your peak falls, you're at the soft-peak stage and should continue whipping. Watch carefully, because heavy cream can easily be overwhipped.

Pumpkin Pie

I love pumpkin. Each fall I roast pounds and pounds of sugar pumpkins, puree them, and store the gorgeous orange flesh in the freezer so I can eat it all year long. I actually like it right out of the jar topped with Greek yogurt, stevia, and cinnamon. The holidays give me an excuse to make this pie, and the pecan crust gives it a rustic feel.

makes 1 (9-inch) pie, serves 8 to 12

1¾ cups pumpkin puree (about one 15-ounce can)

½ cup low-fat milk

½ cup half-and-half

2 large eggs

1 teaspoon vanilla extract

1 teaspoon ground cinnamon

½ teaspoon freshly ground nutmeg

½ teaspoon ground allspice

¼ teaspoon liquid stevia

¼ teaspoon salt

1 (9-inch) Pecan Pie Crust (page 149), baked

Preheat the oven to 375°F.

In a large bowl, whisk together the pumpkin puree, milk, half-and-half, eggs, vanilla, cinnamon, nutmeg, allspice, stevia, and salt. Pour into the baked pie crust. Cover the edges of the crust with aluminum foil to prevent them from overbrowning. Place the pie on a baking sheet and bake for 50 minutes, or until the filling has slightly puffed and set in the center. If you want the crust a bit browner, remove the foil during the last 5 to 10 minutes of baking.

Let cool before slicing. Store covered in the refrigerator.

Variation—Sweet Potato Pie: To make a sweet potato pie, replace the pumpkin puree with 2 cups mashed sweet potato, increase the milk to ¾ cup, and replace the nutmeg with ground ginger. Separate the eggs, reserving the whites. Put all ingredients except the egg whites into the bowl of a food processor fitted with the steel blade and puree until smooth. Transfer to a large bowl.

In a medium bowl, beat the egg whites until stiff peaks form. Stir one-fourth of the whites directly into the sweet potato mixture. Fold the remaining egg whites into the mixture in 2 or 3 additions. Gently turn the sweet potato filling into the baked pie crust. Bake at 375°F for 30 to 40 minutes, until the pie filling has puffed and the center is set. Cover the crust during the last 15 minutes of baking to prevent overbrowning. Let cool before slicing. Store covered in refrigerator.

Quick Tip: Pumpkin pie can be made a day ahead. Or, bake the crust and prepare the filling the night before. Then assemble the pie and bake it the day you plan to serve it.

Apple Pie with Pecan Crumb Topping

When baking an apple pie, the fruit sinks as the juices are released. I pile the apples a little higher in the middle so when it comes out of the oven the pie looks full, which is why I call for 6 to 7 cups of apples. If you need more to get the same result, use more. And if you need less, use less. It all depends on the depth of your pie plate.

makes 1 (9-inch) pie, serves 8 to 12

Filling:

6 to 7 cups peeled and thinly sliced baking apples

juice of ½ small lemon

½ cup palm sugar

1 tablespoon tapioca starch

1 teaspoon ground cinnamon, plus ¼ teaspoon for sprinkling

¼ teaspoon freshly ground nutmeg

pinch of salt

1 (9-inch) Flaky Pie Crust (page 150), unbaked

Crumb topping:

¾ cup Basic Flour Blend (page 212)

¼ cup palm sugar

pinch of salt

6 tablespoons cold unsalted butter, diced

¼ cup coarsely chopped pecans

Preheat the oven to 375°F.

To make the filling, put the sliced apples in a large bowl and squeeze the lemon juice over them. Add the palm sugar, tapioca starch, 1 teaspoon cinnamon, the nutmeg, and salt. Toss to combine and set aside.

To make the crumb topping, mix together the flour blend, sugar, and salt in a medium bowl. Use your fingertips to cut the butter into the flour until it resembles the consistency of coarse, mealy pebbles. Mix in the pecans.

Scrape the filling and all the juice into the unbaked pie crust. Top with the crumb mixture. Cover the edges of the pie crust with aluminum foil to prevent overbrowning and bake for 35 to 40 minutes. Uncover the pie crust edges if you'd like them a bit browner, and bake for 15 to 20 minutes longer, until the apples are fork tender.

Quick Tip: Fill a large bowl three-quarters full with water and stir in the juice from half a lemon. Put the peeled apples into the bowl to prevent browning. As you slice the apples, put them back into the lemon water until you're ready to toss them with the sugar mix.

Fresh Fruit Tart

I haven't met anyone who doesn't love this tart, which makes it a go-to recipe when I have company. It makes preparing a big meal simpler because the entire tart can be assembled a day ahead of time.

***makes 1 (8-inch) tart,
serves 8 to 12***

4 cups Opera Cream (page 157)

1 (8-inch) Pecan Pie Crust
(page 149), baked in a tart pan and
cooled completely

2 tablespoons no-sugar-added
apricot or apple preserves

2 tablespoons water

assorted fresh fruit, such as berries,
grapes, kiwifruit, and oranges

Spread the opera cream evenly in the baked pecan pie crust.

Combine the preserves and water in a small saucepan and bring to a simmer to melt. Strain if necessary to remove any pieces of fruit.

Slice the berries and grapes in half lengthwise. Peel the kiwi, cut them in half, and slice thinly. Peel the oranges and remove the membrane. Lay the slices on paper towels with the cut-sides down to absorb any juices that would otherwise mar the top of your tart. Create an attractive pattern with the fruit on the surface of the opera cream. Brush the top of the fruit with the melted preserves to give the tart a professional, finished look. Chill before serving.

Quick Tip: When cutting this tart, use a good-quality, sharp serrated knife and let the knife do the cutting. If you press down into the tart, you'll smash the gorgeous crust.

Pastry Cream

I learned how to make pastry cream in Fundamentals of Baking at culinary school. Of course, we used whole milk and white sugar. I came home determined to make it refined sugar–free and found that it's quick and simple but requires constant focus for a good result. It's imperative to gather all your equipment and ingredients before beginning because you can't stop the cooking process once it's started. This has been adapted from the Culinary Institute of America's Mastering the Art of Baking and Pastry.

makes about 3 cups

2 cups low-fat milk, divided

pinch of kosher salt

5 tablespoons cornstarch

3 large eggs, beaten

1½ teaspoons vanilla extract

1½ tablespoons unsalted butter, cubed

3 tablespoons agave nectar, or as needed

Prepare an ice bath to cool down the pastry cream by putting some ice in a bowl large enough to surround the bowl you'll use to store your final product. Cover the ice with water, but don't add so much that it will overflow when the bowl of pastry cream is added. You'll need a whisk, a spatula, a 4-quart or larger stainless steel saucepan, a clean bowl to store the final pastry cream, and plastic wrap.

In the saucepan, bring 1½ cups milk and the salt to a boil, stirring with the spatula. The milk will start to foam up, so watch it carefully. If you don't pay attention, you'll have a mess on your hands. While the milk is coming to a boil, whisk the cornstarch into the remaining ½ cup milk in a medium bowl. Add the eggs and vanilla to the milk and cornstarch mixture and whisk until combined.

Once the milk comes to a boil, temper the egg and milk mixture by pouring about one-third of the boiling milk directly into the egg mixture, whisking constantly. Don't stop whisking or your eggs will curdle. Then pour the whole tempered egg mixture into the saucepan with the milk, whisking constantly. Bring the mixture back to a boil while whisking. As it comes to a boil, it will start to look like scrambled eggs. Don't stop whisking or the eggs really will scramble.

Once the mixture thickens and comes to a boil, take it off the heat and immediately add the butter while still whisking. Don't stop whisking until all the butter is melted into your pastry cream. Add the agave. Taste the cream; if you want it a little sweeter, go ahead and add more agave, but do it quickly.

Turn the hot pastry cream into a clean bowl and put plastic wrap directly on the cream. This will keep it from forming a skin. Wrap the bowl with plastic wrap to protect it from absorbing any odors while in your refrigerator. Place the pastry cream in the ice bath, then put it, surrounded by the ice bath, in the refrigerator to cool completely.

Variation—Lemon Pastry Cream: Add the grated zest from half a small lemon when you add the agave.

Variation—Opera Cream: Prepare the pastry cream and let it chill completely. Combine 1 cup heavy cream with $1/8$ teaspoon powdered white stevia and beat to stiff peaks. In a large bowl, whisk 2 cups pastry cream to break it up so it's smooth. Stir ¼ cup whipped cream directly into the pastry cream. Fold the remaining whipped cream into the pastry cream in 2 additions. This opera cream is the consistency of a light mousse. Total heaven. It makes a very light filling. If you want your opera cream thicker, use 1 part whipped cream to 3 parts pastry cream.

Cupcakes & Cakes

Carrot Cupcakes

A favorite every time they're served, these cupcakes are packed with carrots and light on flour, so they're a little healthier than most. Top them with whipped cream cheese frosting or spread raw cashew cream on top. **dairy-free**

makes 12 cupcakes

½ cup agave nectar

⅓ cup canola oil

2 tablespoons freshly squeezed orange juice

½ teaspoon vanilla extract

2 large eggs

½ cup plus 2 tablespoons sorghum flour

2 tablespoons tapioca starch

1 teaspoon gluten-free baking powder

½ teaspoon baking soda

½ teaspoon ground allspice

½ teaspoon salt

1½ cups grated carrots (3 to 4 carrots)

½ cup coarsely chopped toasted pecans

1 recipe Whipped Cream Cheese Frosting (page 172) or Raw Cashew Cream (page 176)

Preheat the oven to 350°F. Line a standard 12-cup muffin tin with cupcake papers or lightly mist the cups with cooking spray.

Whisk the agave, canola oil, orange juice, vanilla, and eggs together in a large bowl until well mixed. In a medium bowl, whisk together the sorghum flour, tapioca starch, baking powder, baking soda, allspice, and salt.

Add the dry ingredients to the wet ingredients and stir with a rubber spatula until just combined. Do not overmix. Fold in the carrots and pecans.

Use a spring-release ice cream scoop to divide the batter evenly among the prepared cups. Bake for 25 to 30 minutes, until a toothpick inserted into the center of a cupcake comes out clean. Let cool in the pan for 5 minutes, then transfer the cupcakes to a wire rack lined with a paper towel to cool completely. Once cool, top with frosting or cashew cream.

Quick Tip: A food processor fitted with the grating disk makes fast work of preparing the carrots. Make sure to feed the carrots into the feed tube vertically to get short pieces of grated carrot. If you don't have a food processor, grate the carrots on the large holes of a box grater.

Chocolate Sour Cream Cupcakes

Pairing sour cream, chocolate, and coffee creates layers of flavor in these moist cupcakes.

makes 12 cupcakes

½ cup warm low-fat milk

½ cup Dutch-processed cocoa powder

½ cup low-fat sour cream

6 tablespoons unsalted butter, at room temperature

½ cup agave nectar

¼ cup palm sugar

1 large egg

1 teaspoon vanilla extract

1¼ cups Basic Flour Blend (page 212)

1½ teaspoons gluten-free baking powder

¾ teaspoon instant decaf coffee granules

½ teaspoon kosher salt

½ teaspoon xanthan gum

1 recipe Whipped Coffee Frosting (page 179) or Whipped Cream Cheese Frosting (page 172) or Caramel Glaze (page 180)

Preheat the oven to 325°F. Line a standard 12-cup muffin tin with cupcake papers or lightly mist the cups with cooking spray.

In a medium bowl, whisk the milk and cocoa powder together until smooth. Whisk in the sour cream and set aside.

In the bowl of a stand mixer fitted with the paddle attachment, beat the butter on medium speed for about 3 to 5 minutes, until light and fluffy. Beat in the agave. Once combined, add the palm sugar and beat until light and fluffy. Add the egg and vanilla and beat on medium speed until the egg is fully incorporated. Stir in the sour cream mixture on medium-low speed.

In a medium bowl, whisk together the flour blend, baking powder, instant coffee, salt, and xanthan gum. On the lowest speed, mix the dry ingredients into the wet ingredients just until smooth.

Use a spring-release ice cream scoop to divide the batter evenly among the prepared cups, filling them about three-quarters full. Bake for 15 to 20 minutes, until the cupcakes spring back lightly when pressed and a toothpick inserted into the center of a cupcake comes out clean. Allow to cool for 5 minutes in the pan, then transfer the cupcakes to a wire rack lined with a paper towel to cool completely. Store in an airtight container for up to 2 days. Frost the cooled cupcakes with Whipped Coffee Frosting or Whipped Cream Cheese Frosting, or dip the tops in Caramel Glaze before serving.

Quick Tip: Liquids and semiliquids, like sour cream, should be measured in a wet measuring cup for the most accurate results.

Applesauce Spice Cupcakes

I couldn't resist making a version of this old-fashioned cupcake because I love the rich spices. They're perfect for a chilly fall day.

makes 12 cupcakes

¼ cup unsalted butter, at room temperature

¾ cup palm sugar

1¾ cups Basic Flour Blend (page 212)

1½ teaspoons gluten-free baking powder

1 teaspoon baking soda

1½ teaspoons ground cinnamon

½ teaspoon ground allspice

½ teaspoon freshly grated nutmeg

½ teaspoon xanthan gum

¼ teaspoon ground ginger

¼ teaspoon kosher salt

2 large eggs

¾ cup unsweetened applesauce, at room temperature

1 recipe Caramel Glaze (page 180)

toasted chopped pecans (optional)

Preheat the oven to 350°F. Line a standard 12-cup muffin tin with cupcake papers or lightly mist the cups with cooking spray.

In the bowl of a stand mixer fitted with the paddle attachment, beat the butter on medium speed for about 3 to 5 minutes, until light and fluffy. Add the palm sugar one-half at a time, scraping down the bowl as needed, and let the stand mixer run while you prepare the other ingredients.

In a medium bowl, whisk together the flour blend, baking powder, baking soda, cinnamon, allspice, nutmeg, xanthan gum, ginger, and salt.

Once the butter and sugar mixture is light and fluffy, add the eggs one at a time letting the first incorporate fully before adding the second, scraping the bowl between additions. On low speed, beat in the dry ingredients in three parts, alternating with the applesauce, beginning and ending with the dry ingredients. Mix just until smooth.

Use a spring-release ice cream scoop to divide the batter evenly among the prepared cups. Bake for 15 minutes, or until the cupcakes spring back lightly when pressed in the center or a toothpick inserted into the center of a cupcake comes out clean. Let cool in the pan for 5 minutes, then transfer the cupcakes to a wire rack lined with a paper towel to cool completely. Store at room temperature in an airtight container for up to 2 days. Top with caramel glaze just before serving. If desired, dip the glazed cupcakes into toasted, chopped pecans.

Quick Tip: Keep a mini nutmeg grater handy so you'll have freshly ground nutmeg on hand. It has much more flavor than its store-bought ground counterpart.

Almond Butter Cupcakes

Moist and light, these cupcakes can be filled with chocolate and topped with coconut (see variation below) or, for a fun kid-friendly twist, top with Banana Cream Frosting (page 181).

makes 16 cupcakes

⅓ cup unsalted butter, at room temperature

¾ cup palm sugar

½ cup almond butter

2 large eggs

1 teaspoon vanilla extract

2 cups Basic Flour Blend (page 212)

2 teaspoons gluten-free baking powder

½ teaspoon kosher salt

½ teaspoon xanthan gum

¾ cup unsweetened almond milk

1 recipe Chocolate Whipped Cream Frosting (page 182) or Chocolate Glaze (page 180)

Preheat the oven to 325°F. Line a standard 12-cup muffin tin and 4 cups of a second tin with cupcake papers or lightly mist the cups with cooking spray.

In a stand mixer fitted with the paddle attachment, beat the butter on medium speed for 3 to 5 minutes, until light and fluffy. Add the palm sugar one-third at a time, allowing the sugar to incorporate between each addition. Scrape the bowl down as necessary. In a microwave-safe bowl, microwave the almond butter for 20 seconds to warm it, then add it to the butter mixture and beat until smooth. Add the eggs one at a time, allowing the first to fully incorporate before adding the second. Mix in the vanilla.

In a medium bowl, whisk together the flour blend, baking powder, salt, and xanthan gum. On low speed, beat the dry ingredients into the batter in three parts, alternating with the almond milk, starting and ending with the dry ingredients. Mix until smooth.

Use a spring-release ice cream scoop to divide the batter evenly among the prepared cups. They should be about two-thirds full. Bake for 15 to 20 minutes, rotating the tins halfway through, until the cupcakes spring back lightly when pressed in the center or a toothpick inserted into the center of a cupcake comes out clean. Let cool in the pan for 5 minutes, then transfer the cupcakes to a wire rack lined with a paper towel to cool completely. Frost with Chocolate Whipped Cream Frosting or dip the tops in Chocolate Glaze.

Variation—Chocolate Filled Almond Butter Cupcakes with Toasted Coconut: Prepare 1 recipe Chocolate Filling for Cupcakes (page 184) and 1 recipe Vanilla Whipped Cream Frosting (page 182). Toast 1 cup coconut flakes by spreading them on a baking sheet lined with aluminum foil and baking in a preheated 350°F oven for 3 to 5 minutes, stirring after 3 minutes. Fill the cupcakes with the chocolate filling and frost them with the whipped cream. Sprinkle the toasted coconut over the tops.

Quick Tip: If you're filling cupcakes, you can make the filling a day ahead, but for frosting, whipped cream pipes best on the day it's made. You can quickly make a batch while the cupcakes are cooling.

Flourless Chocolate Torte

This classic flourless torte is simple to make, but it tastes like you slaved over it.

makes 1 (9-inch) cake

4 tablespoons unsalted butter, plus more for greasing

2 tablespoons hot water

1 teaspoon instant espresso powder

4 large eggs, separated

½ cup agave nectar, divided

½ cup Dutch-processed cocoa powder, sifted, plus extra for garnish

Preheat the oven to 350°F. Very generously grease the bottom and sides of a 9-inch springform pan with butter.

In a small bowl, mix the hot water and espresso powder. Set aside. In a microwave-safe bowl, melt the 4 tablespoons butter and set aside.

In a medium bowl with a handheld mixer or in the bowl of a stand mixer fitted with the whisk attachment, beat the egg yolks for about 5 minutes, until thick and light yellow in color. Your beaters should leave a trail in the yolks for a couple of seconds before the yolks meld back in. Gradually add ¼ cup agave to the yolks and beat for several more minutes until well combined. Stir in ¼ cup cocoa powder with a spatula. Once it starts to incorporate, add the remaining cocoa powder. Continue stirring with the spatula, scraping the sides of the bowl as needed. When the cocoa is mostly incorporated, add the espresso water and melted butter. Stir until smooth.

In a large bowl, beat the egg whites on medium speed, until they are almost at the soft-peak stage. Gradually add the remaining ¼ cup agave and beat until soft peaks form. Add one-fourth of the egg whites to the chocolate mixture and stir in well. Don't worry about deflating the whites—this will lighten the chocolate mixture enough to allow you to fold in the remaining egg whites.

Fold in half of the remaining egg whites. Once they are mostly incorporated, add the remaining egg whites and continue folding until the batter has a consistent color.

Transfer the batter into the prepared springform pan. Place the pan on a baking sheet and gently place the sheet in the center of the oven. Bake for 18 to 22 minutes, until the center is set. Let cool on a wire rack for 15 minutes. Using a thin metal spatula, loosen the torte from the edges of the pan and remove the outer ring. Serve warm or at room temperature, garnished with a light dusting of cocoa powder.

Quick Tip: You can make this the day before, wrap and refrigerate, then allow to come to room temperature before serving.

Peanut Butter Hot Fudge Cake

I've seen versions of this cake in so many places and could never shake the "I gotta try that!" feeling. I'm so glad I did—it's a fun, gooey mess to eat. As the cake bakes, it rises and sits on top of a bed of thick hot fudge sauce that forms below. I use almond milk to make this dairy-free for those chocolate lovers who can't have milk, but any nondairy, neutral-flavored milk will work well, as will cow's milk. **vegan, slow cooker recipe**

serves 6 to 8

½ cup Basic Flour Blend (page 212)

½ cup plus 1 tablespoon palm sugar, divided

¾ teaspoon gluten-free baking powder

¼ teaspoon kosher salt

1/8 teaspoon xanthan gum

1/3 cup unsweetened almond milk

1 tablespoon canola oil

½ teaspoon vanilla extract

¼ cup smooth sugar-free peanut butter

¼ cup Dutch-processed cocoa powder

¼ teaspoon instant decaf coffee granules

1¼ cups very hot (not boiling!) water

Coat a medium (4-quart) or large (5- to 6-quart) slow cooker with cooking spray. The smaller your slow cooker, the thicker your cake will be and the longer it will need to cook.

In a large bowl, whisk together the flour blend, ¼ cup palm sugar, the baking powder, salt, and xanthan gum. In a medium bowl, whisk together the almond milk, oil, and vanilla. In a microwave-safe bowl, microwave the peanut butter for 20 to 30 seconds, just until softened and easy to stir. Add the wet ingredients to the dry ingredients, then stir in the warm peanut butter.

Evenly spread the batter in the bottom of the prepared slow cooker. The batter will be thick.

In the same bowl you used to mix the batter, whisk together the cocoa powder, remaining ¼ cup plus 1 tablespoon palm sugar, and coffee granules. Carefully pour the hot water into the cocoa mixture and whisk until smooth. Pour on top of the batter in the slow cooker. Do not mix.

Cover and cook on high for 1 to 2 hours, checking after 1 hour. The cake is done when a toothpick inserted into the center comes out clean. Serve warm or cold.

Quick Tip: Though mixing the batter and the fudge in the same bowl may at first seem like the wrong thing to do, it doesn't harm the recipe at all. All the ingredients are going in the same place, and it saves dishwashing time later on.

Vanilla Bean Sponge Cake

My friend Kelly Broznya from The Spunky Coconut *(www.TheSpunkyCoconut.com) is known for her Vanilla Bean Cake. This is my version. I tested this recipe in a cooking class I taught, and the overwhelming response was that it's almost like a sponge cake. I smiled while I watched my students gobble it up and then ask to take home the last couple of pieces. Note: There's no added salt in this recipe because most canned beans are high in sodium. If you use home-cooked or low-sodium canned beans, add ¼ to ½ teaspoon salt with the dry ingredients.* **dairy-free**

makes 1 (8-inch) cake

1 (14.5 ounce) can white beans, drained and rinsed well

¼ cup unsweetened applesauce

¼ cup agave nectar

4 large eggs

2 tablespoons non-hydrogenated shortening, melted and cooled

1 tablespoon vanilla extract

¼ teaspoon liquid stevia

½ cup Basic Flour Blend (page 212), plus extra for dusting the pan

1 teaspoon gluten-free baking powder

½ teaspoon baking soda

1 recipe Chocolate Avocado Frosting or Whipped Chocolate Avocado Frosting (page 174)

Preheat the oven to 350°F. Line an 8-inch round cake pan with parchment paper. Lightly mist the bottom and sides of the pan with cooking spray, then coat it with extra flour.

In a food processor fitted with the steel blade, pulse the beans and applesauce several times to combine, then puree until almost smooth. Add the agave and puree until completely smooth, scraping down the bowl as needed. Add the eggs, shortening, vanilla, and stevia. Process until combined.

In a medium bowl, whisk together the flour, baking powder, and baking soda. Add to the food processor and pulse until combined. Pour the batter into the prepared cake pan. Bake for 25 to 30 minutes, until the cake is lightly golden brown and a toothpick inserted into the center comes out clean. Let cool for 15 minutes in the pan. Carefully run a thin metal spatula between the cake and the pan, then turn the cake onto a wire rack lined with a paper towel to cool completely. Frost with Chocolate Avocado Frosting or Whipped Chocolate Avocado Frosting.

Quick Tip: For a successful bean cake, the beans must be rinsed very well. Shake the excess water off the beans before adding them to the food processor. Don't try to save time by skipping the parchment paper and not flouring your pan—this cake will stick if the pan isn't properly prepared.

Lemon Poppy Seed Cake

The flavors in this cake remind me of spring and summer. To make an impressive dessert, bake two cakes and use a knife to level the tops. Frost the tops of the cakes with Raspberry Ricotta Frosting (page 177), then stack the cakes to create a torte. Decorate the top with fresh raspberries.

makes 1 (8-inch) cake

¼ cup unsalted butter, at room temperature

½ cup plus 2 tablespoons palm sugar

1 large egg

1 cup Basic Flour Blend (page 212)

½ teaspoon gluten-free baking powder

½ teaspoon xanthan gum

¼ teaspoon baking soda

¼ teaspoon kosher salt

½ cup low-fat milk

¼ cup part-skim ricotta cheese

1 tablespoon freshly squeezed lemon juice

1 tablespoon grated lemon zest

1 tablespoon poppy seeds

1 recipe Raspberry Ricotta Frosting (page 177)

Fresh raspberries (optional)

Preheat the oven to 350°F. Line an 8-inch cake pan with parchment paper and lightly mist the bottom and sides of the pan with cooking spray.

In a stand mixer fitted with the paddle attachment, beat the butter on medium speed for about 3 minutes, until light. Add the palm sugar one-third at a time, letting it incorporate before adding more. Continue beating for about 5 minutes, until the palm sugar starts to dissolve and the butter incorporates more air. Add the egg and beat until thoroughly combined, scraping down the bowl as needed.

In a medium bowl, whisk together the flour blend, baking powder, xanthan gum, baking soda, and salt. Set aside. In another medium bowl, stir together the milk, ricotta cheese, and lemon juice. Set aside.

On low speed, beat in the dry ingredients in three parts, alternating with the ricotta and milk mixture, beginning and ending with the dry ingredients. Mix just until smooth. Fold in the lemon zest and poppy seeds.

Transfer the batter into the prepared pan and bake for 25 to 30 minutes, until the cake springs back lightly when touched in the center and a toothpick inserted into the center comes out clean. Let cool for 20 minutes in the pan, then carefully run a thin metal spatula between the cake and the pan and turn the cake onto a wire rack lined with a paper towel to cool completely. Frost the cake with Raspberry Ricotta Frosting and decorate with raspberries, if using.

Quick Tip: Lining wire racks with a paper towel helps reduce indentations on the cake.

Banana Walnut Cake

Once it's cooled, frost this cake with Whipped Cream Cheese Frosting, or keep it dairy-free with light and airy Whipped Chocolate Avocado Frosting. **dairy-free**

makes 1 (9-inch) cake

½ cup canola oil

½ cup agave nectar

¼ cup palm sugar

2 eggs

¾ cup fork-mashed very ripe banana

¼ cup unsweetened almond milk

1 teaspoon vanilla extract

2 cups Basic Flour Blend (page 212)

2 teaspoons gluten-free baking powder

1 teaspoon baking soda

1 teaspoon ground cinnamon

½ teaspoon ground ginger

¼ teaspoon kosher salt

¾ cup chopped toasted walnuts

1 recipe Whipped Cream Cheese Frosting (page 172) or Whipped Chocolate Avocado Frosting (page 174)

Preheat the oven to 325°F. Line a 9-inch round cake pan with parchment paper, and lightly mist the bottom and sides with cooking spray.

Beat the oil and agave in the bowl of a stand mixer fitted with the paddle attachment on medium speed for about 3 minutes, until combined and light. Add the palm sugar one-half at a time and beat for about 3 minutes, until the mixture is lighter in texture.

Add the eggs one at a time, waiting until the first egg has fully incorporated before adding the second. Add the banana, almond milk, and vanilla. Beat until combined.

Meanwhile, whisk together the flour blend, baking powder, baking soda, cinnamon, ginger, and salt in a medium bowl. Once the liquid ingredients are combined, add the dry ingredients all at once, mixing on low speed until smooth. Fold in the toasted walnuts.

Transfer the batter to the prepared pan and bake for 35 to 40 minutes, until the cake springs back when lightly touched and a toothpick inserted into the center comes out clean. Let cool in the pan for 20 minutes, then carefully run a thin metal spatula between the cake and the pan and turn the cake onto a wire rack lined with a paper towel to cool completely. Frost with Whipped Cream Cheese Frosting or Whipped Chocolate Avocado Frosting.

Quick Tip: Toast the walnuts on a sheet pan at 325°F for 5 to 7 minutes, just until fragrant, while you assemble the other ingredients.

Chocolate Teff Cake

This supermoist cake uses nutritious teff flour, one of my favorites to pair with chocolate. The dense, tender crumb is perfect for filling with pudding or Whipped Cream Cheese Frosting and fresh strawberries.

makes 1 (8-inch) cake

½ cup unsweetened almond milk

½ cup unsweetened applesauce

1 teaspoon vanilla extract

¼ teaspoon liquid stevia

½ cup teff flour

1 ounce unsweetened baking chocolate

¼ cup canola oil

½ cup palm sugar

1 large egg

1 large egg white

½ cup Dutch-processed cocoa powder

1 teaspoon gluten-free baking powder

½ teaspoon baking soda

¼ teaspoon kosher salt

¼ teaspoon xanthan gum

1 recipe Whipped Cream Cheese Frosting (page 172) or 1 recipe Fluffy Meringue Frosting (page 183)

Preheat the oven to 350°F. Line an 8-inch round cake pan with parchment paper and lightly mist it with cooking spray.

In a medium bowl, stir together the almond milk, applesauce, vanilla, stevia, and teff flour until smooth. Set aside.

Chop the chocolate into several pieces and put into a microwave-safe bowl with the oil. Microwave for 30 seconds and stir to melt. Microwave for another 15 seconds if necessary and stir again.

Put the melted chocolate and oil in the bowl of a stand mixer fitted with the paddle attachment. On medium speed, add the palm sugar one half at a time and beat for about 3 minutes, until cool and lighter in texture. Add the egg and the egg white and beat until combined.

In a medium bowl, sift together the cocoa powder, baking powder, baking soda, salt, and xanthan gum. On low speed, beat the dry ingredients into the palm sugar mixture in three parts, alternating with the applesauce mixture, beginning and ending with the dry ingredients. Beat just until smooth. Transfer the batter to the prepared pan and bake for 22 to 28 minutes, until the center of the cake springs back when pressed lightly and a toothpick inserted into the center comes out clean.

Let cool in the pan for 20 minutes, then carefully run a thin metal spatula between the cake and the pan and turn the cake onto a wire rack lined with a paper towel to cool completely. Frost with cream cheese frosting or meringue frosting.

Quick Tip: Teff flour can lend a light crunch to baked goods. Soaking it in the almond milk and applesauce mixture before adding it to the batter eliminates that issue.

Fast Frostings

Whipped Cream Cheese Frosting

Pair this slightly sweet frosting with almost any cake or cupcake, including Chocolate Teff Cake (page 170), Carrot Cupcakes (page 159), or Banana Walnut Cake (page 169). It makes a great cake filling, too. **egg-free**

makes about 4 cups

8 ounces light (Neûfchatel) cream cheese, at room temperature

2 tablespoons agave nectar

1 teaspoon alcohol-free vanilla extract

pinch of salt

1 cup cold heavy cream

In the bowl of a stand mixer fitted with the paddle attachment or with a handheld mixer, beat the cream cheese, agave, vanilla, and salt on medium speed for about 3 minutes, until smooth and light.

In a medium bowl, use an immersion blender fitted with a whisk attachment or a handheld mixer with clean beaters to whip the heavy cream on medium-high speed to stiff peaks. Stir one-fourth of the whipped cream into the cream cheese mixture. Gently fold in the remaining whipped cream until combined. This can be made one day ahead and refrigerated until ready to use. Spread or pipe onto a cooled cake or cupcakes.

Quick Tip: Chill the bowl and beaters in the freezer for 10 minutes before whipping the heavy cream. This helps the cream to whip properly.

Chocolate Cream Cheese Frosting

This versatile frosting pairs well with Vanilla Bean Sponge Cake (page 167), Chocolate Sour Cream Cupcakes (page 160), Almond Butter Cupcakes (page 162), and Banana Walnut Cake (page 169). **egg-free**

makes about 1½ cups

4 ounces light (Neûfchatel) cream cheese, at room temperature

1 cup heavy cream, divided

6 tablespoons Dutch-processed cocoa powder

½ cup Powdered Palm Sugar (page 185)

1 teaspoon alcohol-free vanilla extract

In the bowl of a stand mixer fitted with the paddle attachment or with a handheld mixer, beat the cream cheese and 2 tablespoons heavy cream on medium speed for about 3 minutes, until smooth and light. Sift in the cocoa powder and powdered palm sugar and mix together on the lowest setting, then add 2 more tablespoons heavy cream and the vanilla. Beat until light and smooth. In another bowl, whip the remaining 6 ounces heavy cream on medium-high speed to stiff peaks. Stir one-fourth of the whipped cream directly into the chocolate cream cheese mixture. Fold in the remaining whipped cream until combined. Refrigerate until ready to use. Spread or pipe onto a cooled cake or cupcakes.

Quick Tip: Refrigerate this frosting before piping to help firm it up.

Chocolate Avocado Frosting

I love watching people eat this frosting—no one ever knows that it's made with avocados. The amount of sweetener you need will depend on the flavor and size of your avocados. This recipe has a great starting point, but please use more or less agave depending on how your frosting tastes. If you choose to increase the stevia, do so 5 drops at a time and taste it before adding more. Too much stevia can lend a bitter taste. **vegan**

makes about 1 cup

3 small ripe avocados

¼ cup plus 3 tablespoons Dutch-processed cocoa powder

¼ cup agave nectar, or more

20 to 25 drops of liquid stevia, or more

Seed, peel, and chop the avocados. Place the avocado in the bowl of a food processor fitted with the steel blade. Add the cocoa powder and agave nectar and pulse several times to combine, then process until smooth. Taste and add agave and/or stevia as needed. Refrigerate overnight before using to achieve the best flavor. Let it come to room temperature before use for best results.

This frosting can be frozen. When ready to use, thaw it in the refrigerator and then beat it on medium-low speed with a handheld mixer or in the bowl of a stand mixer fitted with the paddle attachment until smooth.

Variation—Whipped Chocolate Avocado Frosting: For a supercreamy nondairy chocolate frosting, prepare 1 recipe Chocolate Avocado Frosting and 1 recipe Whipped Coconut Cream (page 175). Stir one-fourth of the whipped coconut cream directly into the chocolate avocado frosting. Fold in the remaining three-quarters coconut cream until thoroughly combined. Cover and refrigerate until ready to use. This frosting can also be frozen, but it won't be as light once it thaws.

Quick Tip: To quickly seed and peel avocados, use a sharp knife to cut around the seed from top to bottom. Open the avocado like you would a peach by twisting the two halves in opposite directions. Hold the side with the seed in it in one hand. Use a sharp knife to whack the seed; your knife will get stuck. Turn the knife and the seed will pop out. Cut each piece in half and peel the skin away.

Whipped Coconut Cream

A dairy-free version of whipped cream, this frosting is not quite as sturdy as traditional whipped cream, but it's just as delicious. If you can find coconut cream instead of coconut milk, it will work just as well. **vegan**

makes about ¾ cup

1 (15-ounce) can full-fat coconut milk

½ teaspoon alcohol-free vanilla extract

8 to 15 drops of liquid stevia, or more

Refrigerate the coconut milk overnight. The next day, carefully open the can and remove the coconut fat that has solidified in the top portion of the can, being careful not to mix it with the liquid underneath. Discard the liquid. In a medium bowl, use an immersion blender fitted with a whisk attachment or a handheld mixer to whip the coconut cream for 3 to 4 minutes, until soft peaks form. Mix in the vanilla and stevia. Cover and refrigerate until ready to use.

Quick Tip: Coconut cream has a natural sweetness to it, so use a light hand when adding stevia. Taste after adding 8 drops and add more as needed.

Raw Cashew Cream

This cream can be used as a cupcake frosting or as a spread for your favorite nut bread or a slice of toast.

makes about 2 cups

1 cup raw cashews

3 cups water, divided

3 large pitted Medjool dates

1 teaspoon alcohol-free vanilla extract

pinch of kosher salt

In a small bowl, cover the cashews with 2 cups water. In a second small bowl, cover the dates with 1 cup water. Soak both for 20 minutes. Drain the cashews, discard the soaking water, and add the cashews to a blender. Add the dates with their soaking water, and add the vanilla and salt. Start the blender on low speed and increase to high. Blend for 1 to 2 minutes, until creamy. Cover and refrigerate for several hours before serving. The cream thickens slightly in the refrigerator. Keeps for 5 to 7 days.

Quick Tip: This recipe works best with a high-powered blender. My good friend Maggie Savage from *She Let Them Eat Cake* (SheLetThemEatCake.com) shared that this can also be made with a regular blender if the cashews are soaked overnight. You'll get a smoother consistency.

Raspberry Ricotta Frosting

Raspberry puree gives this frosting a light, fresh flavor. Pair it with Lemon Poppy Seed Cake (page 168), Vanilla Bean Sponge Cake (page 167), or Chocolate Sour Cream Cupcakes (page 160). It also makes a great cake filling. **egg-free**

makes about 3½ cups

½ teaspoon unflavored gelatin

1 tablespoon water

1 cup frozen raspberries, thawed

½ cup part-skim ricotta cheese

3 tablespoons agave nectar

1 cup heavy whipping cream

15 drops of liquid stevia

In a small microwave-safe bowl, microwave the gelatin and water for 20 seconds, or until the gelatin is dissolved. Set aside to cool. If the gelatin sets up firm before you add it to the other ingredients, return it to the microwave for 10 seconds.

Puree the raspberries in the bowl of a food processor or mini food chopper. Push the puree through a fine-mesh strainer into a medium bowl and discard the seeds. Add the ricotta and agave to the puree, and mix with a rubber spatula until smooth. In a second medium bowl, use an immersion blender fitted with a whisk attachment or a handheld mixer to whip the heavy cream and stevia to soft peaks. Add the cooled gelatin and whip to stiff peaks. Stir one-fourth of the whipped cream directly into the raspberry mixture. Fold the remaining whipped cream into the raspberry mixture until uniform in color. Cover the frosting with plastic wrap and chill in the refrigerator until thickened.

Variation—Jam: Use ½ cup of your favorite all-fruit preserves in place of the frozen raspberries. If the preserves have seeds, heat the jam slightly in the microwave and push it through a fine-mesh strainer. Discard the seeds. Adjust the amount of agave based on the sweetness of the preserves. Some all-fruit preserves, such as strawberry, are dull in color. Add 6 to 8 drops of natural food coloring to make the frosting bright and attractive.

Variation—Fresh Fruit: Use your favorite fresh fruit in place of the raspberries, making sure to strain the puree before adding it to the ricotta.

Quick Tip: Use a flexible rubber spatula to press the raspberry puree quickly through the strainer. Make sure to scrape the puree hanging onto the bottom of the strainer to get as much flavor as possible.

Whipped Ricotta Cream

Ricotta adds an extra dimension of flavor and texture to desserts, which is why I like to use it in frostings. It's perfect on cupcakes, cakes, or with any fruit dish.

makes about 1½ cups

½ cup heavy cream

½ teaspoon vanilla extract

10 drops liquid stevia, or as needed

½ cup part-skim ricotta cheese

Whip the heavy cream with an electric whip until it starts to thicken. Add the vanilla and stevia, and whip until soft peaks form. Add the ricotta and whip until combined. Taste and add stevia as needed. Refrigerate until ready to use.

Whipped Coffee Frosting

Make your chocolate cupcakes into a coffee-lover's delight—fill them with Vanilla Whipped Cream (page 182) before topping them off with this frosting. It'll bring out the kid in even the most serious grown-ups.

makes about 1½ cups

1 tablespoon water

½ teaspoon unflavored gelatin

1 cup heavy cream

1½ teaspoons instant espresso powder

¼ cup Powdered Palm Sugar (page 185)

Combine the water and gelatin in a small microwave-safe bowl. Microwave for 15 to 20 seconds, until the gelatin has dissolved. Set aside to cool. If the gelatin sets up firm before you add it to the other ingredients, return it to the microwave for 10 seconds.

In a medium bowl, stir the heavy cream and espresso powder together until the powder has dissolved. Whip with an immersion blender fitted with a whisk attachment or a handheld mixer until the cream begins to thicken, almost to soft peaks. Add the powdered palm sugar and cooled gelatin mixture. Whip until stiff peaks form. Refrigerate until ready to use.

Quick Tip: If you want to pipe this frosting onto cupcakes instead of spreading it, double the recipe.

Chocolate Glaze

This glaze is thick, sticky, and delicious. Immediately after dipping your donut or cupcake in the glaze, dip it again in your choice of toasted nuts or unsweetened coconut for an extra layer of texture and flavor. **egg-free**

makes about ¾ cup, enough for 6 donuts or 12 cupcakes

½ cup palm sugar

2 tablespoons low-fat milk

1 teaspoon vanilla extract

¼ cup Dutch-processed cocoa powder

1 cup finely chopped toasted nuts or shredded toasted coconut

In a small heavy-bottomed saucepan, bring the palm sugar, milk, and vanilla to a boil over medium heat. Once the mixture begins to boil, remove from the heat and whisk in the cocoa powder. Return to the heat and whisk until the cocoa powder is fully incorporated and the glaze is smooth.

Working quickly, dip the tops of your donuts or cupcakes into the warm glaze. If the glaze gets too thick to easily dip the tops of your donuts or cupcakes, simply return the pan to the heat and whisk until the glaze thins. After dipping in the glaze, immediately dip in the nuts or coconut.

Variation—Caramel Glaze: Use heavy cream instead of milk, omit the cocoa powder, and add 2 tablespoons butter.

Make It Dairy-Free: Use nondairy milk instead of cow's milk; use coconut milk instead of heavy cream; omit the butter and use a nondairy butter substitute.

Quick Tip: Have your cooled cupcakes or donuts and choice of nuts or coconut ready in assembly-line fashion before making the glaze. The glaze is easiest to work with when it's warm.

Banana Cream Frosting

Here's a kid-friendly frosting perfect for spreading on cupcakes or a single layer cake. It's got a light, mousselike texture, so it's not the best choice for frosting the sides of cakes. Don't worry if you have a little extra left over—this is light enough to eat all by itself.

**makes about 4 cups,
enough for 24 cupcakes or
1 (9 x 13-inch) cake**

1 tablespoon water

½ teaspoon unflavored gelatin

1 ripe banana

1 tablespoon freshly squeezed lemon juice

1 recipe Vanilla Pudding (page 193)

1 cup heavy cream

In a small microwave-safe bowl, microwave the water and gelatin for 20 to 30 seconds and stir to melt. Repeat if necessary to fully melt the gelatin. Set aside to cool, but don't let it harden. If the gelatin sets up firm before you add it to the other ingredients, return it to the microwave for 10 seconds.

In a medium bowl, beat the banana and lemon juice with a handheld mixer on medium speed until smooth. Add the vanilla pudding and mix briefly, just until combined. In another bowl, whip the heavy cream to soft peaks. Add the cooled gelatin and beat until stiff peaks form. Stir one-fourth of the whipped cream directly into the banana pudding mixture. Fold the remaining whipped cream in until fully incorporated. Refrigerate until ready to use.

Quick Tip: One of my favorite kitchen tools is my handheld lemon juicer. It's an enamel-coated metal press that quickly juices half a lemon or lime. If you don't have one, put it on your wish list.

Vanilla Whipped Cream Frosting

This whipped cream can be piped and will actually hold its shape. You won't have to worry about it melting, either. It will hold up nicely in the refrigerator for several days, but for the best results, use it immediately. **egg-free**

makes about 2 cups

1 tablespoon water

½ teaspoon unflavored gelatin

1 cup heavy cream

½ teaspoon alcohol-free vanilla extract

15 to 20 drops of liquid stevia, or more

In a small microwave-safe bowl, microwave the water and gelatin for 20 to 30 seconds and stir to melt. Repeat if necessary to fully melt the gelatin. Set aside to cool but don't let it harden. If the gelatin sets up firm before you add it to the other ingredients, return it to the microwave for 10 seconds.

In a medium bowl, use an immersion blender fitted with a whisk attachment or a handheld mixer to whip the heavy cream to soft peaks on medium speed, then add the cooled gelatin, vanilla, and 15 drops of stevia. Whip to medium-stiff peaks. Taste and adjust the sweetness with stevia as needed. Use this whipped cream immediately to frost cakes or cupcakes, or as a cake filling.

Variation—Vanilla Whipped Cream: Follow the directions for Vanilla Whipped Cream Frosting, but omit the water and gelatin. Use this recipe for topping pies, cobblers, and ice creams.

Variation—Chocolate Whipped Cream Frosting: Follow the directions for Vanilla Whipped Cream Frosting, but increase the heavy cream to 1 ½ cups and stir in 3 tablespoons cocoa powder and 3 tablespoons Powdered Palm Sugar (page 185) once the cream is nearly at the soft-peaks stage, then add the gelatin and vanilla. Omit the stevia. Proceed as directed.

Variation—Mocha Whipped Cream Frosting: Dissolve 1 teaspoon instant decaf coffee granules or ½ teaspoon instant espresso powder in the heavy cream before you start whipping it. Proceed as directed for making Chocolate Whipped Cream Frosting.

Fluffy Meringue Frosting

A traditional meringue has 2 parts sugar to 1 part egg whites. Since agave is much sweeter than sugar, I opted to use equal parts by weight. After many, many attempts I discovered that gelatin will keep the agave from weeping out of the meringue so that it stays in place on your cakes and cupcakes. You can pipe this frosting with a large tip, but it won't hold up for fine detailed decorations. **dairy-free, vegetarian**

makes about 4 cups, frosts 1 (8-inch) cake

1 teaspoon unflavored gelatin

2 tablespoons water

½ cup pasteurized liquid egg whites

½ teaspoon cream of tartar

pinch of salt

⅓ cup agave nectar

1 teaspoon alcohol-free vanilla extract

If you don't have a double boiler, make one by using a 4-quart saucepan and a stainless steel or glass bowl that will fit snugly on top of the pot. Add 1 inch of water to the saucepan, bring to a boil, then reduce to a gentle simmer. Set the bowl on the saucepan; it should not come in contact with the water.

While the water is coming to a boil, combine the gelatin and 2 tablespoons water in a small, microwave-safe bowl and the microwave for 20 seconds. Stir the gelatin to melt, and if necessary return it to the microwave for another 15 to 20 seconds, until dissolved. Set aside to cool. It's important that the gelatin stay in liquid form. If the gelatin sets up firm before you add it to the other ingredients, return it to the microwave for 10 seconds.

In the bowl set over simmering water, beat the egg whites, cream of tartar, and salt with a handheld mixer until stiff peaks form. Add the agave a little at a time, each time beating until stiff peaks form before adding more. Beat in the liquid gelatin, and continue beating until stiff peaks form. Remove the bowl from the simmering water and set on a kitchen towel to keep it steady. Beat in the vanilla and continue beating on high speed until the frosting has cooled and thickened and is spreadable. Use immediately.

Quick Tip: Using pasteurized egg whites for this frosting is safer than using regular egg whites because any salmonella that may have been present has been killed. This is especially important when serving children, the elderly, and anyone with a compromised immune system.

Chocolate Filling for Cupcakes

Even adults love biting into a cupcake to find a creamy, chocolatey filling.

**makes about 1 cup,
enough to fill 12 to 15 cupcakes**

1 cup low-fat milk, divided

1¾ tablespoons cornstarch

2 teaspoons agave nectar

⅛ teaspoon liquid stevia

⅛ teaspoon salt

½ teaspoon alcohol-free
vanilla extract

2 tablespoons Dutch-processed
cocoa powder

Combine ½ cup milk and the cornstarch in a small bowl and set aside. Pour the remaining ½ cup milk into a small heavy-bottomed saucepan and add the agave, stevia, salt, and vanilla and stir to combine. Heat over medium heat. When the milk mixture begins to heat up, whisk in the cocoa powder. Once small bubbles begin to form around the edge of the pan, whisk in the milk and cornstarch mixture. Stir until the pudding thickens and boils. Transfer to a bowl and place plastic wrap directly on the surface of the pudding. Chill for several hours or overnight.

To fill the cupcakes, use an apple corer to cut out the centers of the cupcakes without cutting through to the bottom. Spoon the filling into a sealable plastic bag, seal the bag, cut a small hole in one corner, and squeeze the filling directly into the cupcake holes until they're filled. Frost as usual. Keep the cupcakes refrigerated until served, as this is a milk-based filling.

Make It Dairy-Free: Replace the low-fat milk with your favorite nondairy milk.

Quick Tip: Alcohol-free vanilla uses vegetable glycerine as a base instead of alcohol. It's slightly sweet and doesn't impart any alcohol flavor to puddings and other stovetop and noncooked recipes.

Powdered Palm Sugar

I keep a jar of powdered palm sugar in my pantry at all times to use in frostings and for making candied nuts. It's simple to make and works beautifully. Though this is a powdered sugar, keep in mind that it has a brown sugar–like flavor and color and works best in chocolate, caramel, and other flavored applications. **vegan**

makes 1 generous cup

1 cup palm sugar
1 tablespoon cornstarch

In a high-powered blender or a clean coffee grinder, whirl the palm sugar and cornstarch together until light and powdery. (If using a coffee grinder, mix only half the ingredients at a time.) Store in an airtight container until ready to use. If it clumps during storage, sift before using.

Quick Tip: Cornstarch serves two purposes in this recipe: It reduces clumping and also helps thicken frostings and glazes.

Mousses, Puddings, & Custards

Easy German Chocolate Mousse

This is a lighter version of a classic dessert, but it's still luscious enough to please anyone. Once assembled and adorned with grated carob chips, toasted coconut, and pecans, its stunning presentation makes it a great holiday or dinner party dessert. You don't have to tell anyone how simple it was to make.

makes 4 servings

¾ cup low-fat milk

1½ teaspoons unflavored gelatin

¼ cup agave nectar

1 teaspoon vanilla extract

¼ teaspoon instant decaf coffee granules

¼ cup Dutch-processed cocoa powder

1 cup heavy whipping cream

1 handful unsweetened carob chips, or more

½ cup toasted pecans

½ cup toasted coconut flakes

4 toasted pecan halves, for garnish

Pour the milk into a medium heavy-bottomed saucepan and sprinkle in the unflavored gelatin. Let sit for a few minutes to soften the gelatin. Heat over medium-low heat and stir in the agave, vanilla, and instant coffee. Once the mixture begins to heat up, whisk in the cocoa powder until smooth. Let the mixture heat until it nearly boils. Remove the pan from the heat and strain the mixture through a fine-mesh strainer into a large bowl. Cover and refrigerate for 20 minutes, or until cool and thickened. Don't chill too long, or it will be too thick to incorporate the whipped cream.

While the chocolate mixture is chilling, pour the heavy whipping cream in a medium bowl. Whip on medium-high speed using a stand mixer or handheld mixer until stiff peaks form. Cover and chill until the chocolate mixture is ready.

Stir one-fourth of the whipped cream right into the chocolate mixture until completely incorporated. Fold the remaining whipped cream into the chocolate in 2 or 3 additions, adding more when the previous addition has started to incorporate. Once you add the last of the whipped cream, grate the carob chips directly over the mousse with a rotary cheese grater (see Quick Tip), then continue folding until the mousse is well combined.

Just before serving, crush the toasted pecans and coconut with your fingers. Spoon mounds of chocolate mousse into four beautiful stemmed dessert dishes and top with a sprinkling of pecans and coconut. Place a toasted pecan half on top of each as final garnish. Chill until served.

Quick Tip: If you don't have a rotary cheese grater, whirl the carob chips in the bowl of your mini food chopper. Of course, these can be finely chopped with a knife as well.

Baked Quinoa Pudding with Raisins

My dad loved rice pudding and my Grandma Ruth made it for him quite often. When I was growing up, I remember him standing at the kitchen counter eating it right out of the baking dish. Every time I make my protein-packed quinoa version, I find myself standing at the counter, eating it right out of the baking dish, too. Like father, like daughter.

makes 6 to 8 servings

1½ cups cold water

1 cup quinoa

3 large eggs, lightly beaten

1½ cups low-fat milk

½ cup half-and-half

⅓ cup agave nectar

1 teaspoon vanilla extract

¼ teaspoon kosher salt

1 cup raisins

½ teaspoon ground cinnamon

½ teaspoon freshly grated nutmeg

Vanilla Bean Ice Cream (page 197) (optional)

Preheat the oven to 325°F. Set a kettle of water to boil for the bain-marie (water bath). Once it boils, reduce the heat and keep the water very hot.

Pour the 1½ cups cold water into a medium heavy-bottomed saucepan and bring to a boil. Meanwhile, rinse the quinoa in a fine-mesh strainer until the water runs clear. Once the water in the pan is boiling, add the quinoa, cover, and reduce the heat to a simmer for 15 to 20 minutes, until all the water is absorbed. Remove the pan from the heat and let the quinoa cool slightly.

While the quinoa is cooking, whisk together the eggs, milk, half-and-half, agave, vanilla, salt, and raisins. Mix the cooled quinoa into the egg mixture. Pour the pudding mixture into a 1½- to 2-quart casserole dish. Make a bain-marie by placing the filled baking dish into a deep 4-quart casserole dish that's set on a large baking sheet. Put the baking sheet with the pudding in the oven and, with the oven door open, pour hot water from the tea kettle into the larger casserole dish until it's halfway up the side of the smaller dish. Bake for 25 minutes.

While the pudding is baking, mix the cinnamon and nutmeg together in a small bowl. After 25 minutes, stir the pudding and sprinkle the top with the cinnamon and nutmeg. Bake for 25 to 35 minutes longer, until a knife inserted in the middle of the pudding comes out clean.

Carefully remove the pudding and the bain-marie from the oven. Remove the smaller dish with the pudding from the larger dish and let cool slightly on a wire rack. Serve warm or cold, plain, or with ice cream. Store covered in the refrigerator.

Make It Dairy-Free: Use your favorite nondairy milk instead of cow's milk and use full-fat coconut cream or other rich nondairy milk instead of half-and-half.

Quick Tip: Never attempt to pour boiling water. Instead, use very hot—but not boiling—water for your bain-maire.

Tapioca Pudding

Warm, creamy tapioca pudding is one of my guilty pleasures. I love the simplicity, the taste, and the texture. The slight nuttiness imparted by unsweetened almond milk is delicious. For an almost butterscotch-nutty flavor, use palm sugar. If you don't have almond milk on hand, low-fat milk also works well; just reduce the vanilla to 1 teaspoon. **dairy-free, slow cooker recipe**

makes 4 servings

2 cups unsweetened almond milk

¼ cup agave nectar or palm sugar

2 teaspoons vanilla extract

¼ teaspoon kosher salt

¼ cup small pearl tapioca
(not quick-cooking)

1 egg, beaten

Optional toppings:

2 strawberries, sliced

4 teaspoons toasted sliced almonds

Vanilla Whipped Cream (page 182), Whipped Coconut Cream (page 175), or Raw Cashew Cream (page 176)

Combine the almond milk, agave or palm sugar, vanilla, and salt in a small or medium (2- to 4-quart) slow cooker. Add the tapioca and stir well. Cover and cook on low for 1 hour and 40 minutes.

Add 4 tablespoons of the hot tapioca to the beaten egg 1 tablespoon at a time, mixing well between additions. Stir the egg and tapioca into the pudding in the slow cooker. Cover and cook on low for 20 minutes longer, then stir the pudding again. The pudding is done when it's thick and the center reaches 165°F on an instant-read thermometer. Let the pudding sit partially covered for 5 minutes before serving. Serve with your choice of toppings.

Make It Egg-Free: If you can't have the egg, leave it out. Your pudding will still be scrumptious.

Quick Tip: There's no need to soak the tapioca before cooking it; it gets all the soaking it needs in the slow cooker.

Hodge Podge Bread Pudding

In culinary school, I saw one of my chef instructors throw a varied mess of baked goods into a bread pudding mix. I was horrified but didn't dare say a word. Later, when we served the bread pudding, it was clear he was onto something. Our guests came back for seconds and thirds. I decided to create a universal bread pudding recipe, the perfect way to use up all the too-dry-to-serve and leftover baked goods stored in my freezer. Regardless of what I put into this pudding, there are never any leftovers.

makes 6 to 8 servings

4 cups gluten-free leftover baked goods, your choice

2½ cups low-fat milk, divided

¼ cup plus 2 tablespoons palm sugar

2 tablespoons unsalted butter, melted

2 large eggs

1 teaspoon vanilla extract

Optional toppings:
Bread Pudding Sauce (page 192)
Vanilla Bean Ice Cream (page 197)

Lightly spray a 1½-quart baking dish with cooking spray.

Crumble the baked goods, leaving some chunks bigger than others. Add to the prepared baking dish.

Combine ½ cup milk and the palm sugar in a microwave-safe bowl. Microwave for 45 seconds and stir until the palm sugar is mostly dissolved. In another medium bowl, whisk together the remaining 2 cups milk, the melted butter, eggs, and vanilla. Whisk in the warm milk and palm sugar. Pour the mixture over the baked goods, stir to combine, and let soak for 20 minutes, or until the baked goods are fully saturated. Meanwhile, preheat the oven to 350°F.

Place the baking dish on a baking sheet and bake for 50 minutes to 1 hour, until the pudding is puffed, golden brown, and set in the center. The center of the pudding should read 165°F on an instant-read thermometer.

Serve warm with your choice of toppings.

Make It Dairy-Free: Use your favorite nondairy milk instead of cow's milk and nondairy butter or unsweetened applesauce instead of butter.

Quick Tip: Pull out frozen baked goods the night before you want to make this dish and let thaw in your refrigerator.

Bread Pudding Sauce

I love bread pudding covered with sauce, but it's usually just butter, heavy cream, and sugar. I wanted another option that was a little lighter than a traditional sauce that would balance out the sweetness of the pudding. Yogurt does the trick—it's smooth, creamy, and healthier and adds just enough tang. **egg-free**

makes about 2 cups

¼ cup unsalted butter

½ cup low-fat milk

½ cup palm sugar

1 teaspoon alcohol-free vanilla extract

½ teaspoon ground cinnamon

pinch of salt

1 cup plain low-fat yogurt

Melt the butter and milk in a heavy-bottomed saucepan over medium-low heat. Add the palm sugar and heat until dissolved, whisking occasionally. Mix in the vanilla, cinnamon, and salt. Remove the pan from the heat and let the mixture cool slightly. Whisk in the yogurt one-third at a time, making sure each addition is incorporated before adding more. Return to the stove to warm gently over low heat, stirring, just until warm. If the sauce gets too hot, the yogurt will curdle. Serve over warm bread pudding.

Quick Tip: This sauce can be made ahead of time and very gently reheated.

Vanilla Pudding

Recently, I read that pudding is back in style. I was shocked, of course, because I didn't know it had fallen from grace. Who doesn't love a good bowl of pudding? I use low-fat milk, but if you want a richer pudding, use whole milk.

makes 4 servings

2 cups low-fat milk, divided

2½ tablespoons cornstarch

1 tablespoon agave nectar

1½ teaspoons alcohol-free vanilla extract

¼ teaspoon kosher salt

¼ teaspoon liquid stevia

Heat 1½ cups milk on medium heat in a heavy-bottomed saucepan. In a small bowl, combine the remaining ½ cup milk and the cornstarch. Set aside. Add the agave, vanilla, salt, and stevia to the milk in the saucepan and stir. When tiny bubbles start to form around the edge of the pot, add the remaining milk and cornstarch mixture while whisking constantly. Continue whisking until the pudding thickens and boils. Remove the pan from the heat, transfer the pudding to a large bowl, and cover by placing plastic wrap directly on the surface of the pudding. Chill before serving; the pudding will thicken while in the refrigerator.

Variation—Chocolate Pudding: Follow the recipe above, but whisk ¼ cup cocoa powder into the 1½ cups milk while it heats. Reduce the cornstarch to 2 tablespoons and the vanilla extract to 1 teaspoon; increase the agave to 1½ tablespoons.

Make It Dairy-Free: Use your favorite nondairy milk in place of cow's milk. (I happen to love the flavor of almond milk pudding!) Increase the cornstarch to 3 tablespoons for both vanilla and chocolate nondairy pudding.

Quick Tip: Though tapioca starch will thicken this dish, I don't recommend it. It doesn't result in a velvety pudding.

ana Blueberry
ipped Gelatin

...d Jell-O when I was a kid and still do. It's simple to make and fun to eat. This version is a little ...althier, sweetened with fruit and real juice instead of refined sugar. It's light and airy and looks stunning when served in fancy glasses and topped with Vanilla Whipped Cream or Raw Cashew Cream. **vegan**

makes 6 to 8 servings

2 cups apple juice, divided

1 tablespoon unflavored gelatin

1 large banana

1 cup frozen blueberries,
not thawed

Optional Toppings:
Vanilla Whipped Cream (page 182)
or Raw Cashew Cream (page 176)

fresh blueberries

Put ½ cup apple juice and the gelatin in a microwave-safe bowl. Microwave for 20 seconds, stir, then microwave for 20 seconds longer. Repeat if the gelatin isn't completely melted. Set aside to cool.

Put the banana, blueberries, and 1 cup apple juice in a blender. Start on low speed and increase to medium until the mixture is pureed. With the blender running, add the gelatin mixture and the remaining ½ cup apple juice. Transfer to a large bowl, cover, and refrigerate for 15 to 30 minutes until the gelatin is the consistency of a milk shake. If the mixture sets completely, you won't be able to whip it.

Using a handheld mixer, beat the mixture until it doubles in volume. Transfer to serving dishes or a gelatin mold. Refrigerate until set. Serve with your choice of toppings.

Quick Tip: If by chance your gelatin sets before you can whip it, it will still be delicious. You can use an immersion blender or a handheld mixer to beat it to a mousselike consistency.

Yogurt with Chocolate Sauce and Berries

This just might be the perfect dessert—it's filled with good probiotics from the tart yogurt, there's sweetness from the sauce, and it's super creamy. I find myself scraping the bowl to get every last yummy bite. **egg-free**

makes 4 servings

½ cup heavy cream

2 tablespoons Dutch-processed cocoa powder

2 tablespoons palm sugar

½ teaspoon vanilla extract

2 cups Greek yogurt

¼ cup fresh raspberries

Add the heavy cream, cocoa powder, palm sugar, and vanilla to a small heavy-bottomed saucepan and whisk until combined. Heat over medium heat, stirring, until the sauce starts to boil. Remove from the heat.

Divide the yogurt into 4 bowls. Drizzle each bowl of yogurt with 2 tablespoons chocolate sauce and top with raspberries.

Quick Tip: This versatile chocolate sauce is delicious on ice cream, cake, or even as a fondue.

Frozen Desserts

Vanilla Bean Ice Cream

My refined sugar–free kitchen obsession started with ice cream. It's my favorite thing to make. I've tried every combination I can think of, and this is my favorite vanilla ice cream. It's soft enough to scoop right out of the freezer and fabulously creamy. I use low-fat milk to make it a little healthier, but feel free to use whole milk if you want a richer ice cream.

makes about 2 quarts

2 cups low-fat milk

1 teaspoon arrowroot powder

1½ teaspoons unflavored gelatin

2 vanilla bean pods
or 2 tablespoons vanilla extract
or 1 vanilla bean pod and
1 tablespoon vanilla extract

4 large egg yolks

½ cup agave nectar

2 cups heavy cream

Pour the milk into a medium heavy-bottomed saucepan. Put the arrowroot powder into a small bowl. Take 1 tablespoon milk from the saucepan and stir it into the arrowroot. Set aside. Sprinkle the gelatin across the milk in the saucepan and let it soften for several minutes.

If using vanilla beans, split them lengthwise and add to the saucepan. Heat the milk to scalding over medium heat, stirring until the gelatin is dissolved. Once the milk reaches the scalding point and tiny bubbles start to form on the edge, turn the heat down to medium-low and remove the milk from the heat.

While the milk is heating, in a medium bowl use an immersion blender fitted with a whisk attachment or a handheld mixer to beat the egg yolks on medium speed for about 2 minutes, until light yellow and thick. Add the agave to the egg yolks and beat until smooth, about 1 minute. Add the heavy cream and beat for another minute. Add ⅓ cup warm milk to the egg yolk mixture, stirring constantly. Add the egg mixture to the saucepan with the milk, whisking constantly, and return the pan to medium-low heat. Add the dissolved arrowroot and stir.

Cook for 3 to 5 minutes, stirring constantly, until the mixture has thickened. Do not boil. There are two ways to see if the mixture is finished cooking: One is to dip a spoon into the ice cream base and quickly remove it. Using your finger, draw a line in the base on the back of the spoon. If the base holds the line and does not run, then it's finished. If not, cook for 30 seconds to 1 minute longer and test again. Or use an instant-read thermometer to test the temperature; the ice cream base will be cooked at 165°F. Remove from the heat.

If you used vanilla bean pods, scrape the beans from the softened pods by holding the pod on the edge of the pot and scraping the beans directly into the milk with a rubber spatula or flat-edged wooden spoon. Discard the empty pods. Stir in the vanilla, if using. Strain the ice cream base into a medium bowl using a fine-mesh strainer. Cover immediately, placing plastic wrap directly on the ice cream base; this prevents it from forming a skin. Refrigerate for at least 4 hours, preferably overnight. The ice cream base will thicken considerably.

Stir-freeze the base in an ice cream machine according to the manufacturer's directions. Transfer to a freezer-proof container and freeze for 2 hours before serving.

Variation—Cinnamon Ice Cream: Omit the vanilla beans. Use 1 tablespoon vanilla extract and add 1 teaspoon ground cinnamon with the vanilla.

Make It Dairy-Free: Coconut milk makes the creamiest nondairy ice cream. Use 1 (15-ounce) can light coconut milk and 1 (15-ounce) can full-fat coconut milk in place of the low-fat milk and heavy cream. Omit the arrowroot and eggs. Dissolve the gelatin in 1 cup coconut milk over medium heat on the stovetop, then strain into a medium bowl. Whisk in the remaining coconut milk, 1 tablespoon vanilla extract or seeds from 1 vanilla bean, and ¼ cup agave nectar. Taste and add 1/8 to ¼ teaspoon liquid stevia, if desired. Chill for 4 hours or overnight before stir-freezing the mix in an ice cream machine. Makes about 4 cups.

Quick Tip: The gelatin helps the ice cream incorporate more air as it freezes and makes it more like store-bought ice cream. Arrowroot helps make it easy to scoop. Both make this a fabulous homemade ice cream.

Lighter Vanilla Ice Cream

Vanilla is my husband's favorite ice cream flavor—he eats a bowl every night. I wanted to make him a healthier ice cream that would still taste good enough for him to want to eat it and not feel deprived. This is the result. He actually prefers this to the fuller fat version. I usually use ¼ teaspoon liquid stevia in this recipe, but the amount can vary depending on the brand you use.

makes about 2 quarts

2½ cups low-fat milk

1 teaspoon arrowroot powder

1½ teaspoons unflavored gelatin

2 large eggs

¼ cup agave nectar

1½ cups heavy cream

2 vanilla beans or 1 tablespoon vanilla extract

¼ to ½ teaspoon liquid stevia

Pour the milk into a medium heavy-bottomed saucepan. Put the arrowroot powder into a small bowl. Add 1 tablespoon milk from the saucepan and stir it into the arrowroot. Set aside. Sprinkle the gelatin across the milk and let it soften for several minutes.

If using vanilla beans, split them lengthwise and add to the saucepan. Heat the milk to scalding over medium heat, stirring until the gelatin is dissolved. Once the milk reaches the scalding point and tiny bubbles start to form on the edge, immediately turn the heat down to medium-low and remove the milk from the heat.

While the milk is heating, in a medium bowl beat the eggs with an immersion blender fitted with a whisk attachment or a handheld mixer on medium speed for about 2 minutes, until light yellow in color and double in volume. Add the agave to the eggs and beat for 1 to 2 minutes, until light in color and foamy. Add the heavy cream and beat for 1 minute. Add ⅓ cup warm milk to the egg mixture, stirring constantly. Add the egg mixture to the saucepan with the milk, whisking constantly, and return to medium-low heat. Add the dissolved arrowroot and stir.

Cook for 3 to 5 minutes, stirring constantly, until the mixture has thickened. Do not boil. There are two ways to see if the mixture is finished cooking: One is to dip a spoon into the ice cream base and quickly remove it. Using your finger, draw a line in the base on the back of the spoon. If the base holds the line and does not run, then it's finished. If not, cook for 30 seconds to 1 minute longer and test again. Or use an instant-read thermometer to test the temperature; the ice cream base will be cooked at 165°F. Remove from the heat.

If you used vanilla bean pods, scrape the beans from the softened pods by holding the pod on the edge of the pot and scraping the beans directly into the milk with a rubber spatula or flat-edged wooden spoon. Discard the empty pods. Stir in the vanilla, if using. Add the stevia, starting with ¼ teaspoon and adding up to ¼ teaspoon more as needed. Strain the ice cream base into a medium bowl using a fine-mesh strainer. Cover immediately, placing plastic wrap directly on the ice cream base; this prevents it from forming a skin. Refrigerate for at least 4 hours, preferably overnight. The ice cream base will thicken considerably.

Stir-freeze the base in an ice cream machine according to the manufacturer's directions. Transfer to a freezer-proof container and freeze for 2 hours before serving.

Dark Chocolate Ice Cream

Baking chocolate with Dutch-processed cocoa powder creates great flavor with less fat and calories than traditional chocolate ice cream. The espresso powder brings out the chocolate even more.

makes about 1½ quarts

1½ cups low-fat milk

1 teaspoon arrowroot powder

1 teaspoon unflavored gelatin

2 ounces unsweetened baking chocolate

⅓ cup Dutch-processed cocoa powder

1 teaspoon vanilla extract

1 teaspoon instant espresso powder

2 large eggs

⅓ cup agave nectar

1 cup heavy cream

Pour the milk into a medium heavy-bottomed saucepan. Put the arrowroot powder in a small bowl. Take 1 tablespoon milk from the saucepan and stir it into the arrowroot. Set aside.

Sprinkle the gelatin over the milk. Chop the chocolate into pieces and add to the pan. Heat over medium heat, stirring until melted. Whisk in the cocoa powder, then add the vanilla and espresso powder. Once the cocoa is fully incorporated, turn the heat to medium-low and remove the pan.

Whisk the eggs in a medium bowl with an immersion blender fitted with a whisk attachment or a handheld mixer for about 2 minutes, until light in color and doubled in volume. Add the agave and continue mixing until thoroughly incorporated. Whisk in the heavy cream and beat for 1 minute. Temper the eggs by adding ⅓ cup of the warm milk mixture to the eggs while whisking. Pour the egg mix into the chocolate mixture, whisking constantly. Whisk in the arrowroot, and cook for 3 to 5 minutes, until the ice cream base has thickened.

There are two ways to see if the mixture is finished cooking: One is to dip a spoon into the ice cream base and quickly remove it. Using a finger, draw a line in the base on the back of the spoon. If the base holds the line and does not run, then it's finished. If not, cook for 30 seconds to 1 minute longer and test again. Or use an instant-read thermometer to test the temperature; the ice cream base will be cooked at 165°F. Remove from the heat.

Strain the ice cream base into a medium bowl using a fine-mesh strainer. Cover by placing plastic wrap directly on the surface of the ice cream base; this prevents it from forming a skin. Chill for at least 4 hours, preferably overnight. The base will thicken considerably. Stir-freeze the base in an ice cream machine according to the manufacturer's directions.

Quick Tip: Store your ice cream base in 1-quart Mason jars to save refrigerator space. To chill it down quickly, place the sealed jar in a tall bowl and surround it with an ice bath.

Five-Minute Blueberry Banana "Ice Cream"

This is one of my favorite summertime snacks. I've made it with any frozen fruit I have on hand—cherries, peaches, and strawberries, to name a few. I don't recommend raspberries or blackberries, as they'll make your "ice cream" seedy.

makes 1 serving

½ banana, frozen and chopped into ½-inch pieces

½ cup frozen blueberries

½ cup low-fat cottage cheese

1 tablespoon chopped toasted nuts

Put the banana and blueberries in a small food processor or blender. Process until it's in small chunks. Add the cottage cheese and process until smooth, scraping down the sides of the bowl as necessary. Put your ice cream in a serving bowl and top with the nuts. If a firmer texture is desired, put the ice cream in the freezer for 5 minutes or so before eating.

Quick Tip: Keep your freezer stocked with ripe, frozen bananas to make quick frozen treats like this one or to use in smoothies. Peel them, cut each one in half, and wrap them up. Before you wrap and freeze the bananas, if you slice them into segments without cutting all the way through, it makes it easier to cut them into chunks before adding to the blender or food processor.

Roasted Walnut and Maple Syrup Ice Cream

Though I don't generally use evaporated milk in ice cream, it works great in this recipe. You'll be able to put together a scoopable, no-cook ice cream base in less than 10 minutes. This ice cream is just slightly sweet. I prefer it this way, as the toasted walnuts perfume the entire ice cream with their rich, earthy flavor. If you want a sweeter dessert, add some stevia or a little more maple syrup.

makes about 1 quart

1 cup walnuts

1 cup cold low-fat or regular evaporated milk

1¼ cups heavy cream, divided

⅓ cup grade-B maple syrup

⅛ to ¼ teaspoon liquid stevia

Preheat the oven to 350°F. Line a baking sheet with aluminum foil. Spread the walnuts in a single layer on the baking sheet and toast for 5 to 8 minutes, until fragrant. The nuts will continue to cook after being removed from the oven, so be careful not to overcook them. Let cool. Coarsely chop and store in an airtight container until you're ready to stir-freeze your ice cream.

While the nuts are toasting, place the milk in the bowl of a stand mixer fitted with the whisk attachment. Beat on medium speed until the milk doubles in volume. Slowly pour in half of the heavy cream with the mixer running. In a small bowl, combine the maple syrup with the remaining heavy cream and gently fold it into the whipped milk mixture. Taste, and if a sweeter ice cream is desired, add stevia.

Transfer to a medium bowl, cover, and chill for at least 4 hours or overnight. Stir-freeze the base in an ice cream machine according to the manufacturer's directions. When the ice cream is nearly frozen, add the toasted walnuts. Transfer to a container and let harden up to 2 hours before serving.

Pineapple Mint Sorbet

I fell in love with sorbets after reading Martha Rose Shulman's cookbooks. Her passion for healthier food has inspired me countless times in the kitchen. This recipe is adapted from a sorbet in her book Fast Vegetarian Feasts. The flavors here are so simple but fully exquisite. The sweetness is based solely on the fruits you use, so make sure they're very ripe and in season. **vegan**
makes about 1 quart

½ large pineapple, peeled, cored, and cut into chunks

2 large very ripe bananas

½ cup freshly squeezed orange juice

1 tablespoon freshly squeezed lime juice

4 large mint leaves

Put the ingredients into your blender in the order listed. Starting on low speed and increasing to high, blend until the mixture is liquefied. Stop to scrape down the blender if necessary. Transfer to a container and chill for at least 4 hours, or overnight.

Stir-freeze the sorbet base in an ice cream machine according to the manufacturer's directions. Scoop the sorbet into a freezer-proof container and let it firm up in the freezer for 30 minutes before serving. The sorbet will get hard if left in the freezer overnight. To serve once it's frozen solid, microwave the sorbet for 30 seconds. Use a sharp knife to cut it into large chunks. Place the chunks into the bowl of a food processor fitted with the steel blade. Pulse several times, then process until smooth. Serve immediately.

Quick Tip: A high-powdered blender will create the best consistency for this sorbet. If you don't have one, blend the ingredients separately and then mix them together in the blender once they're pureed.

Strawberry Jam Bars
with Ice Cream

My husband ate these night after night until they were all gone, which speaks volumes because he's a plain-vanilla kind of guy. The apricots and lemon zest give these frozen treats a real pop of flavor.

makes 16 (2 x 2-inch) bars

½ cup firmly packed dried apricots

1¼ cups raw almonds

½ teaspoon grated lemon zest

¼ teaspoon ground cinnamon

¾ cup all-fruit strawberry preserves

2 cups Vanilla Bean Ice Cream (page 197)

Lightly coat an 8 x 8-inch pan with cooking spray. Place the apricots in a microwave-safe bowl and cover with water. Microwave for 1 minute. Set aside.

Place the almonds in the bowl of a food processor fitted with the steel blade. Pulse several times to break them up and then process until coarse. Drain the dried apricots and add them with the lemon zest and cinnamon to the food processor. Process until the nuts are finely ground and the ingredients stick together. Press into the bottom of the prepared pan. Spread the jam evenly over the crust. Wrap with plastic and place in the freezer for at least 4 hours, or preferably overnight.

Let the ice cream sit out for 20 minutes, or until softened, then spread across the top of the bars. Wrap with plastic and return the pan to the freezer for 1 hour, or until frozen. Cut into bars and serve. Use a sharp knife dipped in hot water and wiped dry to get the cleanest cut.

Quick Tip: If you plan to remove the entire block of bars from the pan before slicing them, line the pan with parchment paper and let it hang over the edges. This will give you an easy way to lift the bars out to a cutting board.

Apple Spice Granita

Apples and cinnamon are one of the most comforting flavor pairings for me. It's probably because of the apple pies my grandma baked when I was growing up. This simple granita brings a little bit of fall into the hot summer months. Don't worry about telling anyone how healthy it is . . . it's better to let them think they're indulging. **vegan**

makes 4 (½-cup) servings

2 cups unsweetened applesauce

1 teaspoon ground cinnamon, or more

¼ teaspoon freshly grated nutmeg, or more

Toppings:
yogurt, Crème Fraîche (page 50), or Vanilla Whipped Cream (page 182)

Mix the applesauce, cinnamon, and nutmeg in an 8 x 4-inch glass loaf pan. Taste and add more cinnamon or nutmeg if desired. Cover and place in the freezer for 1 hour. Remove and stir. When the applesauce is very firm, scrape it with a fork to create ice shavings. Return it to the freezer for 1 hour and repeat the scraping process. If needed, return to the freezer for 1 more hour and scrape again. Serve with a dollop of yogurt, crème fraîche, or whipped cream.

Nutty Carob-Covered Bananas

Frozen banana has a deliciously creamy, almost ice cream–like texture that makes these taste like they're much more sinful than they really are.

makes about 2 dozen banana bites

1 cup unsweetened carob chips

2 tablespoons non-hydrogenated shortening

2 large firm ripe bananas

½ cup finely chopped roasted salted peanuts or unsweetened shredded coconut

Using parchment paper, line a baking sheet that will fit in your freezer. Set aside.

Place the carob chips and shortening in a heatproof bowl that fits nicely on top of a saucepan. Bring ½ inch of water to a gentle simmer in the saucepan, set the bowl on top, and turn the heat off. Let the carob and shortening sit on top of the pan of water for 5 minutes, then gently stir until the carob has melted completely.

While the carob is melting, slice the bananas ½ inch thick. Spread the peanuts or coconut on a plate.

Once the carob has melted, use a fork to gently cover the banana slices in the carob, one slice at a time. Don't use the fork to spear the banana slice; instead, use the fork to move the banana slice around in the carob, slide under a flat side of the banana slice, lift it out of the carob, and move it in a circular motion to help any excess carob come off. Use a toothpick to help slide the fruit off the fork and into the nuts or coconut. Coat with the nuts or coconut, then transfer to the prepared baking sheet. Repeat with remaining banana slices.

Place the banana bites in the freezer for 1 hour, until solid. Quickly transfer to a freezer-proof container. Store in the freezer until ready to serve. When ready, remove the banana bites from the freezer and serve immediately. Once the bites are thawed, you can't refreeze them without changing the appearance of the carob.

Variation—Nutty Carob Banana Pops: Cut each banana into halves or thirds, depending on the size. Put a popsicle stick lengthwise in the middle, and proceed as directed.

Orange Creamsicle Ice Cream Sundaes

I was at a cooking demo where the chef served liquor-soaked berries with ice cream. Obviously, I couldn't try it. Everyone else loved it, though, so I came home and made my own version that's a little healthier. This light, refreshing dessert served with Lemon Cornmeal Biscotti (page 133) would be perfect for a ladies' luncheon.

makes 6 to 8 servings

1 cup freshly squeezed orange juice or no-sugar-added bottled or frozen orange juice

¾ cup Vanilla Bean Ice Cream (page 197), plus 1 to 2 scoops per serving

½ cup blueberries

½ cup raspberries

½ cup sliced strawberries

juice of ½ lime

1 to 2 tablespoons chopped fresh mint (optional)

Combine the orange juice, ¾ cup ice cream, blueberries, raspberries, strawberries, and lime juice in a medium bowl. Cover and refrigerate for several hours or overnight. The ice cream will melt into the orange juice. Stir. Place 1 to 2 scoops of ice cream in each serving bowl. Top with some juice and berries. If desired, sprinkle with a little mint.

Quick Tip: I prefer freshly squeezed orange juice for this recipe. If you use a store-bought orange juice, make sure it doesn't have a bitter aftertaste.

Chocolate Almond Butter Popsicles

Who doesn't love popsicles? These are perfect for a hot summer day. Made with healthier ingredients and completely fruit-sweetened, these are treats you can feel good about giving to your kids, or you can enjoy one (or two) on your own. **vegan**

makes 6 (4-ounce) pops

1¾ cups cold unsweetened chocolate almond milk

2 large ripe frozen bananas, cut into pieces

2 tablespoons almond butter

2 tablespoons cocoa powder

½ teaspoon alcohol-free vanilla extract

pinch of powdered stevia (optional)

Place all the ingredients except the stevia into a blender in the order listed. Start on low speed and increase to medium. Scrape down the bowl if necessary and keep the speed on medium until well blended. This keeps the popsicles from incorporating too much air. Taste and add stevia as needed. Too much stevia will bring out the bitterness in the chocolate, so add lightly.

Pour into 6 (½-cup) popsicle molds. Freeze for 4 hours, or until solid. Unmold by running under warm water for 5 seconds.

Quick Tip: Using chilled almond milk and frozen bananas helps these popsicles freeze faster, which creates smaller ice crystals and a smoother texture.

Banana Raisin Dessert Crepes

You can certainly use butter instead of cooking spray to get a richer taste and a little more caramelization on the bananas. With the ice cream, though, these crepes are rich enough for me.

makes 2 servings

1 tablespoon raisins

1 heaping tablespoon walnuts

2 medium bananas, sliced

sprinkle of cinnamon

2 (10-inch) Buckwheat Crepes (page 20)

2 scoops Vanilla Bean Ice Cream (page 197)

In a small microwave-safe bowl, cover the raisins with water and microwave for 30 seconds. Set aside.

Heat a nonstick 10-inch skillet over medium heat. Add the walnuts and toast, stirring often, until fragrant, about 5 minutes. Remove from the pan and allow to cool.

Spray the skillet with cooking spray. Add the bananas in a single layer and cook until lightly golden brown. Flip the bananas. Drain the raisins and reserve the soaking liquid. Add the raisins to the pan with 1 tablespoon soaking water. Sprinkle with cinnamon. The bananas are done when they're soft and the liquid in the pan is syrupy. Add more soaking liquid, if needed. While the bananas are cooking, use your fingers to crumble the walnuts into small pieces.

Split the banana mixture between the two crepes. Put the bananas in one-fourth of each crepe. Fold the crepes in half, then fold them into quarter-circles. Top each crepe with a scoop of ice cream and walnuts.

The Simply Sugar & Gluten-Free Kitchen Guide

Flour Blends

When baking gluten-free, there are so many different flours available. For my recipes, I've chosen the ones that I've found to be the most reliable and produce the best results. Personally, I prefer a blend of flours that aren't too starchy. Including some starch, though, is necessary for creating the best overall product. I use Bob's Red Mill products for sorghum flour, garbanzo–fava bean flour, potato starch (not potato flour!), and occasionally for tapioca starch.

There are many quality commercially prepared flour blends available on the market today. I use them on occasion and they perform well. Each one functions a little differently because of the flours used and the amount of xanthan gum included, if any. I am a big supporter of many of these products because I know the companies are working hard to improve the quality of life for those eating gluten-free.

Gluten-free products can be pricey, and making your own flour blend can help keep your costs down. I'm frugal by nature and keep a careful eye on my grocery bill, which in my opinion is big enough. One day I sat down and figured out the cost of making my own flour blend, and it's about $8 for four pounds. I know, $2 a pound for flour is a little costly. But if you compare that with the price of store-bought gluten-free flour blends, you'll find that by mixing your own you save about 50 percent. By my standards, that's a great deal.

The recipes in this book have all been tested with my Basic Flour Blend. Since different flours have different weights by volume and getting the proportion correct is important to a good flour blend, this recipe includes both volume and weight measures. I use my digital kitchen scale to quickly and accurately weigh the ingredients and mix up a batch. I fill my flour container and store any extra in a 1-gallon sealable plastic bag.

Basic Flour Blend

4 cups (480 grams) garbanzo–fava bean flour

4 cups (452 grams) sorghum flour

2 cups (324 grams) potato starch

1 1/3 cups (156 grams) tapioca starch

Mix well and store in an airtight container, preferably in the refrigerator.

Sugar-Free, Gluten-Free Kitchen Essentials

White Sugar Alternatives

Agave Nectar   This low-glycemic syrup is made from the agave plant, and it's similar in texture to honey. It's twice as sweet as sugar, so you can generally use half as much. It's neutral flavored, so it works great in recipes that need sweetness without additional flavors. My favorite brand is Wholesome Sweeteners.

Dates   I think of dates as nature's candy. They're incredibly sweet and packed with fiber. To use them in baked goods, soak the dates in warm water until soft, then puree. Date purees, and other dried fruit purees, can be used to add moisture and replace some of the fat in your baked goods. They can also be processed with grains or nuts to make a crust.

Dried Fruit Soaking Liquid   Dried fruit generally works best in recipes when it's soaked first in warm liquid, usually water or milk. This liquid can then be used to sweeten recipes. Use it to replace some or all of the liquid called for in a recipe. Store it in an airtight container in the refrigerator for up to 2 weeks.

Grade-B Maple Syrup   With manganese and zinc and fewer calories than white sugar, this healthier alternative can be used to sweeten cakes, cookies, and breads. I use it sparingly and in small amounts.

Honey   I went years without using honey, but today I can tolerate it in small quantities. All honey will crystallize at some point; if this happens, you can melt the crystals by setting the bottle in warm water.

Palm Sugar (Coconut Palm Sugar)   This low-glycemic unrefined granular sweetener has quickly become one of my favorite sweeteners because it's easy to use and tastes great. It's made from the sap of coconut tree blossoms and is rich in potassium, magnesium, zinc, and iron. It's also a natural source of vitamins B1, B2, B3, B6, and C. It's lower in calories than honey or agave nectar. I think of it as the healthier brown sugar alternative. My favorite brands are Sweet Tree Sustainable Sweeteners Coconut Palm Sugar and Navitas Naturals Palm Sugar.

Stevia   A no-calorie, super-sweet powder or liquid made from the Stevia rebaudiana plant, stevia is 30 to 45 times sweeter than sugar. Some brands have a bitter aftertaste, but there are great products on the market. I use stevia to reduce the overall amount of added sweeteners in my baking and in any beverage I want to sweeten. It's important to add it to recipes in small amounts and taste after each addition because too much can cause a slight aftertaste. NuNaturals Stevia is my favorite brand.

Unsulphered Blackstrap Molasses   When white sugar is refined, the by-product is molasses, so most of the sucrose has been removed. It contains manganese, iron, potassium, copper, calcium, and vitamin B6. I use it occasionally for gingerbread, cookies, and cakes. It also has fewer calories than agave or honey.

Gluten-Free Flours

Blanched Almond Flour   This flour is made from finely ground blanched (skinned) almonds. Store in the refrigerator or, for long-term storage, keep in the freezer. Due to its high fat content, it can go rancid quickly if stored at room temperature for extended periods of time. I occasionally add it in small amounts to baked goods to improve the tenderness and structure.

Buckwheat Flour   One of my favorite gluten-free flours for its hearty flavor and ease of use, this flour isn't wheat at all. It's made from the triangular seed of the buckwheat plant and has a rich, nutty flavor that's delicious in breakfast foods and baked goods. Store at room temperature.

Cocoa Powder, unsweetened   There are two types of cocoa powder: regular and Dutch-processed. I prefer Dutch-processed because the flavor is more intense. I haven't found a brand of Dutch-processed cocoa powder that I'm not fond of. If you can't find Dutch-processed cocoa powder, use Hershey's or Ghirardelli's regular unsweetened cocoa powder instead. Store at room temperature.

Cornmeal   Since it is ground dried corn, some varieties of cornmeal are ground coarser than others. I like to use stone-ground cornmeal with a fine texture. Store at room temperature.

Cornstarch   Made from the endosperm portion of the corn kernel, this thickener is used in sauces, frostings, and also some baked goods. Store at room temperature.

Garbanzo Bean Flour   Made from dried garbanzo beans, also known as chickpeas, this flour has a distinct taste that becomes milder, even unnoticeable, when baked. Store in the refrigerator.

Garbanzo–Fava Bean Flour   A blend of garbanzo bean flour and fava bean flour, this has become one of my favorites. The protein in the flour helps create structure in baked goods. It's healthy, it works great, and there's no beany taste. I prefer Bob's Red Mill brand. Store in the refrigerator.

Millet Flour Millet is a grain that can be ground into flour at home in a high-powered blender, but the flour can also be purchased already ground. It has a light color when baked. Store in the refrigerator.

Potato Starch Don't confuse potato starch and potato flour. They're two different products. I was hesitant to use potato starch for quite some time, but once I did I was sold. It helps to thicken gluten-free batters and create structure in baked goods. I use Bob's Red Mill brand in my recipes. Store in the refrigerator.

Quinoa Flour Quinoa is actually a seed, though many people think it's a grain. It has a distinct flavor and works beautifully in baked goods. I've used Bob's Red Mill brand consistently with good success. Store in the refrigerator.

Sorghum Flour This is another favorite, a heartier grain that works incredibly well in gluten-free baking. It's not at all fussy, it's high in protein and fiber, and it creates results similar to wheat flour's. Bob's Red Mill brand makes this flour. Store at room temperature.

Tapioca Starch/Flour Sometimes called tapioca starch flour, this starch works to thicken batters and create structure. I like the Bob's Red Mill and Ener-G brands. Tapioca starch should be flavorless and odorless. If it has a baking soda smell, take it back to the store and don't use it in your baked goods. It will create a metallic aftertaste. Store at room temperature.

Teff Flour Ground from the tiniest grain in the world, teff flour contains protein, calcium, and iron. It creates delicious chocolate and spiced baked goods.

Pantry Staples

Always read labels when buying shelf-stable products—you can never be sure whether a product contains white sugar or gluten. My personal rule of thumb for white sugar when it comes to products like mayonnaise and salad dressings: If sugar isn't listed in the first five ingredients, the concentration is so low it won't affect me. Note that the same is not true for gluten when dealing with celiac disease and gluten-intolerance. In these cases, the products must be completely gluten-free.

Applesauce, unsweetened Use unsweetened applesauce to increase moisture and replace 25 to 50 percent of the fat in your baking.

Baking Chocolate, unsweetened Because it's 100 percent chocolate, baking chocolate is dairy-free. It is too strong to be substituted 1 to 1 in recipes calling for semisweet or even bittersweet chocolate. I find that even with added sweeteners, the results are best when I use 25 to 50 percent of the sweetened chocolate called for in a recipe. I regularly use Ghiradelli as they make a great-tasting unsweetened baking chocolate that is also frugally priced. Other excellent brands include Dagoba and Green & Black's, though they're a little more expensive. Find them in the baking section of your grocery store.

Beans, canned and dried   I regularly stock garbanzo beans, black beans, cannellini beans, pinto beans, and navy beans. I keep canned beans on hand for their convenience, but I prefer home-cooked beans for most recipes because they have more flavor. Often, though, I don't have any cooked beans on hand or no time to prepare them and am always grateful I can open a can and easily add them to a recipe. If you forget to soak dried beans the night before, like I often do, quick-soak them by covering the beans with 1½ inches of water, bringing them to a boil for 5 minutes, then removing from the heat. Let them soak for 1 hour, covered, then drain, rinse, and proceed as if you'd soaked the beans all night. I generally find that quick-soaked beans take a little longer to cook than beans I soak overnight.

Broth   My absolute first choice is always homemade stock or broth. The difference is that stock is made from just bones, while broth is made from meat or meat and bones. While I love a great stock, I generally have flavorful homemade chicken broth in my freezer from Make Ahead Chicken (page 97). I do keep store-bought broth in the pantry as a backup. Often, store-bought low-sodium chicken broth contains sugar or evaporated cane juice to enhance the flavor. For this reason, when I buy broth I choose the full sodium version and keep in mind that I'll likely need to use a light hand when salting my dishes. Also, not all broths are gluten-free—be sure to check the label.

Brown Rice   I prefer brown rice instead of white rice because it includes the bran and germ, which contain the majority of the grain's nutrients. When substituting, take into consideration that brown rice takes longer to cook than white rice.

Brown Rice Bread Crumbs   Made by Hol-Grain, these work just like bread crumbs but are made from brown rice.

Canned Tomatoes   A great convenience product, canned tomatoes taste much better than out-of-season fresh tomatoes.

Carob Chips, unsweetened   Because I can't eat white sugar, I use unsweetened carob chips instead of chocolate chips as I've yet to find a sugar-free chocolate chip without sugar alcohols. Sweetened carob chips contain barley malt, which contains gluten. If you can't find unsweetened carob chips or if you don't like carob, feel free to use your favorite brand of chocolate chips. Some people who can tolerate small amounts of white sugar find that chocolate with 70 percent or more cacao works well for them.

Coconut Milk, regular and light   Regular coconut milk can be used in place of heavy cream in many recipes. It also makes a creamy dairy-free ice cream. Use light coconut milk when you want the flavor of coconut milk but not all the fat and calories.

Dairy-Free Milks, unsweetened   My favorite dairy-free milk is almond milk because it's naturally sweet and adds great moisture to baked goods. It's also much lower in calories than cow's milk and it's low-glycemic. Other nondairy milks include hemp milk and rice milk, which are more neutral-flavored than almond milk but also much higher in calories.

Dried Fruits   Raisins, dried figs, and dates all add sweetness to baked goods. For a gourmet feel in recipes, try using currants, which taste much like raisins but are smaller.

Flaxseed   Flaxseed is a great source of omega-3 fatty acids. I often use flaxseed meal in my baking, but it can go rancid quickly because of the high fat content. Instead of buying flaxseed meal at the store, I buy whole flaxseed and grind it in a clean coffee mill. This way, my flaxseed meal is fresher and frugal.

Non-Hydrogenated Shortening   Conventional vegetable shortening contains harmful trans fats produced during hydrogenation; non-hydrogenated shortening is manufactured without trans fats and is healthier. My favorite brand is Spectrum Organics. Look for it at your local health store.

Nuts   I buy almonds, pecans, and walnuts in large quantities at my local warehouse store and keep them in the freezer. They go rancid quickly at room temperature.

Oats, gluten-free certified   To be gluten-free, oats must be certified gluten-free because they are often processed on equipment that also processes wheat products.

Pasta   There are great gluten-free pastas on the market today. My favorite brands are Tinkyada and Ancient Harvest. See Six Tips for Perfect Gluten-Free Pasta (page 223).

Pepitas (Hulled Pumpkin Seeds)   These seeds are a tasty alternative to nuts if you're allergic. You can buy pepitas raw or toasted. I use toasted, salted pepitas on my salads instead of croutons.

Quinoa   This seed behaves like a grain and must be rinsed before cooking, as it has a natural coating that can taste bitter. Rinse in a fine-mesh strainer until the water doesn't bubble over the quinoa and runs totally clear.

Sunflower Seeds   Sunflower seeds are a great alternative for those who can't eat nuts. They can also be ground into a homemade nut butter substitute using a high-powered blender.

Vanilla Extract   It was previously thought that vanilla extract contained gluten because of the alcohol; however, it's now generally accepted that the gluten is removed during the alcohol's distillation process, and vanilla extract is considered gluten-free. Most vanilla extract contains sugar, so I prefer using sugar-free vanilla, but if it's alcohol based, it has an overt alcohol taste because there's no sugar to balance the flavor. Glycerin-based, sugar-free, alcohol-free vanilla extract works really well, especially in recipes where the food isn't cooked after it's added to the recipe.

Wild Rice   Actually a long-grain marsh grass that is now cultivated, wild rice is a healthier white rice alternative. Keep in mind that it takes longer to cook than white rice.

Must Be Gluten-Free!

Make label reading a habit. It's important to take full responsibility for everything that you cook, eat, and serve to others. Though some products don't contain wheat, they can be processed in a way that cross-contaminates them. These items are often mistaken to be gluten-free:

- Baking powder
- Oats and oat products
- Store-bought broths
- Soy sauce
- Teas

Xanthan Gum   In wheat-based baking, gluten, the protein found in wheat, is the main binding agent; but in gluten-free baked goods, xanthan gum is used to bind and provide structure. Guar gum can also be used in place of xanthan gum. My general rule for using xanthan gum is ¼ teaspoon per 1 cup flour when making cupcakes, cookies, and muffins, and ½ teaspoon per 1 cup flour for cakes. Yes, xanthan gum is expensive. If you're like me, you might have a heart attack in the baking aisle when you see that it's $12 for one 8-ounce bag, but it's an essential ingredient in quality gluten-free baked goods. Don't worry, that 8-ounce bag will last at least nine months, if not longer.

In the Refrigerator

Butter, unsalted   Using unsalted butter in your baking and cooking will allow you to control the amount of salt in the final product.

Cream Cheese   I use light cream cheese instead of full-fat for most applications because the taste is nearly the same while contributing fewer calories and less fat.

Eggs   My recipes have been tested with large eggs, but extra-large eggs will work as well. Bring eggs to room temperature before adding to baked goods. You can do this quickly by putting your eggs in a glass or stainless steel bowl and covering them completely with warm water for 5 minutes.

Heavy Cream   Heavy cream helps give structure to sugar-free frostings and adds flavor and texture to ice cream.

Milk   I buy 1 percent fat milk, but feel free to use your favorite type.

Yogurt   I use plain low-fat yogurt, but use whatever your family enjoys most. Yogurt can also be used to add moisture and replace 25 to 50 percent of the fat in your baking.

In the Freezer

Bananas   Use these to increase sweetness and moisture and reduce fat in baked goods. Cut overripe bananas in half, wrap, and pop in the freezer. They'll continue to get sweeter, and you'll always have bananas on hand for muffins and breads.

Berries and Fruit   Use your favorites; I like to keep frozen blueberries, raspberries, and peaches on hand.

Bread Crumbs   Save any extra waffles, stale gluten-free bread, and even cornbread. Let leftovers dry out, whirl them in your food processor, and you'll have bread crumbs. Store in the freezer to keep fresh.

Leftover Baked Goods   Perfect for quick snacks or an unexpected visitor, leftover baked goods can also be used to make Hodge Podge Bread Pudding (page 191).

Meat   I watch for sales and buy large quantities of meat when I see a good deal. To save time later on, I clean any meats that need it, such as trimming extra fat from chicken thighs, and wrap in meal-size portions. I keep pork loin and chops, chicken breasts and thighs, ground turkey, and whole chickens stocked in my freezer.

Vegetables   I prefer fresh vegetables but keep frozen on hand for nights when I'm short on time. I often hear from cooks who feel bad about not being able to prepare everything from scratch and do it all perfectly. Don't fall into this trap and opt for a drive-through meal. Take the shortcuts where you need to.

My Favorite Kitchen Tools and Supplies

Quick and simple cooking can be made easier with the right kitchen appliances. I rely on my favorite kitchen equipment for efficiency and simplicity. Don't worry if you don't have something on my list. The great thing about cooking is that you can achieve the same results many different ways. Below I'll share how to use alternative equipment. Because I use my stand mixer for baking, I have specified that in the recipes along with which attachment I use. If you don't have a stand mixer, use a handheld mixer with beaters. You can achieve the same result; it'll just take a few minutes longer.

Aluminum Foil, both regular and heavy duty   Make your cleanup easy by lining baking sheets with foil.

Baking Sheets   I use rimmed 11 x 17 (half sheet pan) baking sheets. I prefer light-colored sheets because dark ones attract more heat and cause the bottoms of cookies to brown quicker.

Blender   A high-powered blender, like a VitaMix, is perfect for making Powdered Palm Sugar (page 185), ice cream bases, sauces, and smoothies. If you don't have a VitaMix, Oster has a reasonably priced blender that's powerful enough.

Bowl Scraper   This thin, flat plastic tool is perfect for scraping bowls, cleaning work surfaces and rolling pins, and moving chopped food from your cutting board to a pan or mixing bowl.

Cast Iron Pans   I use my cast iron pans for baking quick breads and cakes, and also for getting a great sear on meats.

Cookbook Stand   I love my cookbook stand! It saves lots of counter space because my cookbooks sit upright instead of laying flat on the countertop. I also keep a pen with my stand so I can easily make any notations about changes to the recipe I'm making while cooking.

Cookie Scoop   Using a spring-release cookie scoop ensures that all your cookies will be the same size and makes quick work of scooping lots of little cookies. They come in various sizes.

Cooking Spray   I use plain canola oil baking spray. Always, always spray baking pans even if they're nonstick. Gluten-free batters need that extra help to release from the pans. You can also butter or grease your pans. Keep the coating light. You want your cakes to bake, not fry.

Cooling Racks   I have a wire set that stacks and also has collapsible legs. Use them to cool anything that comes out of your oven.

Cutting Boards   I have three cutting boards for three categories of food: raw meat, fruits and veggies, and prepared foods. It's just not safe to cut raw meat in the same place you cut fresh veggies. My 12 x 18-inch cutting boards give me ample room to work.

Kitchen Organization

Flour Storage   The best solution I've found for storing flours has been wide-mouth containers from SnapWare. They're airtight and keep flours fresh. I store some in the refrigerator and some in the pantry. See specific flours for storage information.

Grocery List   Like many others on a gluten-free diet, I have to shop at multiple places to get what I need. Creating a grocery checklist was one of the smartest things I've ever done. I included the places I frequent most often with the items I need organized by area. The list hangs in my pantry at all times, and when I notice something running low I simply check it off. Grocery shopping is now a breeze.

Labeling   Keep a roll of transparent tape and a couple of permanent markers in your kitchen. Scotch tape will stick to just about anything and releases easily, and every cook should have a couple of Sharpie markers close by.

Mason Jars   I keep all my dry goods, such as beans, rice, grains, and dried fruit in Mason jars. I can see exactly what's inside and they line up neatly in my pantry. They're also inexpensive, usually about $1 for each 1-quart jar.

Digital Kitchen Scale   It took me a long time to break down and buy a scale because I wasn't quite sure I'd use it. Today I can't believe I ever functioned without one. I use it for everything from mixing flour blends quickly to weighing 8 ounces of fresh tomatoes or pasta.

Dry Measuring Cups   Dry measures are used for anything that's not in liquid or syrup form and come as a set with 1 cup, ½ cup, ⅓ cup, and ¼ cup measures. Don't use your dry measuring cups for liquids because your measurements won't be as accurate.

Food Processor   Use this handy appliance to make dough; to puree fruits, soups, and sauces; and to chop or grate cheese and veggies. Though it's a big upfront investment, I've never regretted the purchase. I've had my Cuisinart since 1995, and it still works like a dream.

Ice Cream Scoop   Get a standard spring-release scoop and use it to quickly and evenly scoop batter into muffin tins. It's worth investing in a good one; the cheaper versions I've bought broke within weeks of bringing them home.

Immersion Blender   These are relatively inexpensive and allow you to puree sauces and soups right in the cooking vessel. I bought a Cuisinart and it also has a whisk attachment so I can quickly beat egg whites or heavy cream.

Instant-Read Thermometer   Use this tool to check the temperature of baked goods, meats, and ice cream bases. If a specific temperature is ideal, I've listed it in the recipe. For most baked goods, a temperature of 200°F indicates that it's done. One exception I've found is low-fat baked goods, which are usually ready at around 185° to 190°F.

Kitchen Knives   Using the wrong knife, or a dull one, is like trying to hammer a nail with a screwdriver. It just won't work. Where I mention specifically to use a sharp serrated knife or a sharp chef's knife, it's because it produces the best result. I got my serrated knife at a local restaurant supply store for $15, and it works just as well as the $100 serrated knife I have. If you're going to invest in good kitchen knives, take your time and test how they feel in your hand. I use Wüsthof knives because they fit my hand and aren't too heavy.

Measuring Spoons   I have several sets because I always find a way to dirty them all. My measuring spoons sit in a small glass jar in my cupboard so I can easily find them.

Muffin Tin   I use a standard 12-cup muffin tin for cupcakes and muffins. Though you can oil your muffin tins, I generally prefer to use cupcake papers for easy cleanup.

Rasp Grater   I use this daily for grating Parmesan cheese, garlic, carrots, and carob—anything that you need to grate quickly and easily. It's easier to clean and much simpler to use than a box grater. They come in different sizes, too, as well as with different blades, such as fine rasp, ribbon rasp, and coarse rasp. Microplane is the brand to have.

Mini Food Chopper   This little gadget looks like a mini food processor. It's great for chopping and pureeing smaller quantities of food.

Oven Thermometer   The simple fact is that most ovens aren't calibrated correctly. Using an oven thermometer allows you to tell if your oven is at the right temperature. Temperature variations of more than 25 degrees warrant a service call. Know, though, that the oven temperature will vary during baking, so don't fret if it's not spot on.

Parchment Paper   I love this silicone-coated paper for easy clean up when baking anything on a baking sheet. I also use it to line the bottom of my cake pans. No stick and no mess.

Plastic Wrap   I often wrap muffins and cookies in individual serving sizes before popping them in the freezer so they're well preserved and easy to pull out for a serving or two at a time. Plastic wrap is also important for covering custards, puddings, and ice cream bases so they don't form a skin when refrigerated.

Pots and Pans   I have a set of both nonstick and stainless steel pans. Some good sizes to have: small and large sauté pans, small and large sauce pans, and a large stockpot. One of my stockpots has a steamer insert, which makes quick work of steaming veggies. It also doubles as a pasta insert, which makes it simple to drain pasta. If you have to stack your nonstick pans for storage, place a layer of paper towels between them so the nonstick coating doesn't get scratched.

Six Tips for Perfect Gluten-Free Pasta

1. Always start your pasta water before preparing the rest of your meal. It's OK if the pasta water sits and boils until you're ready to cook the pasta.

2. Add 1 tablespoon salt per gallon of water to season the pasta.

3. Add 1 tablespoon olive oil to the water right before adding the pasta and stir the pasta well to prevent it from sticking together in the pot. Stir frequently as it cooks.

4. Test the pasta 3 minutes earlier than stated on the package, and continue testing until it's al dente. Some brands will become mushy if overcooked.

5. Gluten-free pasta retains the best texture when it's taken directly from the cooking pot and put into the pan of sauce and tossed or if it's transferred directly to the serving plate and topped with sauce.

6. If you happen to overcook the pasta, try rinsing it with warm water and letting it cool slightly. Some brands will firm up. To reheat the pasta, run it under hot water and top it with hot sauce.

Favorite Brands: Tinkyada Brown Rice Pasta, especially for lasagne noodles, and Ancient Harvest Quinoa Supergrain Pasta, especially their linguini, which tastes just like regular pasta

A Baker's Dozen: Tips for Simply Sugar & Gluten-Free Baking Success

More often than not something calls me away from the kitchen in the middle of assembling a recipe and I can't remember where I left off. I've found myself wondering if I've already added the xanthan gum or the baking powder more times than I'd like to admit. My best solution for this is to set all the unused ingredients at the front of my countertop. As I use them, I move them to the back of the counter. I also go straight down the list of ingredients in a recipe so when I do get pulled away, it's much easier to remember my stopping point. Here are some other tips to keep in mind to create perfect baked goods every time:

1. Trust the recipe. Read all the way through the before beginning to make sure you understand what you need to do and how you should do it. Gluten-free, refined sugar-free batters don't always behave the same way that wheat and white sugar batters do. This is the mistake I see the most often, especially in those cooks new to gluten-free baking.

2. Taste and smell your flours. Flours, even wheat flour, can go rancid. By learning the unique taste and smell of each variety, you'll never use a rancid flour.

3 Have all your ingredients at room temperature unless the recipe calls for cold ingredients. To quickly bring eggs to room temperature, set them in a glass and cover them with warm water for 5 minutes.

4. Always use unsalted butter.

5. Use a dry measuring cup for dry ingredients and a wet measure for wet ingredients. Measure agave, applesauce, sour cream, yogurt, egg whites, ricotta cheese, and other similar ingredients in a wet measuring cup.

Ruler   I have a wooden ruler that I use to measure and cut dough. It's great for getting a straight, clean cut. I put it right in the dishwasher, too. Plastic or metal will work, too.

Sealable Plastic Bags   I keep all sizes of these bags on hand. They're great for storing, mixing, and marinating in the refrigerator and freezer. Cleanup is simple, and they're easy to label, too.

Sifter   This gadget is key for lightening gluten-free baked goods and getting the lumps out of cocoa powder and palm sugar.

Silicone Baking Mats   This ingenious invention keeps your baked goods from sticking and helps keep the bottom from getting too brown. They're reusable and easy to clean.

6. When measuring flour, stir it before measuring. Then use a large spoon to scoop the flour into the dry measuring cup. Use a flat edge to level the flour. Never pack flour or dip your measuring cup into the flour bin and level it off. You'll have more flour than you need. Use a straight edge to level baking powder, baking soda, and xanthan gum as well.

7. Use a stevia brand that you enjoy. Stevia is not a standardized product. The sweetness varies from brand to brand, and some have a bitter aftertaste. If you don't like the flavor of the stevia you're using, it won't get better once you add it to a recipe.

8. Invest in an oven thermometer. Most ovens aren't calibrated correctly and this will ensure you have the right oven temperature. A 25-degree difference is acceptable, and the temperature will fluctuate during the baking process.

9. If a recipe says to bake a dessert for 15 minutes, start checking a few minutes earlier to avoid over baking. If using a dark-colored baking pan or sheets, start checking your food 5 to 7 minutes earlier as they absorb more heat and cause food to bake faster.

10. Splurge on silicone baking mats and parchment paper. My frugal nature made it difficult to spend $20 on a baking mat, but it worked so well that I immediately bought a second, as well as a silicone dough mat for rolling out pie crusts. Parchment paper works for lining baking sheets and is perfect for lining cake pans, too.

11. Using a different-size pan than a recipe calls for means you will have to adjust baking times and sometimes oven temperatures. Yes, you can start with a standard cupcake recipe and make mini-cupcakes instead, but they'll bake much quicker.

12. Bake pies, crisps, crumbles, and any other dish with the potential for "boil over" on a sheet pan. This protects the floor of your oven and also makes them easier to handle.

13. Open the oven only when necessary. Opening the oven too often will increase baking time and the quality of your product will not be as good.

Silicone Rubber Spatulas   I never have enough of these handy spatulas. Gluten-free batters and doughs can be stickier than conventional ones. When spreading cake batter into a pan, I spray my spatula with cooking spray or lightly wet it with water and spread the batter evenly.

Slow Cooker   I have three: small, medium, and large. I know, extreme. I'd actually have more if I had room to store them. I absolutely love being able to throw some ingredients into my slow cooker and walk away, knowing that I'll have a fabulous dinner or dessert with little effort on my part. If you don't have one, consider picking one up the next time you're out. They're inexpensive and will pay for themselves in the time they save.

Spice or Coffee Grinder   I keep a clean coffee grinder on hand to make flaxseed meal, Powdered Palm Sugar (page 185), or to grind spices. Look for one with a removable top so you can put it right in your dishwasher.

Stainless Steel or Glass Bowls   A set of quality bowls in various sizes will give you many options when working on a recipe. For instance, I've never purchased a double boiler—instead, I use a bowl that will fit snugly on top of a pot with about 1 inch of water simmering in the bottom. This is much more versatile than a double boiler because you can remove the bowl and keep working without dirtying another dish.

Stand Mixer   I couldn't live without my KitchenAid stand mixer. (I actually have two.) It frees my hands to do other tasks while it creams butter and mixes dough. Though it's a little pricey, I've had mine since 1995 and it's still going strong. I also love the KitchenAid ice cream maker attachment. I've tested others, and this one creates the lightest, creamiest ice cream.

Waxed Paper   This is different from parchment paper because you can't use it to line your baking sheets, but it helps make cleanup quick if you use it to catch sifted flour or grated fruits and veggies. I use waxed paper to separate certain foods I'm freezing, like hamburger patties, chicken breasts, or even cake layers.

Wet Measuring Cups   These cups are made of glass or translucent plastic and are graded on the side. You can get them from 1 cup to 8 cups in capacity. Use these for any liquid, such as milk, agave syrup, sour cream, and eggs. Don't use your wet measuring cups for dry ingredients or your recipe won't come out right as dry ingredients can't be leveled off in a wet measure.

Whisks   I use both stainless steel and silicone-coated whisks depending on what pans I'm using. The silicone-coated whisks help me whip up sauces in my nonstick cookware without ruining the coating.

Handy Conversions

Measure	Equivalent	Metric
1 teaspoon	--	5 milliliters
1 tablespoon	3 teaspoons	14.8 milliliters
1 cup	16 tablespoons	236.8 milliliters
1 pint	2 cups	473.6 milliliters
1 quart	4 cups	947.2 milliliters
1 liter	4 cups + 3½ tablespoons	1000 milliliters
1 pound	16 ounces	453.49 grams
2.21 pounds	35.3 ounces	1 kilogram
350°F / 400°F	--	175°C / 200°C

Ingredient Substitutions

If I've learned anything from eating refined sugar–free and gluten-free, it's that there is always another way to make a cake. I make thoughtful substitutions knowing that the final outcome will be different, but as long as the proportions of the recipe are the same, the result will still be delicious. For example, if I opt to use apple juice instead of milk, I do so knowing that the flavor and texture of my baked good will be different. Not all substitutions make sense, either. It's challenging to substitute large quantities of certain ingredients, like eggs, without disastrous results. **Note:** All substitutions are 1:1 unless otherwise indicated.

FOR THIS...	SUBSTITUTE...	
Milk	• Any nondairy milk • Fruit juice	• Full-fat coconut milk • MimicCream
Heavy cream	• The top of a refrigerated can of full-fat coconut milk	
Heavy cream, for whipping	• see Whipped Coconut Cream (page 175)	
Butter	• Coconut oil • Nondairy butter	• Non-hydrogenated vegetable shortening
Unflavored gelatin	• Agar-agar	
Agave nectar	• Grade-B maple syrup	• Honey
Melted butter	• Neutral-flavored oil, such as canola or grapeseed	
1 large egg	• 2 egg whites • ¼ cup yogurt • ¼ cup applesauce • 1 tablespoon flaxseed meal mixed with 3 tablespoons warm water or applesauce	• Ener-G Egg Replacer; use as directed on box *Note: eggs add leavening to a baked good, so the baking powder or baking soda will generally need to be increased by ¼ to ½ teaspoon. Also, baking times may be altered.*
Yogurt	• Nondairy yogurt (but most has added sugar in the form of evaporated cane juice)	• Applesauce • Sour cream
Unsweetened carob chips	• Chocolate chips (some people use 70% dark chocolate because it's lower in sugar than others)	
Nuts (in case of allergies)	• Pepitas (hulled pumpkin seeds)	• Sunflower seeds
Instant espresso powder	• Instant coffee granules, decaf or regular; increase the amount to taste	
Large Medjool dates	• Any date (if small, double the quantity)	
Light cream cheese (Neûfchatel)	• Full-fat cream cheese • Nondairy cream cheese	
Xanthan gum	• Guar gum	
Buttermilk	• Regular milk or nondairy milk; add 1 tablespoon lemon juice per cup to sour the milk and let it sit for several minutes before using	
Sour cream	• Yogurt—regular, Greek, or nondairy	• Applesauce

Product Resources

I have come to rely on certain brands because not all products are made the same or produce the same results. Make sure to read labels to ensure gluten-free status.

Agave Nectar   Wholesome Sweeteners (www.WholesomeSweeteners.com)

Almond Milk   Almond Breeze (www.BlueDiamond.com); Almond Dream (www .TasteTheDream.com)

Brown Rice Bread Crumbs   Hol-Grain (www.HolGrain.com)

Flours   Arrowhead Mills (www.ArrowheadMills.com) buckwheat flour; Bob's Red Mill (www.BobsRedMill.com) I use Bob's in 99 percent of my baking. My most-used products: garbanzo–fava bean flour, potato starch, sorghum flour, quinoa flour, and teff flour; Ener-G (www.Ener-G.com) tapioca starch flour, egg replacer

Non-hydrogenated Organic Vegetable Shortening   Spectrum Organics (www.Spectrum Organics.com)

Oats   Bob's Red Mill (Rolled oats, quick-cooking oats; www.BobsRedMill.com); Montana Monster Munchies (www.MtMonsterMunchies.com) rolled oats, quick-cooking oats, and oat bran

Oil   Wesson Canola Oil (www.Wesson.com)

Palm Sugar (also called Coconut Palm Sugar)   Navitas Naturals (www.NavitasNautrals.com); Sweet Tree Sustainable Sweeteners (www.Sweet-Tree.biz)

Pasta   Ancient Harvest Quinoa Brands (www.Quinoa.com) pasta noodles, quinoa flakes; Tinkyada (www.Tinkyada.com) brown rice noodles for lasagna, though all of their brown rice pasta products are delicious

Rice Milk   Rice Dream (www.TasteTheDream.com)

Stevia   NuNaturals, Inc. (www.NuNaturals.com) liquid and powdered stevia with no bitter taste

Vanilla Extract   Frontier Natural Products Co-op for Alcohol-Free Vanilla (www .FrontierCoop.com); Simply Organic (www.SimplyOrganicFoods.com); Singing Dog Vanilla (www.SingingDogVanilla.com)

Purchasing Products

Amazon.com's Subscribe & Save   By enrolling in this free program, you can get many gluten-free, sugar-free products at a 15-percent discount—with free shipping. To qualify, you must buy at least one case at a time (usually four bags of flour). You control when items are shipped and can cancel at any time. Some of my repeat purchases: Bob's Red Mill Garbazno-Fava Flour, Quinoa Flour, Whole Grain Rolled Oats, and Sweet Tree Sustainable Sweeteners Palm Sugar.

iHerb.com   With a huge selection of gluten-free products and white-sugar alternatives, iHerb .com is perfect for anyone who wants to buy smaller quantities at good prices. If you're new to iHerb.com, use the code SIR086 for a discount on your first order. Among many other products, they carry Bob's Red Mill products, NuNaturals Stevia, and Navitas Naturals Palm Sugar.

Stores Dedicated to Gluten-Free Foods   It's more common to find gluten-free products at grocery stores. These are some of the stores I've shopped either at home or while traveling: Central Market (www.CentralMarket.com), Natural Grocers (www.NaturalGrocers.com), Publix (www.Publix.com), Raisin Rack (www.RaisinRack.com), Sprouts (www.Sprouts.com), Trader Joe's (www.TraderJoes.com), Whole Foods (www.WholeFoodsMarket.com).

Recommended Reading

Gluten-Free & Refined Sugar–Free

Amsterdam, Elana. *The Gluten-Free Almond Flour Cookbook.* New York: Celestial Arts, 2009.

Broyzna, Kelly. *The Spunky Coconut Grain-Free Baked Goods & Desserts.* Apidae Press, 2010.

Feuer, Janice. *Fruit-Sweet and Sugar-Free: Prize-Winning Pies, Cakes, Pastries, Muffins, and Breads from the Ranch Kitchen Bakery.* Rochester, New York: Healing Arts Press, 1993. (Some recipes are gluten-free, all are refined sugar–free.)

Heller, Ricki. *Sweet Freedom: Desserts You'll Love without Wheat, Eggs, Dairy or Refined Sugar.* Victoria, British Colombia: Trafford Publishing, 2009.

Pascal, Cybele. *The Allergen-Free Baker's Handbook: How to Bake without Gluten, Wheat, Dairy, Eggs, Soy, Peanuts, Tree nuts, and Sesame.* New York: Celestial Arts, 2009. (Some recipes are refined sugar–free.)

Segersten, Alissa and Tom Malterre, MS CN. *The Whole Life Nutrition Cookbook: Whole Food Recipes for Personal and Planetary Health.* 2nd ed. Birmingham, Alabama: Whole Life Press, 2009. (Some recipes are refined sugar–free.)

Gluten-Free

Hagman, Bette. *The Gluten-Free Gourmet Bakes Bread: More Than 200 Wheat-Free Recipes.* New York: Holt Paperbacks, 1999.

Nardone, Silvana. *Cooking for Isaiah: Gluten-Free & Dairy-Free Recipes for Easy, Delicious Meals.* New York: Sprig, 2010.

O'Dea, Stephanie. *Make It Fast, Cook It Slow: The Big Book of Everyday Slow Cooking.* New York: Hyperion, 2009.

Reilly, Rebecca. *Gluten-Free Baking: More Than 125 Recipes for Delectable Sweet and Savory Baked Good, Including Cakes, Pies, Quick Breads, Pudding, Cookies, and Other Delights.* New York: Simon & Schuster, 2002.

Shepard, Jules E. Dowler. *Free for All Cooking: 150 Easy Gluten-Free Allergy-Friendly Recipes the Whole Family Can Enjoy.* Cambridge, Massachusetts: De Capo Press, 2010.

Other Cookbooks

Beard, James. *Beard on Food: The Best Recipes and Kitchen Wisdom from the Dean of American Cooking.* New York: Bloomsbury USA, 2007. First published 1974.

Flemming, Alisa Marie. *Go Dairy Free: The Guide and Cookbook for Milk Allergies, Lactose Intolerance, and Casein-Free Living*. Henderson, Nevada: Fleming Ink, 2008.

Gelles, Carol. *1,000 Vegetarian Recipes*. New York: Macmillan, 1996.

McGee, Howard. *On Food and Cooking: The Science and Lore of the Kitchen, rev. ed*. New York: Scribner, 2004.

Page, Karen and Andrew Dorenburg. *The Flavor Bible*. New York: Little, Brown, 2008.

Peterson, James. *Baking: 350 Recipes and Techniques, 1500 Photographs, One Baking Education*. Berkeley, California: Ten Speed Press, 2009.

Authors

Though their recipes aren't gluten-free, I have learned so much about good food and cooking from the authors below. Pick up any of their books—you won't be disappointed.

> Ina Garten—The Barefoot Contessa creates the best simple food infused with flavor.
>
> The Moosewood Collective—Vegetarian cooking that's full of flavor.
>
> Rachael Ray—A wealth of information about making good food from scratch in a hurry.
>
> Martha Rose Shulman—Healthier recipes made with foods from all around the world.

Bibliography

The Community Cook Book. *Woonsocket Hebrew Ladies' Aid and Sisterhood of Congregation of B'Nai Israel*. Woonsocket, 1947.

Cook's Illustrated. *The New Best Recipe, 2nd ed*. Brookline, Massachusetts: America's Test Kitchen, 2004.

Coulson, Zoe, editor. The *Good Housekeeping Illustrated Cookbook*. New York: Hearst Books, 1980.

Culinary Institute of America. *Baking and Pastry: Mastering the Art and Craft*. Hoboken, New Jersey: John Wiley & Sons, 2009.

Fairchild, Barbara, editor. *The Bon Appétit Cookbook: Fast Easy Fresh*. Hoboken, New Jersey: John Wiley & Sons, 2008.

Garten, Ina. *Barefoot Contessa Family Style*. New York: Clarkson Potter, 2002.

Hensperger, Beth and Julie Kaufmann. *Not Your Mother's Slow Cooker Cookbook*. Boston: Harvard Common Press, 2005.

Mateljan, George. *The World's Healthiest Foods*. Seattle: George Mateljan Foundation, 2007.

O'Brien, Susan. *Gluten-free, Sugar-free Cooking*. Philadelphia: Da Capo Press, 2006.

Page, Karen and Andrew Dorenburg. *The Flavor Bible*. New York: Little, Brown, 2009.

Shulman, Martha Rose. *The Best Vegetarian Recipes*. New York: HarperCollins, 2001.

———. *Fast Vegetarian Feasts*. New York: The Dial Press, 1982.

———. *Light Basics Cookbook*. New York: William Morrow and Company, Inc.: 1999.

Vita-Mix Whole Foods Recipes for Better Living. Cleveland, Ohio: Vita-Mix Corporation, 2009.

Index

With Gratitude

First, and always, I am deeply grateful to God and the way He has worked in my life. There have been some interesting twists and turns along the way that I didn't understand at the time, but looking back I can clearly see His fingerprints all over my journey.

To my husband and best friend, Joe, who has always made my happiness, hopes, and dreams as important as his, who has generously given me the complete freedom to do what I love most in life. *Simply Sugar & Gluten-Free* would have been just a mere thought without his love and support. In the beginning, it was his gratitude for my feeble attempts to cook without wheat or white sugar that sparked a desire in me to succeed no matter what. I love you, Joe. Always and all ways.

To Helen, who's spent countless hours discussing flavor profiles, textures, and baking ratios, and looking at photos over e-mail. You picked up the phone every time I called and generously helped me find my way before there was any hope of a blog or a cookbook. Thank you for all the hours spent mentoring me about everything including relationships, homemaking, careers choices, and my relationship with God. My prayer is that someday I'll be able to do the same for someone else.

To my mom, Sheila, and my dad, Arthur, who instilled in me the importance of being the best I could be, for teaching me about determination and perseverance, and for showing me that achievement comes from consistent, thoughtful effort. I've inherited Dad's love of sweets and Mom's insistence on healthier foods, which have been my guiding compass for creating the foods I love most with a healthier twist.

To my Grandma Ruth, who let me sit on the blue stool in her kitchen while she deftly peeled apples and I ate the scraps as she talked to me about how to keep them from browning and showed me how to roll out pie crust and flute the edges. I learned from her how to cook from scratch with a whole lot of love.

To my sister Marcia for her loyal support throughout this project. She's shared recipes, tested recipes, and given me a new perspective on vegan cooking. For being excited and prodding me forward on days when I wanted to quit and reminding me what my real purpose was to begin with. And, for having the courage to share my work over and over until someone noticed what I was doing.

To Karen Musa for knowing that good food has no limits and graciously welcoming me into your culinary arts program. And, to Chef Michele Brown, for your willingness to stretch and help me learn to bake without taking a bite, for believing that I could succeed when I didn't yet believe it was possible myself.

To the gluten-free online community, I love you. You welcomed me with open arms, included me, and honored my perspective on food. You've shared with me, laughed with me, supported me, and let me be a part of your life. To all of you, I treasure your friendships.

To the *SS&GF* readers, you've changed my life and my heart. I'm humbled daily by your honesty and insistence on a better life. Thank you for coming back day after day, asking for more, and pushing me to stretch.

And to Ulysses Press, for plucking my blog out of the hundreds of thousands and having enough confidence in my work to put it in print. To Keith, Karma, Lauren, Bryce, and their incredible staff for their patience with a first time author and for putting forth the effort to produce a book that is better than I could have created on my own.

To those who've helped SS&GF along the way, thank you! Alisa Flemming, Alisa Cooks (AlisaCooks. com); Alta Mantsch, Tasty Eats at Home (TastyEatsAtHome.wordpress.com); Elana Amsterdam, Elana's Pantry (ElanasPantry.com); FoodSpring (FoodSpring.com); Glutenista (Glutenista.com); Go Dairy Free (GoDairyFree.org); Jen Caffetry, Gluten-Free Life with Jen (GfreeLife.com); Jenn DiPazza, The Leftover Queen (LeftoverQueen.com); Kalyn Denny, Kalyn's Kitchen (KalynsKitchen.blogspot.com); Karina Allrich, Gluten-Free Goddess (GlutenFreeGoddess.blogspot.com); Katie Fox, Simple Organic (SimpleOrganic. net); Katie Kimball, Kitchen Stewardship (KitchenStewardship.com); Maggie Savage, She Let Them Eat Cake (SheLetThemEatCake.com); National Foundation for Celiac Awareness (CeliacCentral.org); Ricki Heller, Diet, Dessert, & Dogs (DietDessertnDogs.com); Shirley Braden, Gluten-Free Easily (GlutenFreeEasily.com); The Gluten-Free Allergy Free Expo (GFAFExpo.com)

Thank you to my blog designer for a gorgeous site and logo! Rhiannon Cunag, 21RubyLane.com

A huge thank you to all who helped test recipes for this book! Ally Massie, akalife4me.wordpress .com; Alta Mantsch, TastyEatsAtHome.wordpress.com; Amanda Struckmeyer, TeamStruckmeyer.blogspot .com; Amelia Byrnes, GlutenFreebiesByMiel.com; Anne Barfield, ChickenParadise.com; Annette Simpson, ElisLunch.wordpress.com; Cara Lyons, CarasCravings.blogspot.com; Carrie Forbes, GingerLemonGirl .com; Cheryl Harris, GfGoodness.com; Colette Donnelly, CuriousWhy.com; Debi Smith, HuntersLyonesse .wordpress.com; Gigi Stweart, GlutenFreeGigi.com; Hallie Klecker, HallieKlecker.com; Heather Thompson, HealthyGrainFreeLiving.blogspot.com; Helen Adams, MizHelensCountryCottage.blogspot.com; Jamie Lynn, CrankyLittleRedHead.blogspot.com; Jenn DiPiazza, LeftOverQueen.com; Jessica Meyer, ATXGlutenFree .wordpress.com; Karen Michika, KarensMeltingAway.tumblr.com; Kari Romo, KariRomo.com; Katrina Morales, GlutenFreeGidget.blogspot.com; Kim Maes, CookItAllergyFree.com; Kristy Hightower, GetFitByPhone .com; Maggie Savage, SheLetThemEatCake.com; Natalie Kimble, TurtleSoupAndMakeItSnappy.blogspot .com; Paula Jones, bellalimento.com; Renee Euler, BeyondRiceAndTofu.com; Ricki Heller, DietDessertnDogs .com; Ruth Clark, TheWayToHisHeart.blogspot.com; Sunny Jones, FreshAndFiesty.blogspot.com; Tia Hain, GlugleGlutenFree.com; Winnie Abrams, HealthyGreenKitchen.com; Aamina Masood; Abigail Brown; Amy Floyd; Ashley Miller; Audrey Clymer; Barb Ryan; Carrie Wood; Christianne Madonna; Christine Sullivan; Deidra Schultz; Diane Bramos; Diane Janowiak; Dixie Duncan Anderson; Edith Russo; Elizabeth Heironimusb; Emily Fisher; Erika Hulings; Erin Gerih; Felicia Saucier; Gail Doughty; Heather Cramer; Heather Middleton; Holly Hill; Janet Hurley; Jean Skeels; Jeanette Reed; Joyce van den Berg; Julia Foster; Julie Bates; Julie Snow; Karah Palmer; Kathleen McDermott; Katie Cassanova; Katie Gredecki; Kelly Ahti; Kelly Dixon; Kim McLaurine; Kristen Overton; Larissa Dodson; Laura Sterrett; Linda Stiles; Linda Wiltrout; Loralie Tidwell; Melody Mayo; Nancy McDonnell; Neveen Hegab; Rose Gulledge; Shelly Hoffman; Sherri White; Stephanie Tsouloufis; Tanja Funk; Zeljka Hassler

Much love and gratitude,
Amy

About the Author

AMY GREEN authors the popular food blog Simply Sugar & Gluten-Free (www.SimplySugar AndGlutenFree.com), where she shares her passion for healthy living. She has abstained from refined sugars and wheat since 2004 and, as a result, is maintaining a 60-plus-pound weight loss. Over the years, Amy has learned that eating healthier doesn't equal deprivation. In addition to owning a small business, Amy is finishing her pastry arts degree at Collin College in Frisco, Texas, and teaches local sugar-free, gluten-free cooking classes. She holds a bachelor's degree in psychology and a master's degree in education, both from Ohio State University. Previously, Amy taught elementary school and owned one of the premier pet care companies in the North Dallas area. She lives with her husband and four dogs in Dallas, Texas.